The
Ivington
Diaries

The Ivington Diaries

words and pictures by

Monty Don

BLOOMSBURY

LONDON · BERLIN · NEW YORK

For Sarah.
Thank you.

Introduction

In 1991 we bought a derelict house with a two-acre field. There was no garden at all to speak of, although a pile of building rubble sheltered by a curving stone wall had once been a vegetable garden. If this was only a field of dreams, at least it was not cluttered with anyone else's fantasies.

The plot was a long rectangle with the house jammed into one corner so that almost all the land stretched out behind and to one side of the building. One long side of the rectangle was bounded by barns converted into half a dozen cottages, and the other was raised above a water meadow with the river Arrow running through it. The second time we visited the house we looked out of an attic window and glimpsed an otter on the river bank. Curlew call haunted the spring nights. It was awkward, utterly impractical and, of course, irresistible.

The house was very old, with the majority of the extant part fifteenth- and sixteenth-century, and the first year was spent repairing it so that it was habitable. In the process I pored over every inch of it, slowly untangling the architectural evidence. It turned out that its history was much deeper and more fascinating than we could ever have imagined. There is evidence of at least three buildings on the site, with Saxon remains, the footings of a medieval hall house and the existing building – which is itself an amalgam of two separate timber-framed Tudor houses. Whilst the builders worked indoors I did nothing in the garden for that first year beyond clear the scrub and brambles and turn it into a grass field. All the while I dreamed the garden into being, walking the ground, smelling the air. By the time it was ready to begin planting, fully eighteen months after buying the place, I already knew my unborn garden intimately.

I was also rebuilding my own life. Our business had collapsed and we had sold everything we had to bail ourselves out and I felt thoroughly sorry for myself. Then my mother died and I received a small legacy that enabled us to put a deposit on this astonishingly cheap house. To live in a fascinating house with the chance to make two acres of garden on superb soil was the best of all fresh starts. I was not just making a garden. I was making and mending me and us.

It has always been us in this together the whole way. From the very first, Sarah and I have built our lives based upon our home and garden. The children have grown up here. There are three dogs buried in the garden. I have spent almost all my spare time in the garden and Sarah a great deal of hers, but we have been assisted by a series of long-term helpers, all local, and all of whom I regard as lifelong friends. The household has always been a busy place, even chaotic, driven by a

// Summer 1992. The site cleared and woven fences marking future hedges.

communal human energy. However the decisions, down to the last plant, have always been taken by Sarah and myself as an equal partnership and both of us have always had an absolute veto on everything to do with house and garden. On a day-to-day level I spend much more time in the garden than she does, and I have certainly never seen her touch any kind of garden machinery, but her eye for detail is simply much better than mine, whilst perhaps I see the big picture a little more clearly. I tend to do everything edible whilst she spends days in the jewel garden, tending and moving plants, creating a subtle balance. She waits until she knows what she wants to do and then does it very well. I find out what I want to do by trying it out. But there are no demarcation lines and absolutely no sense of any part of the garden belonging to one of us more than the other. It is the sum of our parts and neither of us could or would have done it without the other.

The 'empty' field that became the garden was, of course, no more empty than a wood or stream is empty. It was overflowing with plants, creatures and, above all, a long and complicated history. To ignore any of that when imposing a garden is a failure of imagination, yet to be shackled to a brand of historical purity stifles creativity. At times this can feel like a fine line to tread, but in practice gardens evolve slowly and are very mutable. We have planted, dug up and replanted almost everything, from bulbs to trees and hedges. One of the great virtues of a garden is that it is so temporal and human in scale. A garden seven years old can seem mature and after fifteen years few would be able to date it to closer than a decade. I recall visiting the oldest garden in Britain, Levens Hall in Cumbria, made in the 1690s and famous for its huge and Baroque topiary, and idly asking how long it would take to recreate the garden should it be bulldozed? Thirty years. That is all. Everything after that would simply be holding it in check.

The truth is that creating a mature garden is surprisingly short-term and attainable. For the first three years it is all dreams and schemes. For the next four there is the satisfaction of seeing it come into being, the next seven a gradual maturation and after that it is a rhythm of maintenance and curtailment. Certainly after eighteen years the garden here at Ivington is being radically cut back to tether it to our original scheme.

In practice, we have found that the longer that we garden here, the less we want to impose ourselves on nature. The greatest changes are conceptual as well as physical and have come in the past few years as we have tried to restrict our control and increasingly let the garden run untrammelled. To do this and yet retain the essence of the garden –

The new herb garden being made. The walled garden in its early incarnation. //

which is always a self-conscious control of nature – is tricky, and thus increasingly interesting and rewarding.

Although I had drawn extensive plans of the garden, and the parts appeared bit by bit, the whole scheme was only visible in my own mind. Then, some six or seven years after moving in, we bought the empty barns that separated us from our neighbours and started to repair them. They included a pair of hop kilns with enormously high pyramid roofs and these were scaffolded out. This meant that Sarah and I could climb forty feet and see the entire thing from the air. For the first time it gave a coolly objective view, and in the process translated the garden into something entirely different. It seemed much grander and more grown up than the sensuous struggle that confronted and delighted us daily.

The truth is that this garden has always been a place growing from me and that I have grown into, the earth engrained in my boots and hands rather than viewed dispassionately from afar. I cannot write about it with anything but complete subjectivity. The eye with which I see the garden is the same eye with which the garden sees me.

Practicality is, of course, at the core of gardening, if not gardens. As someone who is happiest when active on his own land, doing something that demands enough skill and expertise to fully engage his attention but not so much as to undermine his competence, the direct, visceral practicalities of gardens and gardening are an essential part of my life. Everything in these pages stems from what I do and have done.

But thought and emotion suffuses every aspect of human life. As a writer it is instinctive to keep a record of events and how they have affected me, and as a gardener a diary is an invaluable tool for future years because otherwise you forget. You think you won't, but you always do. The pattern that builds up from years of a garden diary is a mosaic that can be incredibly detailed even if the entries are very simple. The emotional and intellectual pattern that I have always written down is, in its own way, just as practical. It tempers triumph and comforts despair, both of which run like a river through this place. I have also always recorded the garden with photographs and found the development of the digital camera enormously helpful, so that over the past ten years I have accumulated an archive of tens of thousands of images of it in all its states and dates.

My own obsession with gardening has always been driven by a love of soil and place rather than of plants. I am not, by anybody's stretch of imagination, any kind of plant expert. For many in the British

// By summer 1993 the vegetable garden was growing lustily.

horticultural world this is an admission of failure or incompetence, but it is simply not the driver of my passion. In fact I love many plants for many reasons and by default know a lot about how many of them grow, but the ones I love most are those that strike the deepest emotional and poetic chord within me. I could not care less if they are common, or unfashionable. With plants, as with everything in my garden, I have little sense of objectivity. Everything is personal and all the best moments in my garden are when the sense of self dissolves into grooved movement and flowing, nameless green.

The context for this is a profound hunger for a sense of place and the urge to make a home. The two are not necessarily the same thing. Our home, that we have made from the ruins of a house and a bit of field, is a noisy, rude, scruffy, lovely place with dogs and cats, chickens and music, rows and laughter, food cooking and lights left on. I would forgo all the gardens in the world for home and family – but our garden would always be part of our home and our family.

I realise that this place could, one day, become someone else's home with just as much success. It is transferable. The essence of *place* is fixed absolutely in the thing itself. It is not transferable and can exist in wilderness or public spaces just as much as a garden. So when I visit any garden I always start by looking for the place where it most is itself. Any good garden presents you with this sense of identity from the first. I am sure that the reason one can visit a garden comprised of all the box of horticultural tricks and yet remain strangely unmoved is because it is a space rather than a place. This distinction is the essence of every kind of domesticity. It is what separates a house from a home. It might well be beautiful, botanically fascinating and cared for with supreme expertise but, admirable as they undoubtedly are, none of these things are ever enough.

However you go about it, it is not an idea or technique or any particular plant combination that makes a garden lovely but that sense of place – the indefinable quality that makes you want to be *here* – which the gardener falls in love with. And this book, above anything else, is a love story.

January

One of the surprising effects of a garden is that it never leaves you alone. It stays in your mind like a catchy tune, sometimes naggingly banal but more often magically resolving itself into a perfect harmony. Jobs that in reality are bafflingly hard work and filled with obstructions of every kind are made logical and straightforward in the mind. So soil, spade-jarringly infiltrated with lumps of concrete and rusting metal or clogged with bindweed, becomes sweet loam crumbling off the tireless spade. New borders clear themselves and fill with plants to a primped moment of perfection instead of ending up half done at the critical time of year, misplaced and under-stocked. Then the discrepancy between mind-gardening and reality is cruelly revealed.

You can't stop weaving dreams, but it is a good idea to take stock and make some real plans that can be measured throughout the year. If I do this every year, the same resolutions come up again and again. This need not be an admission of the futility of intention, more a stiffening of the sinews. So here are my New Year's resolutions.

1. The first is to keep a daily gardening journal. I know from experience that this works, but last year there were huge gaps and I regret them already. The journal has a dual purpose. I write in important jobs at set dates in red, if only to nag at my conscience, but also, more usefully, I write down the weather, what plants I ordered and planted, what seeds were sown, what jobs in general were done, and what was noticeable, giving me a complete record of the garden. This need not be fancy in any way. It is a logbook. A simple desk diary suits the purpose admirably. It is much more important to write down truthfully what I have done than to busily fill in all the things I intend to do. An empty page is a reasonable record of inactivity as helpful and meaningful as a page crammed with achievements. If you have a garden book for each year, you can start to compare notes from previous years and my own experience is that this is encouraging rather than depressing.

2. My second resolution is to make a point of learning something new. I seem to be on a permanent cramming course and spend my life surrounded by reference books, but if you have been gardening for a while it is easy to become fixed in your likes and dislikes and to dismiss things of which you are ignorant. This year I want to challenge my own ignorance and apply myself to one specific area. Gardening is such a dauntingly big subject that it is intimidating for all but the nerdish few. Better to focus on one bit at a time and slowly piece the bits together than to tackle the whole lot at once. If I take one subject a year for the

rest of my life and work at it for that year, I might begin to master my craft. This year I want to learn more – much more – about woodland flowers, which I love.

3. This year I will grow as much food for the household as possible. At the moment this is my passion, and I shall indulge it to the hilt. This is all to do with rejecting the anonymity of food. For a society that is so sophisticated about meals, most people are pathetically ignorant about ingredients. The garden is the easiest place to make that direct connection between what we put in our mouths and its provenance. If there is one field of horticulture in which I feel I have genuine expertise it is this, but I have not been using this knowledge fully. I shall grow more soft fruit, more vegetables that are eaten within the hour of picking. Perhaps most importantly, I shall concentrate on what Sarah, myself and the children like to eat, and less on going through the motions of growing certain vegetables simply because I can. I shall be much more particular about varieties and the details of getting them exactly right for our table. Growing vegetables, herbs and fruit should be done in the same spirit as choosing music or clothes: with a mix of precision and adventure.

4. I have always longed for a really grown-up propagating set-up, and this year I am going to make it happen. Our greenhouse is fine (although without tap water or electricity), and we are lucky enough to have an old stable that serves as a potting shed, but one of them is in the wrong place as they are miles apart. I want to move the greenhouse, build cold frames and have a garden yard where the real nitty-gritty goes on. It will be entirely functional and beautiful. The more I garden, the more I realise the importance of an efficient, working propagating system, with electricity, a standpipe as well as a large tank for rainwater, heated benches, a standing area for hardening off, and an area for storing grit, mushroom compost and wheelbarrows. This can be scaled right down to a few square yards in a small garden or given the luxury of space, but, however big, it will be the hub of the garden. I wish I had invested in a set-up like this when we started this garden five years ago rather than muddling along.

5. I am going to grow more annuals. We actually grew quite a lot last year ('we' being mainly Sarah), choosing a wide selection of seed from Thompson & Morgan in scatter-gun fashion, but part of the problem stems from our lack of a proper propagating set-up. Around early May we always have dozens of seed trays in the greenhouse filled with

seedlings and dozens more sitting outside waiting to be planted out. Cold frames should sort us out. We made new borders last year and filled the space with cosmos ('Purity'), sweet peas, zinnias, tithonia 'Sundance' with its extraordinary funnel-shaped stem holding such a vividly orange flower, leonotis (amazing), cornflowers (especially an almost black one), poppies (what a fantastic year it was for poppies), nicotiana (*sylvestris* and *langsdorffii*), molucella, lots of sunflowers (of which the rich russet colours of 'Velvet Queen' were best), eschscholzias and marigolds. The point is not to boastfully list what we did but to catch a hint of the enthusiasm these flowers aroused in me. With careful organisation we can grow many more this year that will flower for a longer period.

6. It is a pathetic admission, but I have to admit that I have never really got to grips with summer bulbs. I want to rectify that because they add a good dimension to any garden. Part of the problem is that I am good at doing what can be done today but hopeless at preparing for what should be done in three months' time. Ordering summer-flowering bulbs is not part of my calendar, and this year I must change that. The reward will be lilies, alliums, iris, galtonia, gladioli and ranunculus represented in the garden through merit and not the occasional fluke.

7. If all the other resolutions are to do with our garden at home, my final one is public. I resolve to take up the fight with more vigour than ever against the pompous dullards who deny gardening the grace, laughter and enthusiastic clumsiness that make it such a joy. I mean the arid pedants who know much of the minutiae of plant nomenclature and diseases but nothing of everyday human life. Gardens are for people of all ages, backgrounds and attitudes, and no one involved in gardening has any right to assume that their audience is hanging on every word. So I promise to do my utmost to entertain and inform, to expose pomposity and dreariness without any allegiance to the horticultural status quo, and to share my love of gardening as enthusiastically and intelligently as I know how.

 Right, let's get on with the year.

4 January 2004
Escape

Sarah and I had a morning in the walled garden. It was cold and the soil both wet and freezing on the hands. Mud stuck. The sort of day when it would be wise to wait for a better moment to work in the borders. But we have been writing a book together for the past couple of months, and it is supposed to be delivered tomorrow and it is not yet done. This means that we should not be doing anything beyond the absolute obligations of sustaining the children and animals other than writing. But it was a clear, frosty Sunday morning after days of oppressively warm, grey weather, and it does one good to play truant from time to time. So, having broken free, we were prepared to break any rules of best horticultural practice just so we could stay outside.

We have been sorting the borders out so they can be planted up with bulbs. It is a chance to review the planting plan as well as to do our border housekeeping. Four years ago we completely dug the walled garden up, divided and discarded where appropriate, cleaned all the bindweed that had worked its way into the roots of the perennials and shrubs, dug it all over and replanted. But it has not had more than a regular weed and an annual mulch since. So we thinned the spread of forget-me-nots, fennel, borage and anthemis, and divided the nepeta, lovage, *Echinops ritro* and *Acanthus spinosus* that have all become thuggish. This is all straightforward enough, but we had real problems with the roses. Originally I planted thirty-odd different types, mainly in threes and fives, all old-fashioned and lovely, but they are all ones that I had brought from our previous garden and which have been moved, in some cases, up to four times. Roses do not like this treatment and many are much the worse for wear. My brain tells me they have to go, but my heart wants to cling to them as the flowers are sublime and they have become old friends. It would be easier if I could simply replace the scrawniest groups, but rose-sickness means that I must wait three years or replace the soil. Perhaps the latter is the least worst option. Either way I used the call of the book and its impossible deadline to dodge the decision for a little longer.

5 January 2002
Decisions

This year I have resolved to change my working habits. To date I have juggled two jobs more or less at random. One is as a broadcaster, which is practically always done away from home. In essence I have to organise myself to be at a certain place at a certain time and then do my stuff. No problem. The other is as a writer, and this is much harder. I do two different types of writing, journalism and books. Journalism is a sprint. So long as it is done well, to the right length and on time, no one minds where or how you do it. Consequently it can be – and often is – fitted round other things. Books, however, are a marathon. They accrue slowly, and at times it can seem as though they will never get written.

The long book I am currently writing is about organic gardening. It is my seventh gardening book, and I have learnt that the secret is to

// The front garden on a frosty morning.

treat it like a conventional job. So I discipline myself to write at set times and to keep writing until I have done a set amount of words. But none of this makes any sense if I don't have time to garden. Gardening is both research and pleasure bundled together.

So my new resolution is to write in the mornings and garden for at least two hours each afternoon before going back to my desk. But this is tricky to keep to. For instance, today was a beautiful clear, frosty morning. The weather forecast said that this would not last, and I itched to go outside and get on with pruning my pleached limes whilst the weather was good. But I resisted and did my twelve hundred words, which took me until two in the afternoon. By which time the weather had changed and it was starting to rain. I still went out, but it was not much fun. Maybe if I wrote over the weekend I could buy a sunny day during the week?

My son Tommy came up with a bright idea the other day whilst we were putting up tomshed mark 2. Tom's first shed had been the heart, soul and workshop of the domestic Tom. I suspect that, in both a very practical and a metaphysical way, he gathered it all up and took it about with him when he was not at home too, and what we were left with, tucked into a corner of the yard, was a chimera, a hologram of the real, internalised thing. However, for his birthday, just before Christmas, he got a bigger shed. This is both a rites-of-passage thing (he is now ten, after all) and a more-space thing. There is all that power equipment to fit in, all those inventions to make. And don't for a second patronise this in your head – these things get made and get made well. But. The first shed was not to be touched. And more space for sheds means less space for gardens. In the end, a position butting on to the potting shed was chosen as being both reachable in the dark, via the illumination of outside lights (vital), and being near power (essential). And being largely out of sight (important to some of us). In the process of putting up tomshed mark 2, Tom had an idea. Why didn't we make the potting shed into the workshop and the workshop into the potting shed? There was, of course, a motive for this – he wanted his shed to butt on to a bigger version of itself rather than a boring potting shed. But it was a radically simple and very good notion and for the past week I have been making it happen.

My outhouses that are potting shed, tool shed and workshop are an essential part of my garden and that is one of the joys of living in the country. The former potting shed was an old stable with a corrugated roof and sloping floor – good for letting the horse muck drain but bad

Red shoots of the pleached limes before their winter prune. //

for standing on whilst pricking out dozens of plants. The new space is bigger, nicer – brick walls, brick floor – and nearer the house. It is further from the greenhouse but not by much, and correspondingly closer to the house. Moving all the pots, the potting bench and the paraphernalia of potting – bags of compost, leaf mould, sieves, trowels, seeds, labels, dibbers, liquid seaweed, watering can and the wind-up radio – is a wonderful way of setting the garden up for the coming year. It feels like real gardening even though the actual soil-stuff is a sneering slick outside in the rain.

The new potting shed has room to make our potting compost with a shovel on the floor – a huge advantage – and the loam, garden compost and sharp sand all get sieved on to the bricks, mixed up (like knocking up mortar) and then shovelled into bags. It is a recipe, a formula. It's a game. I'm playing in my shed and Tom is making proper stuff in his.

8 January 2000
Turfstack

I made the first cut of hellebore leaves in October, another just before Christmas and the last the other day. The idea is to get rid of last year's leaves, which by now have flopped, and cover new growth while at the same time not denying the plants a source of nutrition. I wish I was brave enough to clear the lot in late autumn because they always look horrid. But I love hellebores and don't want to risk harming them.

I have dug out the soil from the cold greenhouse that was filled with tomatoes last summer and topped it up with loam and mushroom compost. The loam comes from the stack of turves that were cut when we made the kitchen garden paths. In fact whenever we cut into the grass – and after all, this entire garden is cut from a grass meadow – the turves are stacked face to face, making blocks about ten by six by six feet. These are then ignored for at least a year. Initially it looks foursquare and sharp-edged, but soon the outside gets a bit shaggy with tufts of grass and the shape slips a little as various animals burrow in and parts rot down faster than others. But when you slice into it, cutting down through the turves with a sharp spade, the loam is lovely rich crumbly stuff that you could eat. We use it for potting compost mainly, but every other year the greenhouse gets a new six inches of topsoil too. Now the soil is prepared, I have covered it with a double layer of fleece to insulate it, and, depending on the weather, I shall sow lettuce, saladini, rocket and perhaps some early carrots at the end of the month.

We had a load of premix the other day with, inevitably, a pile left over, sitting in the yard going hard as we looked at it. We decided to make a pad for deliveries of mushroom compost and/or sharp sand, both of which we use pretty much all the time and it is a pain shovelling up the last bits mixed up with mud, stones and sticks. Now we have a gleaming, smooth surface to scrape and brush clean to our hearts' content.

9 January 1999
Weeds

I am untidy but ordered and Sarah is tidy but disordered. When we work together we make a good team. This winter, for many reasons, we have hardly crossed paths outside, but we had a good day earlier this week reminding ourselves of the intense satisfaction of working together. We didn't do very much of import, tidied up, walked round planning changes, weeded, planted a few things that have been lying around in pots since summer, but it felt entirely happy and of a piece. Indoors I have only experienced this working harmony in the kitchen, but that usually has the added pressure of bored and hungry children, imminent guests or lack of space. This garden is ours, private and yet properly shared, and over the past twenty years our happiest hours have been quietly working in a garden together, perhaps hardly speaking and usually doing separate jobs. It is an important part of our relationship.

I say that we did not do much, but a good weed at this time of year makes a big difference. For much of winter my relationship with the garden is based upon faith. I know and trust that spring will bring beauty, but from November until April memory and hope sustain me more than a coldly objective eye. From time to time I have to face the scruffy facts and try and do something, and a day spent attacking our three main enemies – nettles, couch grass and creeping buttercup – is well spent. This is not glamorous or creative work. All three weeds are particularly bad in amongst the growing hedges and have to be grubbed out on one's knees with a hand fork. The nettles carry a sharp sting and the ground is wet, however dry the day. But by four o'clock, as it began to get dark and the lure of a cup of tea became irresistible, there was a satisfying heap of roots to be burned on the bonfire.

10 January 2004
Moles

I have learnt to live with my moles. Not that I have much choice in the matter – they were here long before I was, and I have done nothing but encourage them. Think about it. Moles like rich, easy-to-dig soil filled with their favourite food, earthworms. As I have spent the last ten years converting two acres of rough pasture into well-dug, manured garden, I have been making an area that was pretty good for moles – there is nowhere in this part of the world where they do not thrive – into what amounts to mole heaven. This is true of all gardens, of course. We complain like mad when molehills appear on our lawns or erupt in the borders, but − short of advertising and offering a bonus prize for admission − we could hardly be doing more to encourage them.

This is not to say that they do not create havoc. There are the molehills themselves, which are unsightly but which provide the raw material for an important part of my home-made potting compost. They also provide hours of pleasure for our Jack Russell puppy, who regards each one as a cross between a sandpit and an affront to his manhood that must be spread as far and as fast as possible. One of these days he is going to discover that there is a hole and the exciting possibility of an animal at the base of it, and the digging will begin in earnest.

The combination of moles and terriers in the garden is worse than a JCB on the loose. But in fact, molehills should be seen as waste heaps from mines rather than as soil thrown up by moles coming to the surface. After a few weeks the subsidence begins. By this time of year, the lawn and paths are corrugated with subterranean tunnels and excavations, just right to turn an ankle or two.

11 January 2004
Labels
....

Labels are a constant problem. In theory we have a rule that every container has its own label bearing all necessary information. This usually means the full name of the plant, when it was sown/planted or taken as a cutting, and perhaps the colour or height. But writing out all these labels − and every year it amounts to thousands − is at best tedious and at worst impossible. So inevitably one starts to label just one pot of a batch or to use shorthand. Then batches get mixed, someone else comes along and misinterprets the shorthand, and things get muddled.

So it has been with some batches of tulips this year. Last year we made a conscious decision to plant many tulips just an inch or so below the surface so they would get all the goodness of the topsoil before being lifted in early summer. This happened to plan. When they had fully dried they were cleaned and put into trays for storage over the summer. Plant labels were slipped into the trays with them. Some must have slipped out again or slipped from one tray to another because when we came to plant them in December we had lost all track of what was what − and it takes a better expert than me to identify the variety of tulip from the bulb alone. So the last tulip job of the year was to line all these hundreds of tulips out into nursery beds and into pots − all labelled 'tulip 1', 'tulip 2' and so on. The pots can be sunk into borders as and where they will best suit, and the lined-out ones can be cut for the house, identified and then *meticulously* labelled for proper planting next year.

// The winter view from my workroom, wet in earth and sky.

12 January 2002
Dream
. . . .

I am one of those people who can go for weeks without a dream crossing the oceans of my sleep, but one recent dream remains firmly in my waking consciousness. I am showing someone round my garden. It is a perfect midsummer day. We come to the orchard. 'I love your blossom,' she says. I laugh: 'That's not blossom, that's the roses.' I then look round and notice that the orchard is filled with roses, climbing into each of the forty-odd trees and in great, sprawling bushes between them, each one heavy with white and soft pink flowers. Mmm, I think, I love that blossom. Then I wake.

Now I am sure this means something profound and informative about my repressed psyche, but for the moment I am more than happy to consider the practical implications. I think roses would be great in my real, daytime orchard. The timing is perfect because the trees – all standards grown on MIII rootstock – are now, after five years, beginning to attain tree-like stature. If I plant climbers now, the trees should be able to support them.

Of course I must not go mad and plant 'Kiftsgate', 'Rambling Rector' or 'Paul's Himalayan Musk' over a spindly apple like 'Lane's Prince Albert'. In a couple of years the tree would be reduced to no more than a tripod for the roses, which would be lovely for a week or so in July but not really the desired effect. I shall start with some less vigorous white climbers like 'Sander's White Rambler', 'Wickwar', 'Félicité Perpétue', 'Madame Plantier' and 'Albéric Barbier', and some soft pinks like 'Blairii Number Two', 'New Dawn', 'Souvenir de la Malmaison' and 'Madame Alfred Carrière'. And in a couple of years, the orchard will have a second, midsummer blossoming. Although, as my daughter is prone to say, Dream on . . .

13 January 2002
Cold
. . . .

The garden has basked in lovely cold sun for days now, frozen day forming layer upon frozen day. But it went down to minus 11 the other night, which was on the cusp between good and disastrous. This time last year we had a night of minus 14, which to my astonishment left the brassicas in their various forms completely blasted. Not one survived. It also broke a couple of valuable pots that I had foolishly left outside, so this year I have brought them all in to an increasingly cluttered potting shed. I also dug up all my wonderful crop of celeriac just before the worst of the frost, so most of it was salvaged. Smugness prevails. But I realised that I may have made a huge mistake with my dahlias, which I had spread out to dry months ago and left them where they lay, under a blanket of fleece. They have not frosted but do seem to

have dried out rather alarmingly. I have since put them in large pots packed with moist coir – time will prove the extent of the damage. That is one of the problems with this sort of weather – most damage is only measurable in two or three months' time. However, I will speak no ill of it as every hour of sub-zero temperatures is a blast against the monstrous regiment of slugs, snails, aphids and fungi that have infiltrated the garden.

Of course the cold has meant that I cannot get a spade into the soil, so I have been thrown back on seasonal tinkering both indoors and out. I have sown rocket, endive, 'Little Gem', mizuna, mibuna and onions, all of which will be grown under cover in the greenhouse. This is still being left open to get as much of a scour from the cold as possible, but it will be closed up very shortly and fleece put over the soil to insulate it so that it will be ready for planting in about six weeks' time. Tomatoes will follow all but the onions. I have cleared barrow-loads of hellebore leaves, which is fiddly pruning I like, although I wish I could recycle them. They will not compost, and end up on the bonfire where they burn with a satisfying spit and crackle. I have also spent much time

Stipa arundinacea and fennel in a frosty corner of the jewel garden. //

redesigning the walled garden, which at the moment is dominated by a trampoline. I am very partial to the occasional bounce myself but dislike the way that it dominates this space, so as soon as the ground softens we will start digging up half the grass to accommodate more borders, all in the soft pastel colours of this part of the garden. The debate is whether to dig up and move some of the roses yet again or buy new plants. Financial sense dictates the former, but I would advise anyone else to do the latter. A healthy new plant will always catch up and do better than a tired transplant.

14 January 2006
Box

For most of my gardening life I have followed the rule that box is best left uncut until Derby Day (not being a racing man, I had to look it up to discover that it was the first Saturday in June) and then again in September. I also followed the precept that September was the ideal time to take cuttings. However, climate chaos (this seems to me a much more accurate description of what is going on than the rather sedate 'climate change') has thrown all this into the air. All rules are now up for questioning.

This is a thoroughly good thing. Gardeners are as prone as anyone else to blindly follow precepts and conventions simply because they are told to do so. This reminds me of a story I heard over Christmas. A highly intelligent and successful woman always boiled a ham for Christmas and swore that the secret of her success was to remove the bone first. When asked why she did this, she admitted that it was what her mother had always done. When her mother was asked why she did it, she said it was what *her* mother had taught her to do. Finally, when the grandmother was asked why she did it, she replied, 'Because when I was first married the largest pan I had was too small to take the whole ham, so I cut the end off to fit it in!'

So when we trimmed all of our box hedges last September, they promptly put on a spurt of vigorous new growth in the exceptionally wet and mild October that we had. This resulted in two things. The first was a shagginess that was the exact opposite effect of what was intended. The second was that all the new growth got frosted by the cold snap we had in November. Result: an ugly, bedraggled garden. So we cut all our box again in December. In the old days – when the weather followed a pattern that our fathers and grandfathers would have recognised – this might have risked a flush of growth in a mild February or March, followed, perhaps, by it all being knocked back by a late frost. That could still happen, of course. But just as they did not used to like to cut later

// *The vegetable garden is starkly defined by its box hedges in winter.*

than early October because that was when the first frosts were likely, now we have to contend with year-round growth interrupted by the occasional cold snap any time between November and May. But by giving the garden its midwinter trim it has a crisp framework around which the season's gentle decay can be held and – in the frost at least – look magical.

I suspect that I complain too much about the wetness of our ground here, but it does dominate everything. If global warning means this pattern of warm, very wet winters with comparatively mild, wet summers, then the marsh that this land was reclaimed from a thousand years ago will reclaim us. At the moment the ground is saturated. Any rain sits on top in dozens of puddles. The only accessible piece is the kitchen garden, which has five years' worth of manure and compost piled into it. This, of course, is the lesson. The more organic matter you can put into or on to your soil, the better it will be for plants and humans alike. But at the moment the ground is too wet to reach the borders and add manure to it. Every footstep sinks and squelches, and a wheelbarrow full of muck is unmovable. So I'm waiting for a dry enough day and then will drop everything to move around on this quagmire.

Ironically the most amenable site is our spring garden, which is the first bit to flood when the river overspills (as now) and which is composed almost entirely of silt. The yellow hamamelis with its spidery flowers is at its best there now and the hellebores are coming through strong. I cut nearly all the leaves from them this week, so that the emerging leaves have light and space to grow. I mulched them all with mushroom compost after their defoliation, which might give them a little extra nutrition to help them on the way but my guess is that they will cope fine.

We got our delivery of sweet pea seeds from Peter Grayson over Christmas, and I have begun to sow them. Expert growers do this in October so the plants develop strong roots and grow away well as soon as the weather warms in spring, but I have never got that organised. We have sixty-six packets, each with about twenty seeds. I sow them in pots, three to a pot, so that is nearly four hundred pots. I know exactly where all the sweet peas are to be planted, and a job to do soon – when the borders resemble soil rather than slurry – is to dig a pit under each wigwam and put in a good load of manure. Sweet peas do like plenty of muck. Finding somewhere for four hundred pots to sit with proper protection is much harder. However, come June it will all be worth it.

Pruning the limes is winter work and can be a bit chilly. //

I have been working flat out for weeks now so my gardening has been limited to a maximum of half an hour a day in the late afternoon if it is not raining. That amounts to roughly three or four brief sessions a week. This is starvation rations and proves to be more tantalising than satisfying any kind of need. So I am very frustrated and long for a few days' uninterrupted work outside. In truth there is not a huge amount that urgently needs doing. The principal job in January is to gradually remove all the hellebore leaves. I have been making several passes at this, taking off any that are affected by *Coniothyrium hellebori*, or black spot. This is getting worse in my garden, which I put down to the combination of damp, mild winters and the way I have allowed self-sown seedlings to spread, thus creating a crowded, poorly ventilated growing area. Anyway, it is not disastrous, and in the short term the best way to deal with it is to cut off any part of the plant that is showing the characteristic brown blotches and burn it. At this time of year I remove any foliage that has fallen below horizontal. There is no science in this – it is just a personal guide that seems to work. And I burn all leaves whether overtly blighted or not, just in case.

The seedling position would appal the hellebore specialist. *H. orientalis* is very promiscuous and will cross-pollinate not just with itself but with other species. Sod's Law dictates that the vast majority of these offspring will combine the worst qualities of their parents coupled with great vigour. In time our hellebores will become overtaken by a mass of muddy-coloured oriental hybrids. The proper way to deal with them is to thin the seedlings radically, keeping any with dark staining on the stems as they tend to be darker-flowering, or any that surround a particular favourite in the hope that they might show some of this parent's qualities. Of course I do none of this.

When I asked my grandfather what the secret of old age was, he said, 'Eat breakfast, lunch, tea and dinner at the same time every day. And avoid butter and gravy.' As he was over ninety at the time and went on to a robust, not to say cantankerous, ninety-seven, there must have been something in it, although I am rather partial to gravy myself. I have inherited his love of habit and routine. The more every day is like its predecessor the better I like it. The truth is that I do a number of different jobs, each with varied demands, so no one week is ever like another, but I hanker after blind repetition. Sarah, who hates the shackles of routine, says that I am like an old dog, blindly shuffling through my daily rituals. Up and straight to my desk to write, breakfast, open and water

An early hellebore sugared with frost. //

the greenhouses, feed the chickens, write, coffee at eleven, write, lunch on the stroke of one, write, feed the chickens...

But in winter it gets dark so early that the late-afternoon chicken run comes mid-afternoon, throwing the whole delicate fabric of life into turmoil. Get absorbed in your work and leave them until after 4 p.m. and the chickens are going to bed, responding instinctively to the falling light. Not that I care too much about the bloody birds. I am much more concerned that within the plodding ritual of walking up to the end of the garden at the same time of every day is the heart of my relationship with the garden. I look at it intensely and need some light to do that. Even in the depths of winter when practically nothing is showing any growth (except the snowdrops and the aconites and the hellebores and the winter honeysuckle and the leaves of the primroses – it is all gently happening...) the falling light changes everything.

How far does the light have to fall before the garden disappears? Whilst walking in the deep blue darkness of a June night can be beautiful, blundering through the wet of a black January evening is usually less than aesthetically illuminating. For most of us the whistle blows for full-time outside once the light falls.

It is not just the timing of my chicken run that sets me thinking about this. Over Christmas we hung a couple of strands of fairy lights around the four Portuguese laurels in the beds around the paved area by the herb garden. Cheesy, dinky, clichéd – all those things but undeniably beautiful as well. It transformed that piece of garden from the house looking out and, even better, sitting outside muffled and gloved.

Occasionally we light the path to the front door with garden torches – the wax kind that you stick in the ground on a cane and that look like fireworks. There are always one or two that will not stay alight, but they still look lovelier than any electrical alternative. I once went to a party with a marquee a walk away from the house and the route was lined with night lights in brown paper bags weighed down with sand. Magical. Bonfires are best in the dark for the light they create as much as for the heat, and if we have had one during the day I always stoke it up when I go out last thing for my nightly perambulation with the dogs just for the glow. Even the torch I use casts a whole new light on the garden and isolates things in a way that is impossible during the day. But best of all are the nights when a torch is not necessary and we can do the whole walk by moonlight.

For most people there is already too much ambient light from street lights, garages and shops. Even where I live, slap in the middle of the country, the night sky is stained with the horrible Agent Orange of a

supermarket on the edge of Leominster that leaves its vast car park brilliantly lit even when closed. Why? Despite this my clear night sky is filled with stars. Most people do not have that luxury.

I spent a good hour yesterday playing in the compost heap.

This kind of therapy depends upon all ingredients being to hand. To wit: some milky January sunshine, all the frosted vegetation cleared away after the mini ice age between Christmas and New Year, a dustbin full of kitchen waste, a bale of straw that got left out in the rain for a month, three barrow-loads of mushroom compost from the lorry-load delivered last September to counteract the acidity of all the Christmas tangerine peel in the kitchen waste, a pile of gritty sand that gets added to every time the paths are swept, all the cardboard from Christmas, a bucket of (old, very powdery) lime plaster and the contents of the chicken house. I just mix it all with a layering action, keeping the heap as box-like as possible. It works every time.

21 January 2001
Compost

22 January 2006
Peregrine
. . . .

This morning I got up, put the kettle on and wandered outside to see if the milk had been delivered, which means going down the garden path. As I tried not to slip on the frosty flags I felt the presence of something in the sky behind me, turned and saw a peregrine falcon flying over the house, beating bent-backed scimitar wings in that idiosyncratic muscular, direct manner. If you know anything at all about birds there are certain rules that always apply. One of them is that if there is any doubt then it isn't. When you see the real thing, you *know*. If you are unsure whether it is a buzzard or a golden eagle, it is always a buzzard.

So it is, in this part of the world at least, with peregrines. You see them with a thump of shocked recognition. For a breathless minute, one the fiercest and most feral of creatures on the planet beat straight above my primped garden, and until it had disappeared into a dancing mote in my eye, we alone shared the tentative dawn sky, the carefully edged path, the clipped yews, the family sleeping indoors, the everything known and unknown of that minute. Then it is gone and, with the pang of loss, a great flush of experience and excitement that lights up the rest of the day on into memory, and, if you have any shred of wonder about you, the rest of your life.

23 January 2004
Freedom
. . . .

It's a funny thing. I spent all of Christmas and new year chained to my desk finishing a book. I started every morning long before it got light, and some nights did not finish until after midnight. The only times I went outside were after breakfast to check the greenhouses and feed the chickens, and around 3.30 in the afternoon to do the same but in reverse. It is no sort of life. Yet each day was spent living in the garden inside my head, through the digital pictures on my computer screen, and from my gardening notebooks and diaries. In other words, although I did not do a single piece of gardening for weeks on end, I was experiencing the garden as intensely as I possibly could.

When you finish a book there is a sense of emptiness and a low that is countered by the exhilaration and freedom of having rid yourself of its shackles. Freedom! But freedom to do what exactly? The truth is that you are all used up and not good for much. So I have been pottering about, doing some desultory weeding and pruning, and wishing that someone would come and tidy up the resulting mess. No change there then.

Most of all I have been relishing these first few hours spent outside in the thin wintry sunshine. It has given me the chance to look at the garden in a gentle, relaxed kind of way rather than with the fixed focus of the writer. The snowdrops are coming into their own and ribboning the path of the spring garden, and the first hellebores are in flower. This is always an anxious few weeks for the hellebores. They look rather naked and inadequate without their leaves but are filling out daily. The primroses are coming too, much, much earlier than in my childhood thanks to global warming but not, according to my records, quite so early as last year. What could this mean? Nothing much, other than I at last have time to look at real flowers rather than just pictures or words about them.

I was quietly digging over the artichoke borders the other day, happy to be dealing with earth again, albeit feeling a little frozen-fingered, when amongst the odd yellow-rooted nettle and rash of creeping buttercup, I hit a writhing infestation of bindweed roots. I know every inch of this garden intimately but have absolutely no memory of bindweed in that spot, the artichoke side of the hornbeam hedge dividing the vegetable garden and this strip. But the evidence of the roots was unavoidable, yards of white, fleshy worms lurking under the surface and going down about eighteen inches into the ground. They ran for about ten yards, down the hedge, in amongst the hornbeam roots and filling a whole barrow by the time I had dug them out. Digging out an unforeseen stash of bindweed roots is a bit like squeezing a spot – there is a kind of ghastly satisfaction, but you wish that it had never been there in the first place. Bindweed, like couch grass or horseradish, will sprout from a tiny section of root left in the ground, so every scrap must be removed. This was tricky in the failing light and I bet there were bits I did not see.

24 January 1999
Bindweed

'It's brutal out there this morning,' Sarah said, and my spirits soared. For the past few days it has barely risen above minus 5, and the car won't start, and the heating in my workroom seems to have conked out, and I can hardly feel my fingers to type, but none of this can dampen my enthusiasm. Just to walk around outdoors on the rock-hard ground in my indoor shoes is a treat, and if I need warming up there is a huge pile of logs to be split.

There is nothing like a good hard dose of winter weather to keep the gardener happy. Not snow of course. Filthy stuff snow, albeit entertaining for an hour or so, but I view it as little more than solid flooding. We, like so many other people around the country, had real flooding over new year, and the ground has been impossible to get at.

25 January 2003
Cold

Wet, wet, wet. Even an empty wheelbarrow carves a rut an inch or so deep. The flood water, like snow, is beautiful in itself, and I am not such a heartless philistine that I don't appreciate it, but we are getting to that time of year when there are things to be done and the clock is ticking.

I am happy to let the garden sleep for most of December, knowing that little will suffer for being left until the new year. But the work I do get on with when the weather is cold at this time of year (and it is an indication of how global warming has pervaded our consciousness that cold weather should be remarkable in January or February) is winter pruning. This involves cutting back the late-summer growth of the espalier pears in the vegetable garden to their now established carbuncles of knobbly spurs and removing the worst of the ever-present canker; cutting the autumn raspberries to the ground; and pruning the standard apples in the orchard – but only to remove crossing or broken branches. By far the biggest job is pruning the pleached limes that run right round the vegetable garden. This can be cold work but there is something about the combination of crisp, clean air and the crisp, clean bite of secateurs on lime wood that is unmatched by any other pruning work, and which I find exhilarating. It takes about a week to complete, so I am hoping it will stay brutal out there for a while yet.

The other day my youngest son was taken to one side by one of his teachers. 'I was wondering, Tom,' he said, 'when is the best time to plant garlic?' 'Oh, about now,' said Tommy, aged nine and a quarter, and moved away before attention was drawn to his unpolished shoes, lack of cap or, for that matter, a week's worth of undone homework. It goes without saying that he hasn't a clue when one might plant garlic, but the teacher went away apparently satisfied. The merriment in the Don household at this story is heightened by the knowledge that I often find myself in the same position. I get mugged with a question as I'm crossing the road, buying a postcard or paying for a cup of coffee. The mugger is invariably friendly but has probably wound themselves up to put the question for a minute or two. In the time it takes to make enough connections to realise what is going on and to think vaguely about the question, all my fight-or-flight instincts kick in. Invariably my mind blanks. Invariably the answer is so simple as to fall inside any possible definition of common sense or so complex as to fall outside any sound bite. And occasionally, just occasionally, it is hard to care even a tiny bit. But, like Tom's mad teacher, people never want the right answer. A confident response, a smile and a hasty retreat fit the bill.

We have been digging up hedges – good, healthy hornbeam hedges but planted in the wrong place. There were four short hedges that divided the artichoke walk into two. Now it runs, unbroken, from one side of the garden to the other, which is one of those changes that has an inevitability when done. The artichokes and cardoons are mulched with straw as frost protection. Every day for the last week the hens have come and carefully scratched this away, exposing the plants to the cold. And every day I have replaced it, thinking murderously of roast chicken.

29 January 2000
Roast chicken

One of the necessary tasks for the book I have just completed was to go through all the old photos, diaries and notebooks I have kept about this garden since it began in November 1991. There was a whole shelf of notebooks and thousands of photos stuffed at random into cardboard boxes – yes, I know that it would have saved time and been better in every way to have carefully sorted them as they were developed and then stuck them into ordered and annotated scrapbooks. But you must be true to your nature. I am a stuffer and stacker, not a sorter and sticker.

30 January 2004
Memory

41

I reckon that I have a pretty good memory. I like to think that I can remember what I did and where I did it to the day. But this is vanity. I can't, and the photos and notes often contradicted my absolute certainties. So much for memory. Obviously the hard evidence helped trace what we did when in the making of this garden. Most of the pictures had been unlooked at for years – a dozen large cardboard boxes packed with random snaps is daunting at the best of times. So it was astonishing to face the fact that much of the garden had evolved in a jerky, almost disjointed fashion. I had planned the whole thing in my head years ago and had conveniently smoothed over all the snags and delays in executing this plan.

Take the lime walk. This is the avenue of pleached limes that leads from the house. It has tulips ('White Triumphator') flanking the brick path in spring, followed by white foxgloves and *Alchemilla mollis*. It seems like an institution. That is the way it is and has always been.

Yet I now know that I planted only half the limes back in April 1993. The biggest was no thicker than my arm. I bought another five to extend the avenue in 1996 and moved a lime from somewhere else in the garden to make the numbers even. And then in 1997 I added a final two. The hornbeam hedge that forms a wall up to the lowest level of pleaching was only planted in January 1995. The brick path was laid in the autumn of that year. The tulips were first planted in December 1999. The limes are pleached every winter and trimmed every July.

So this small section of the garden has actually been assembled, changed, adjusted and generally fiddled with pretty consistently over the past ten years. The idea that you can fix any part of a garden in time or even in place is doomed to fail. Nothing stays exactly as you want it to, and nothing is ever finished. That is the beauty of making a garden.

31 January 1999
Canals
....

It flooded again this week, water filling all the trenches that had been dug for hard paths. If I were doing this garden again, I would incorporate canals – which, after all, are no more than lined trenches and have a wonderfully calming, surreal presence. I think they are much more beautiful than any pond.

We potted up a new batch of lilies, all Asiatic hybrids, chosen for their various shades of orange. Lilies like a well-drained but coarse compost, so I mixed up a third horticultural grit, a third organic potting compost and a third sieved mushroom compost, which seemed to work last year. They get planted quite deep – with at least four inches from the top of the bulb to the surface of the compost – watered lightly and then put in a sheltered spot covered with fleece.

February

The first crocuses appear like timid bunches of grass or a green shaving brush. These are *Crocus tommasinianus* that Maureen gave us ten years ago and which I planted in the little circular bed around the hazel in the spring garden. It wasn't the 'spring' or any other kind of garden then, just a small area I dug over amongst the roots of the only tree in the entire garden. That circular bed is long gone, although the path still curves around its ghost.

I love my spring garden, which is really just two borders divided by a very narrow sinuous path, but the price we paid for it was the loss of the circular bed with the hazel in its centre and edged with woven hazel. Everyone liked that. The garden is layered with good things that were sacrificed for better things and, sometimes, irrevocably done away with for worse things. Maureen would bring us something from her garden almost every week, from a few bulbs to shrubs or a batch of cuttings, and each and every one was treasured. These are the very best plants to have in a garden, ones that have a personal meaning and provenance. That kind of identification with individual plants transforms a garden from a display into a life.

Spring always limbers up in this garden across the back yard through a door into a triangle of ground that we call, appropriately enough, the spring garden. A narrow path made out of all the odds and sods we had left over from building work snakes through it. All the rest is border. It is my favourite bit of the entire garden, but it has a very limited season, retiring into unvisited anonymity from July through to October. Perhaps this is why I savour every day of it from the middle of January, when the first snowdrops start to change from a mass of sharp points to reveal white dewdrops of flower and eventually the hanging white bells they are now.

Much of the planting is taken up with oriental hellebores – nothing fancy, just a mixed bag, many self-sown and varying from almost purple to almost white. The more precious Ballard Group are planted elsewhere, in the jewel garden, which is much more self-conscious and controlled. But I want the spring garden to appear effortless, as though a wood has just exploded softly into flower. In actual fact, it takes an awful lot of work, all of it squatting on my heels, going over each patch of ground literally inch by inch, all the time trying not to crush seedlings or shoots coming up. I have tulips and fritillaries in here, and crocuses round the big hazel that was here before we were, and Solomon's seal, pulmonarias, euphorbias and loads of aquilegias, which seed everywhere, not to mention the forget-me-nots. I have *Rosa hugonis* and *R.* 'Cantabrigiensis', and *Clematis alpina* and *Clematis cirrhosa* 'Freckles' (which always gets caught by the frost) – but this is all jumping the gun. For the moment it is enough to relish the snowdrops and first primroses and wait for the hellebores to have their day. But I don't have to wait for spring any more; I just go out the back door, through the door on to the funny path, and I am in the middle of it.

3 February 2001
Voles

My garden is like Gruyère cheese at the moment, riddled with holes. This is down to *Microtus agrestis*. Or is it *Clethrionomys glareolus*? It's hard to know. They both undermine everything I do in the garden. Literally. I am talking voles. The cats catch them by the dozen, bite their heads off and leave them on the path outside the front door. Owls love them. The other night I was startled by a huge hoot at what seemed to be my shoulder. The torchlight caught a tawny owl as it took off from a sweet pea tripod six feet away. But owls and cats cannot contain them. They should not be hard to catch as they hardly move more than a few yards from their base camp. All they do is eat and breed. They eat their own weight in dry food every week. And they can pass more than a thousand droppings a day. I suppose I should be grateful for the manure.

The very worst thing about voles is not the damage done to roots, not the fact that they nibble at bark and shoots causing death and destruction to beloved plants, not that the ground gives way beneath one's feet causing a twisted ankle. I can almost live with these things. The very worst things about voles is the reaction that they provoke in Poppy. Poppy is a Jack Russell terrier whose obsession in life is to dig out as many voles as she can. As often as she can.

Despite having legs the length of a half-smoked cigarette, the mere whiff of a vole turns her into a mini-JCB, excavating huge holes. If the vole damage is bad, the Poppy damage is horrendous. It is double-edged too, because not only do you have a bloody great pit where plants used to be but also a bloody great heap of soil where more plants used to be. It is sheer vandalism. But at least Poppy feels guilty when caught in the act of vole-digging and runs and hides behind a hedge whilst I roar my hatred for her. The voles, no doubt, merely laugh.

4 February 2002
Bulbels

What little spare time I have had over the past week has been spent crouching awkwardly, slowly shifting my weight so that I can reach just another three inches without having to move. Daintiness is not really

// The spring garden shines through February mist.

my forte. I can do robust and enthusiastic and sometimes careful, but poised grace and balance elude me. Weeding the spring garden has always been a tricky business, but it gets worse as the years accumulate. This is because the snowdrops have begun to spread appreciably and I have let the hellebores seed themselves indiscriminately, meaning that there is simply less room to put my feet to get at the weeds – which also have a knack of getting right in amongst everything.

This slice of garden is on the fringes of the flood plain, and even in the driest year it floods to a greater or lesser degree. This means that it has richer soil than the rest of the garden, a fine silty black loam that drains fast and *wants* to grow things. It is also replenished every year with the seeds of nettles, creeping buttercup and lesser celandine. Nettles are the least of my worries because they are so relatively clumsy in their attempts to colonise, but the lesser celandine is now a horror, with tiny leaflets appearing everywhere. Trying to get every bulbel out of the ground is impossible, so I shall smother them with a thick layer of mulch, although there is an element of hiding them under a carpet in this. Creeping buttercup is another major problem, but I have found that a trowel levered under it is sufficient to get it to release its grip. In the wetter, more clayey bits of the garden, it clings to the soil with roots that clutch like avaricious fingers.

One of the biggest invaders cannot be blamed on the flooding. It is the deadnettle, *Lamium maculatum*. This was carefully planted, by me, just a couple of years ago. Perhaps all ground-cover plants should have a big sticker saying, 'Be careful – this plant does precisely what it claims.' It didn't help that I planted them much closer together than I should, to try and speed up their ability to cover some ground. For the first year they are useless, and the second year little more than a token sprawl happens. But then they kick in, and before you know it your spring garden is hidden under a blanket of dead nettle. It has taken me hours and hours chasing each runner and digging out each set of roots, which completely resist being pulled up. The moral of the story is never to plant ground cover of any kind in a border. It never coexists with any satisfactory mix of plants. Better to use it as an end in itself or not at all.

Lately Sarah has been accusing me of becoming too linear and regimented in my gardening. Too many straight lines – of thought as much as of plants. This is a coded message whose subtext rings like a bell: Where is the poetry? And if there is no poetry, what is the point? Well, I am sure that the massed ranks of the horticultural trade, parks departments and

Catkins of the purple hazel, Corylus maxima 'Purpurea'. //

indeed most of the people who earn their livings from some aspect of gardening would have a snorted word or two to say about that, but for most amateur gardeners, it does not need elaboration because it is so tied up with the inarticulate pleasure of gardening.

Am I getting all straight-lined? Have I lost the ability to let things wend and weave as the spirit moves them – and me? Is it age, weariness, business? You need time to think, to let things happen at their own pace to do any decent work. Whether making a garden or writing anything that is not purely instructional, most of the best stuff is done when you are waiting, apparently not doing anything at all.

It all comes back to the cricket pitch. Names stick. The last ball bowled here was six years ago, before my shoulder got crocked and before cricket fell away from the rather clumsy father/son play matrix. (I was the one always grumbling about not having the time, always bestowing the game like a gift, and I am the one now who remembers those times with most pleasure and misses them much more than him. You always end up with what you deserve.) The cricket pitch got hedged in, and moles went berserk beneath it and reduced the regularly mown grass to a switchback ride. Last year we left just a mown strip down the middle and let two long 'beds' on either side grow into long grass. They were bright yellow for a week with buttercups and the grasses all had violet heads for another week in June. The plan was to fill them this autumn with bulbs – species tulips perhaps – but it is wet, heavy ground. Anyway, nothing was done. Other plans have included digging the grass beds and using them for dahlias or pumpkins; the latest involves topiary hawthorn and low, very thick hawthorn blocks – a bit like mini agricultural hedges. I like this last notion and want to do it sometime – but it is all a bit clipped and straight. A bit effable when the ineffable is so much more interesting.

Perhaps I should just leave it. Let it do its thing. Influence a little but not control. For the first year the grass would just grow long. Thistles and docks and creeping buttercup would flourish. By late summer the grass would be looking tussocky and unglamorous compared to the billowing meadow of midsummer. The second year, a few hawthorn and elder seedlings would appear and a few brambles might creep in. These would grow year on year, and a stray oak, cherry, hazel, ash or field maple seedling could well pop up too, protected from the rabbits by the brambles. It would look much like a railway siding with the brambles, elders and hawthorns doing best and the more 'interesting' trees seemingly suffocated by the untrammelled growth. Not so. The 'wasteland' of brambles, elder and buddleia is the modern version of the pre-Romantic wilderness – something to be tidied or tamed at every opportunity – but in fact it is a vital stage in the development of woodland, providing shelter for slower-growing trees, which in turn will shade them out. So if I left this strip – about the size of many an urban back garden – it would become a little wood. In five years the grass would scarcely be visible, in ten the elders and hawthorns would be small trees, and in thirty the oaks, ashes, field maples, etc. would be well established. In a hundred years most people would not know that it had not always been here.

I won't do that. It feels too much like an academic exercise. But it would be an interesting one, not least because the end result would be dominated by indigenous plants in a way that hardly any garden ever is. Most gardens are like those restaurants that cover a dozen cuisines, filled with an eclectic and at best an idiosyncratic mix of plants from all over the globe.

Thank God for a sustained piece of dry weather. Having taken out fifty metres of hornbeam hedging to expand the jewel garden, which is rapidly colonising half the plot, we have been preparing the ground for planting. Gareth has dug out the nettles that were entwined in amongst the roots of the species roses, which in itself would have been impossible if it had been wet. We spread four tons of sharp sand over the wettest piece, but that amount goes a surprisingly little way once it is spread. I am a great fan of sharp sand, although I know that the official line is that it is too insubstantial to do much good and disappears into the general mix of the soil within a few years. Only horticultural grit will do the job apparently. Well, if it is a small area or you are very wealthy I would agree wholeheartedly, but for those of us with largish expanses of heavy clay soil, horticultural grit at a price in excess of £5 for a small bag is prohibitive. Sharp sand works very well in the short term, and is very cheap and easy to barrow about. We also spread thirty-odd barrow-loads of mushroom compost, rotted down so that it was a cross between molasses and soot. Most significant of all, the 'we' consisted of myself and my two sons, Adam and Tom.

I guess that there is a stage in childhood when 'helping' crosses the line from childcare to real assistance. That line was nonchalantly hurdled. The three of us did the job at least twice as fast as I could have done it alone, and it was much more fun. This – and I realise that I am exposing my inadequacies as a father here – is a milestone for me. Gardening has until now been something that I have done either despite

the children or knowing that half the time I am wilfully choosing to spend time in the garden rather than with them. There is nearly always conflict, albeit often internal. To integrate things successfully, even for a couple of hours, is wonderful. I think that they quite enjoyed it too.

7 February 2004
Weather
· ·

One of the things I like best about British weather is its locality. This has nothing to do with climate, which takes in great swathes of land and knows no national boundaries. I am talking about the physical manifestation of weather which changes from parish to parish. The other day I drove my son to the local train station and a blizzard appeared out of the grey morning sky. I had just listened to the weather forecast where rain was assured everywhere, some showery and some heavy, but snow was not even mentioned. That will put a cat amongst the pigeons, I thought – motorways seizing up, trains abandoned, and egg on all the weathermen's faces. By the time I got the three miles home the countryside was white and the air thick with snowflakes. Sarah was setting off in the opposite direction with more children to different

// Aconites shut tight in the snow.

schools and I almost put a shovel in the back of the Land Rover for her. But when she got home she said that there was not a trace of it just a few miles away from us. Later that day I had a visit from someone who had crossed the country and said they had been through lots of rain, some showery and some heavy, but that this pocket of snow was unique. In fact it started to melt within an hour or so, and for the rest of the day the ground was sodden – although we had not had a drop of rain.

I suppose for the gardener the only weather that counts is what is actually happening on or above your own plot. Over the years I have learnt that every garden has its own reliable weather system. It might have been a freakish batch of snow we got the other day but I bet if I went over my records I could have predicted it from the signs and reactions of plants. Even within a modest-sized garden there are distinct meteorological zones. There is a patch in the jewel garden where two paths cross that always gets the first touch of frost of an evening. I walk it every night in the dark and on a chilly evening the grass either side will still be soft, but just for those few square yards it will be crisp and frosted. There is another frost line further up the garden which you can literally step over. One side is frosty and the other still above freezing. Spooky.

The snowdrops are in their prime and the hellebores are nakedly appearing, heads down and leafless. But the best thing in the garden happened before I got up. At 6.45 a.m. the light began to open up, and a robin and then a wren sang modestly for fifteen minutes and then were quiet. Not much. Hardly a dawn chorus. But I got the message. Gently, quietly, stepping over rain and ice, springtime is coming in.

8 February 2001
Dawn

I recently bought a new chainsaw and have christened it with a dramatic pruning of the large hazel that provides the nucleus of our spring garden. As a rule I am a very enthusiastic pruner, trusting in the regenerative powers of most shrubs and the added stimulus that a good hard cut back provides. This tree defines and shapes the whole of that piece of garden and is certainly the oldest plant we have. So over-enthusiasm with the chainsaw could have ruined everything. As a rule I treat this hazel almost exactly the opposite to a normal coppice one. I cut off all new growth and nurture the old, hoping for a kind of sculpted shade. The problem is that both shade and branches had increased to the point where everything beneath was overwhelmed. A woodland garden is always a matter of juggling the demands of light

9 February 2003
Chainsaw

and shade of the various plants that live there – in this case, and at this time of year, predominantly hellebores, snowdrops, pulmonarias, euphorbias and emerging daffodils and tulips. But no garden ever remains static. You have to cut back in order to maintain the effect you have patiently waited for. It is a hard lesson.

10 February 2002
Shadows

I got up for a pee at 2.30 the other morning and was entranced by the shapes that the topiary yew cones and their shadows made in the bright, frosty moonlight. A breeze rippled the dark like a river and the silvery monochrome stripped away everything but shape from the yews. Twenty-six cones, each different but for that moment each perfect and each with its shadow like an echo. This was an image that I had never imagined when I planted them nine years ago. But how many absolutely clear, frosty days are there a year when there is also a full moon? One? Two? And how often are you likely to be up at 2.30 in the morning to enjoy them? It felt like a door had opened and shown me a parallel garden in another dimension.

11 February 2000
Dogiculture

The dogs think that this garden exists solely for their benefit. Red is deeply in love with a yellow tennis ball (an emotion transferable to any tennis ball as long as it is yellow), and the paths serve only to act as runways for her to gallop down to fetch it. This involves me throwing it. I do this unthinkingly as I garden. Anyone watching will therefore see me, weeding, digging, planting, even mowing, stopping every minute or so to hurl a yellow, disgustingly slobbery object with a large, clumsy dog in hot pursuit. I have learnt to protect the garden by becoming extremely accurate at throwing down the dead centre of the paths – without breaking horticultural stride. I am proud of this sporting feat. Poppy contributes to the exercise by attacking Red as she sets off. The ensuing fracas is harmless to dogs but usually does for a few plants in the mêlée.

Even I, obsessive dog lover, occasionally get fed up with this. We then have a strict few days. No tennis balls. No rampant destruction. No careless animals. No fun. I am the first to waver. I adore my garden but love it most when it is full of the leaping, bouncing life that animals (we have various cats as well) and children add to it.

// *Barry Anne posing in his best collar.*

Some years ago I bought a batch of fifty lime trees in a tree auction. There were two sizes, pretty big (fifteen feet) and small (four feet). The big ones were planted in an avenue. Over the years I have pleached them, pruning them hard at this time of year so that they grow in an entirely lateral framework. I love this annual job. It signals the first stages of spring. Lime wood is sweetly resistant to the secateurs so the cuts are clean and authoritative. More importantly they grow furiously fast from a mere bud on the trunk, so any slip will be recovered within a year or so.

The little limes were planted out but without the same conviction. I had a rough idea that I wanted the same pleached effect right round the kitchen garden, but six years ago the trees seemed years and years away from making that. Now their time has come. We have put up a framework of hazel bean sticks lashed together, supported by eight-foot posts firmly in the ground, right round the four sides of the kitchen garden, twenty metres by twenty metres. This alone makes a huge visual difference. The limes must now be pruned and tied into these supports. This first prune takes a lot of ruthlessness with the knife because it means cutting off some of the best branches and putting faith in weedy little shoots. But I know that it will work.

Then I realised that we should put a similar pleached framework round the jewel garden too, thus making two boxes, one filled with veg and the other with flowers, the two divided by the pathway of artichokes and cardoons. This will be structurally very strong – almost barmily so – but exciting. In fact, the framework round the jewel garden is half done, but we have run out of hazel and are waiting for Big Mike, who is a woodman by day and a nightclub bouncer by night, to make his delivery. So, we have moved seven limes that were in the 'wrong' place and will buy another seven to complete the planting. God! I have wasted so much time moving plants from A to B in this garden! But you have to gnaw away at it until it is right.

Mike delivered the hazel for making low woven fences in the kitchen garden, the twelve-foot rods tied up in bundles of ten with orange baler twine, now stacked against the barn. This gives me more pleasure than I can express. I first bought hazel sticks off Mike seven years ago and must have had thousands off him by now, all cut by him from the same wood with the same billhook. Each time he delivers I show him round and he comments on how things have changed since he last came. Each time he brings his son. He was a babe in arms then but is seven now and looks just like his dad. Buying hazel off anyone else wouldn't seem right. All this is an important part of the garden.

Today Sarah gave me two dozen red rose bushes (twelve *R. moyesii* and twelve 'Scharlachglut', both with flowers as scarlet as arterial blood) but also, as a kind of supplement, three plants each of ten different types of species rose. I loved the thought of the bloody two dozen but the species roses are the things that best feed my hungry horticultural heart. This present came bare-root and hot-foot from the nursery, bony, spiny bundles tied together with string sticking out of used fertiliser sacks. It was rather like receiving a tired and emotional porcupine.

Once heeled in alongside the leeks, my species roses stuck out of the soil like ten bare posies. There was *R. hugonis*, just a bunch of brown twigs; *R.* 'Cantabrigiensis', stems covered with baby bristles and the occasional vicious thorn; and *R. sericea pteracantha*, a curiously drab brown all over, giving no hint of the glorious red fins that its thorns are to become, catching the light like a medieval stained-glass window. *R. willmottiae* has weird and beautiful thorns when bunched all together, each zigzagging away from the one above and below, making a graceful geometric pattern. *R. moschata* and *R.* 'Complicata' are both green-stemmed, even in the heart of winter, but *R. californica* 'Plena' is orange, *R.* x *wintoniensis* red and *R.* 'Nan of Painswick' a deep alizarin. Finally there was *R. pimpinellifolia* 'Double Yellow', so prickly that it was almost bristly. These roses used to be called *R. spinosissima*, which more accurately describes their appearance. Unless you are an expert, only *R. sericea pteracantha* instantly gives itself away for what it is in this raw, unfledged state.

These were a gift, remember, so I did not choose them. To have an influx of unasked-for plants on this scale transforms things. Species roses are tough and easily grown and should last for at least twenty-five years. They will reach 'maturity' in three or four years, but will flower this summer and go on increasing in size for perhaps ten years, all becoming substantial shrubs. So they will make a lasting difference to this place, just as a new wall or staircase would indoors.

There is no reason why species roses should not be mingled carelessly with other plants just like any other shrub rose, but I shall plant most of these all together on the edge of the bit that is called the wild garden. It is actually rather a tame garden at the moment, but a bit of spiky, sprawling, lax habit might make it wilder.

Overleaf. The jewel garden closed for winter. Waiting. //

Today is Sarah's birthday and one of the key dates in our gardening calendar. It is the day that we start our serious seed sowing. I have already been sowing bits and pieces, but more out of frustration than from any real horticultural wisdom. Over the years I have learnt that almost anything sown after 15 February will catch up anything sown before that date and will be healthier for the extra light the seedlings get. Of course this all depends on having a greenhouse and cold frames. Apart from onion sets and broad beans I do not consider sowing outside in a normal year (the sort of year when one does not mow the grass in January) until April. The soil will not have warmed up before then, however mild the odd spell might be.

But before I sow any seeds, the first thing that I do on 15 February is to go outside and pick Sarah a little posy of flowers.

We mulched the borders early this year. Convention has the best time to mulch as early spring, when the soil is moist and starting to warm up, but I ignore this. For a start, all our borders are full of tulips that are too thickly planted to mulch around. If you mulch over them when they are an inch or so tall you do no harm, but more than that and they get flattened. Also I suspect that mulching on cold, even icy, ground does no harm at all. Yes, it is bound to slow down the warming of the soil but only by a day or so. In fact mulching in frosty weather has the huge advantage of having hard ground to push barrows over without making an incredible mess. It takes two ten-ton loads of mushroom compost to mulch our borders and that amounts to an awful lot of barrow-loads, each one wearing a muddy rut in the grass if it is wet.

Mushroom compost does the job very well but is getting increasingly expensive – at least the delivery of it is, which has always cost more than the stuff itself. Garden compost would be best of all but we do not make nearly enough and I cannot see how it is possible for a normal garden to create enough good compost for a mulch over all bare soil two to three inches thick. So I reserve our own compost to use on our edible plants. We do use some cocoa shells every year which are especially good at lightening heavy soil, creating a unique fluffy texture as they slowly rot down.

In the end it matters less what you mulch with than that you mulch at all. It is probably the single most effective job of the year. Organic material will feed the soil, but that is only part of the reason for mulching. Crushed bark, compost, manure, fresh straw, grass clippings, gravel – they will all help keep weeds down and moisture in and

Mushroom compost ready for spreading as mulch in the jewel garden. //

improve the structure of the soil. The only rules to follow are: Never put less than two inches, and never put it on to dry ground. Other than that, anything goes.

17 February 2003
Earth

I think about ghosts a lot. They all live underground. When I was a child I knew that both my great-grandfather and grandfather walked beneath the walnut tree. They were a friendly, gentle presence. This garden too is filled with the people who have cultivated this tiny, particular piece of land, out of sight but as real to me as the pieces of pottery and footings of buildings I scratch against three feet down in the vegetable garden. It is as though the whole landscape is peopled like the buried Chinese armies.

It matters that we are buried in earth, part seed, part compost. From the bones and memories there is the residue of a life force that endures. Soil is land and redolent of place and identity. We are all products of the soil that grew us, our minds filled with ghosts of particular plants and trees and moulded landscape, all dependent on the particular local details of the soil. I remember reading that when the poet Edward Thomas was asked why he was enlisting in the First World War, despite being much too old to be conscripted, he answered by scooping up a handful of earth and saying, 'For this.'

When I dig I am aware that the soil is alive in every way. It is like dough, like air. To treat it with anything other than reverence is mere ignorance, although we are all astonishingly ignorant of life underground, knowing just enough to realise that there is an unimaginable amount that we do not know. Science has hardly begun to scratch the surface, yet I have read that one teaspoon of soil can contain a billion microscopic organisms of more than ten thousand different species. The figures are literally astronomical. We idly muse about life 'out there', but what about the busy subterranean galaxies? What about life down there?

18 February 2002
Flood

As I write this the dawn is lifting to reveal floods right across the landscape. It is like living on the edge of a huge lake. I have not been outside yet but I can see from up here in my workroom that it is a big flood but not a bad flood. How do I know this? Because the water is still a couple of feet short of the path from the lime walk into the vegetable garden. I know that if the flood stays short of that one brick path then it will do no harm.

// Regular floods lap against, and often into, the garden.

Mind you, there is a fair bit of water in the garden. The damp garden is completely submerged – but the ligularias and hostas will love that. Half the spring garden is awash – not so good – and you could swim in the gateway (it is a puddled pool rather than an entrance) into the orchard. Tom, my youngest son, probably will, before the day is out. The broad path from the bottom of the lime walk up to the jewel garden is a canal. It looks lovely but will be a slimy, muddy mess when the water goes.

The point is that I garden on a flood plain. The river is just a hundred yards away and it floods at least twice a year. This is part of the natural rhythm of the landscape and has been so from time immemorial. To try and fight that in any way would be both daft and unsatisfactory. It is not an enemy or a disaster. Much better to try and absorb it somehow into the garden. So the damp garden houses plants that need a really good soak – sometimes for months at a time. The brick paths are effectively flood platforms like the wooden walkways the Venetians use.

19 February 2005
Morning

At this time of year I am woken by birdsong and irresistibly drawn out of bed. I chuck some clothes on, make a quick cup of tea, and then go straight out to the potting shed. It is usually still dark although the light is creeping up from behind the eastern horizon. I don't have long because the children have to be got up ready for school and the household kicks into action around seven, but there are usually about forty-five minutes when I can potter, listening to the radio.

Now, clearly a potting shed is one of the great luxuries of life and every time that I walk into mine, which was a stable housing a very handsome mare until a few years ago, I am aware of that privilege. I have kitted it out exactly as I want it, with two good-sized bays, one for a seed mix and the other for potting compost. Pots and seed trays are stored in racks by size and shape, and there is another bench with card index systems for the seeds. Underneath the bench are large containers for sieved leaf mould, sharp sand, garden compost, molehills and coir.

In my morning sessions I sow seeds, prick out seedlings and mix up compost. The key to these jobs – as with so much in gardening – is little and often. If you just prick out one tray of seedlings or sow one packet of seeds in plugs, it is amazing how it all adds up over the weeks, and that time of morning is ideal for the kind of gentle, quiet concentration that it needs. I am not the most nimble-fingered of people – basically I have hands like hams – but even so I get huge pleasure from handling a tiny seedling and giving it the best possible start in life. I am also passionate about my compost mixes. I constantly try out commercial organic mixes – and some are very good indeed – but in general prefer my own combination of sieved compost, leaf mould, soil and sharp sand. It costs nothing, provides young plants with the right balance and, crucially to my mind, starts the roots off in the same soil and micro-environment that they will be planted out into.

Neglect

I was talking to someone last night about that magical moment when gardens seem to teeter on the edge of collapse or anarchy. Sometimes this stage can last for years but it often is just a matter of weeks or months while things progress inexorably into collapse. Trying to encourage and foster that sense of growing away from the garden and the hand of the gardener is, I think, an essential part of the gardener's skills. The best gardens always seem to have a sense of bunched energy as though their constraints are only partly to do with daily management, and underneath the veneer of order every hedge is ready to become a thicket, every lawn a meadow, and the rose neatly trained against the brickwork will emerge from that straitjacket to become a window-lashing, untrammelled monster.

I have found that with my own garden there is a clear progression that can be monitored at different times of year. Between October and March almost total neglect can be sorted out completely in a weekend. Between April and October harsh experience has shown that two weeks of neglect improve the place enormously, making it shaggier, softer and generally more interesting, rather like a face that has accumulated its age with dignity and not succumbed to the horrendous conceits of Botox and all the various nips and tucks that vain flesh seems increasingly to indulge in.

Pleaching

I have sixty-seven lime trees in my garden, all *Tilia platyphyllos* and all save one pleached to within an inch of their lives. Well, not exactly, as, touch wood, all are robustly healthy, but they are annually reduced to just a clean trunk with three parallel, horizontal branches growing off each side. Everything else is systematically removed. Of these limes, about half are 'Rubra', with plum-coloured shoots, and half are 'Aurea', whose new growth is lime green tipped with bright orange. Both are as ornamental as any dogwood or willow and, being carried high up on their pleached framework, can look spectacular, especially against a dark winter's sky.

But the time has come to remove every last trace of this lovely growth. We all mark our calendar by garden jobs and this is one that is best done in January and February. It is cold work but something that can be done in dribs and drabs, even in snow and ice, and, all things being equal, I should have it done.

'Pleaching' comes from the French word *plessier*, to weave, and it is an inexact art. You simply weave branches together. I was never taught to do it, but just used my common sense and gained a bit of experience along the way. Limes are by no means the only trees that can be pleached, but lend themselves to it because their new growth is very vigorous, soft and sappy so can easily be bent without snapping. This is now my tenth year of pleaching and the only thing that I regret is that I was not fiercer with the trees in their early stages. There is a great temptation to have branches on the diagonal as well as the horizontal and to encourage existing strong growth, even if it is not really where you want it. I have learnt that it is better to be ruthless and remove everything except for three shoots or, if necessary, buds, in the right place and let them grow into position, because they will do this far quicker than you might think.

I trained my branches along hazel bean sticks because that is what I had to hand; bamboo would do as well and be a lot straighter. But in a funny way I rather like my bent and wonky lines and knobbly trees. They have a character of their own that is in high definition for a month or so early in the year, but by June all will be hidden under the cloak of the enormous leaves that such hard pruning produces.

22 February 1999
Deadline

I feel guilty. I have done absolutely no gardening this week at all. I had a book to complete and worked on it all my waking hours to meet the deadline. But Gareth, who is working for us in the garden, has been digging and every three hours I mooch out and look at him and the great wads of soil he is shifting. This makes me confused. I love what he is doing and love the way that he is doing it properly, double-digging large new borders in what was the herb garden and is to be the bouncing garden. Eight tons of mushroom compost are being worked in, and the new beds are raised nearly three feet above the level of the lawn we made last autumn. But I should be doing this. I almost begrudge Gareth the physicality of it, even though it is a fantastic help and he is doing it as well as I could. It is like paying someone to eat your dinner. Odd.

I have promised myself the job of levelling it all and planting the beds up as a reward for finishing the book but experience tells me that

Looking out to the yard with the spring garden beyond the brick wall. //

I will feel useless and unmotivated for a few days. This is to be our private area for eating and playing – the trampoline will go there (hence the 'bouncing garden') – and I shall plant the roses moved last autumn, cardoons, hollyhocks, bronze fennel, sweet peas – all the soft colours that are excluded from the jewel garden. There is a good day coming up when Sarah and I will plant everything which is now standing out in pots. I long for it.

23 February 2004
Bees

I gave Sarah a beehive for her birthday. The bees are yet to arrive because we have not yet got our act together (a refrain that has run through almost every aspect of our lives) but the hive itself is a beautiful thing, a W.B.C. type which is an intricate packaging of trays within a cedar outer box. I have wanted to keep bees for years. The absence of them feels like a lack, although the garden is full of wild bees in the summer. Keeping bees is, like keeping chickens and ducks, the domestic link between farming and gardening that brings out the best in both. The bees will improve the garden, improve your state of mind and provide delicious honey. Seems like a good deal to me. This is nothing to do with a rural idyll. In fact it is probably easier to keep bees in a town than in the country. When we lived in Hackney a man in our street produced huge quantities of excellent honey from his bees that foraged exclusively in inner-city gardens. Ironically, they probably had much richer pollen sources than the average bee living in a contemporary agri-landscape.

I have dealt with animals all my life and my instincts were to get some bees and learn as I went along, but all the advice that I have had suggested that it would be best to do a course in beekeeping at a local college to become familiar with the theory. Hence Sarah is taking them on as I simply do not have time to attend regular classes. Then apparently it is important to find a local beekeeper to guide you through the first year or so until you are familiar and confident with the procedures as well as your bees. This is at the heart of it. Bees have personalities, and every swarm is different. It is hard to think of insects as being sensate beings, but bees show every sign of a subtle, ordered existence that demands at least respect if not wonder.

24 February 2001
Danger

The rhubarb is coming along nicely, pink spikes with delicate lime-green fern-curls of leaf giving no hint of the monsters they are to become. Monsters in more ways than one, because rhubarb leaves are very poisonous. I recall being told as a small child – somewhat bizarrely –

that on no account was I to let the dogs eat the growing rhubarb as it would surely kill them. Many an anxious hour was spent guarding the rhubarb against canine nibbling.

It is not just rhubarb. The garden can be a dangerous place. There are any number of ways to die in pain, and a lot of them happen in the garden. Forty years ago, in pre-strimmer days, my father left his thumb attached to the rest of his hand only by a piece of skin when cutting a bank with a rip-hook. Determined to uphold family tradition, I cut the top of my left index finger off with my secateurs. One of my less pleasant memories but at least I lived to type the tale. The other day a local man fell off a stepladder on to his secateurs, cut his jugular and bled to death. A hideous story but true.

Eat yew and you get ill. Eat laburnum and you get iller, eat deadly nightshade and ... you don't feel very good at all. One can carry this potential of toxicity too far. I have seen labels on bags of daffodil and tulip bulbs in garden centres warning against the noxious effects of eating the bulbs. As if anyone stupid enough to munch their way through a string bag of daffodils does not deserve all the noxious effects

The annual accumulation of winter debris outside the potting shed. //

going. Nevertheless, on a bad day the garden can seem like a nightmare on the roam, waiting to turn that careless moment into horror.

But this is as nothing. Because nothing heals better than the garden. Nothing puts you together again, mind and body, faster than a few days in the thin, early spring sun. Nothing recharges, invigorates or refreshes like fifteen minutes engrossed in soil and leaf and flower.

25 February 2006
Birdsong

The hens are laying again. In fact they started about a month ago, but they are really popping them out now. Putting your hand into the clean straw of a nesting box and taking hold of the smooth, warm, eggy pebble is best of all. That they taste – really properly taste (and this can only be measured by how little bought eggs seem to taste of anything) – is clearly essential. The manure is a useful addition to the compost heap too. In short, they span the garden and kitchen as easily as carrots or the hazel trees (whose catkins are exceptionally vivid and early this year).

The hens are not alone. All the birds are at it. The dawn chorus in February is not as loud or as air-fillingly broad as it is in April, but it is almost unbearably thrilling, starting as a thin reed of sound in the dark which is gradually picked up by individual birds across the garden and fields until it weaves together into an hour of song. You can probably download it for all I know and listen to it on your iPod as you hustle to work with different titles for every day of the year. But it will no more be the real thing without the dark, cold air with that faintest promise of spring (yes, you can smell spring) and a slither of light on the horizon than a pack of supermarket factory eggs are the real thing. The dusk chorus is spectacular at this time of year too, building to a peak in about six weeks' time. It then dies away while the dawn song continues well into summer. I often just stand in the garden at dusk at this time of year and let the sound wash around me. It is as proper a way to garden as anything else that I know.

26 February 2005
Sweet peas

I sowed our sweet peas the other day. Three to a three-inch pot filled with an extra-strong mix of home-made compost but with plenty of sharp sand added so that they drain. It is quite a production line but one of those jobs that marks the season for us.

We used to do this in autumn and you will often be advised that it is best to make an October sowing, but I think that this is a counsel of perfection and does not work best for us. We grow quite a lot of sweet peas – more than sixty wigwams of them, each made of six bean sticks and each bean stick planted with three plants grown together in one pot. So that makes nearly a thousand plants in over three hundred pots. We did not set out to grow so many – it sort of crept up on us. We wanted some in the jewel garden growing up wigwams at strategic points – and because the layout is symmetrical it meant that it was hard to do less than twelve groups to make the rhythmic effect we wanted, and the twelve easily enlarged to double that amount. The jewel garden being a place only for bright and intense colours, it meant that we wanted the lovely whites like 'Cream Southbourne' to go in the walled garden, which is planted entirely in soft pastels and whites. For balance there have to be at least six wigwams there. Then we decided that the long walk would be great for sweet peas and to make that look good it would need another thirty-six wigwams. Megalomania, you see. That is what gardening is for – indulging fantasies of taking over the world and smothering it in sweet peas.

Anyway, all these seedlings take up a lot of space. We used to put them in the greenhouse to germinate and then they overwintered in cold frames. But after a year of that we had to choose between building more cold frames and delaying sowing till spring. No contest. We waited. Even so there is always a period when we have completely run out of room and yet dare not risk putting out the plants because we often get very sharp frosts well into May. The plants get very bushy and strong and, especially if sown in autumn, pot-bound.

I am increasingly thinking that it is worth risking it and planting out in April, having first hardened the plants off well. Come to think of it, logic says that the best thing to do would be to sow the seeds direct in March and bypass the whole potting procedure altogether, maybe sowing just enough backup to infill any failed germination or depredations by the local mouse population.

We are coming to the time of year when the season concertinas and distorts beyond any intelligent guesswork. That, of course, is the joy of it. Years of experience and a jaundiced eye cannot dim the sheer excitement and surprise of the garden opening out into spring. The primroses round my dog Beaufort's grave are flowering in great clumps, tossing and shrugging in the wind. Tom and I planted them after we buried him there, a year ago today. I want this area to be a coppice, but at the moment it is mainly mud with dozens of smallish hazels and a few standard trees. It is heavily planted with bluebells, foxgloves, primroses and violets, but as yet these are barely noticeable. Last year's primroses shine brightest.

27 February 2000
Places

Overleaf. A vole's-eye view of the spring garden. //

71

This business of making places obsesses me. It is certainly at the core of everything I find interesting about gardening. You set out to 'make' a diminutive coppice in a garden but, *pace* garden makeover programmes, it doesn't just happen. Time is an essential part of the mix. Even the time spent not being the place is an important part of becoming the place. It wouldn't work if somehow you could magic it overnight. Faith and a little skill – mainly exercised in knowing what to leave alone – enable you to persevere with the notion of what this space is allotted for. Then one day, quite by surprise, it is there. It is like sunshine breaking through the mist. I know that this is going to happen, but because I don't know when, it remains a desperately exciting and compulsively attractive mystery.

28 February 1999
Visitors
....

Planning out the vegetable garden the other day I suddenly had a wheeze. It would be good to make a long avenue of three-metre-wide beds at the far end of the garden filled with pumpkins and squashes for this autumn. I can see it now, the ground covered by their great trailing leaves and the orange globes sitting there like golden dinosaur eggs. But at the moment these beds-to-be are rough orchard grass, and the job of lifting that all off, let alone of digging it all, requires more time than I possibly have to spare. We cannot spray with glysophate because we are now completely committed to an organic regime. So this week we mowed it (even though it was a frosty morning), collected up the sodden grass and then covered it all with black polythene. It looks horrible. But I hope that this will stop the weeds from growing and when the ground warms up I will rotovate it every couple of weeks until the beginning of June, which is when we plant the squashes out. The idea is to let the weeds germinate and to weaken them by constantly knocking them back. I suppose another option would be to plant through the polythene, but I think that would look bad.

We had American friends over to stay this week and they, of course, are much more familiar with growing squashes and pumpkins than we are. They suggested planting gourds down the avenue and training them over temporary arches. It could look great. Having visitors always puts you on your mettle and I predictably found myself apologising for the garden as they looked round on a completely grey, muddy and dank day. It is a bad habit. It reeks of false modesty and a kind of horticultural competitiveness. We went and looked at two or three other gardens with them, which was an eccentric thing to do in February, but interesting. It means that you look at the garden rather than at flowers, which is actually what most people do when garden-visiting.

March

I've just come back from Morocco, which was heavenly. Never been there before, but for a dose of winter sunshine it was perfect. We visited Jardin Majorelle, Yves Saint Laurent's garden in Marrakech, which popped up in theme-park form at Chelsea a few years ago and was memorable primarily for its Yves Klein-blue paintwork. The real thing was equally dominated by this extraordinarily intense colour but with the huge difference that it shone out under the equally intense, if different, blue of the cloudless sky. Bright paint usually fails in British gardens because of the grey sky rather than any conceptual fault.

Jardin Majorelle was interesting but disappointing. At least that is what I was busy convincing myself until I remembered that it was February. If someone snottily dismissed this garden after a February visit, I would be tempted to ram the entire thing, plant by feeble February plant, down their gullets. So I shall go back in April (oh I wish) before casting judgement.

The best day of the short holiday was spent lying by a pool in hot sun, the snow on the Atlas Mountains rising up on the horizon, planning out this year's vegetable garden. I should have done it earlier, but in truth I have been all over the shop this winter, so it was left undone. Juggling the twenty-four beds so that the succession is healthy and the right things get the most sunshine, and so that it looks good, is a kind of Chinese puzzle I love playing with. For a day my lovely vegetable garden was bathed in Moroccan sun and I lived every seed, every harvest. And now that is in my notebook and – most things being equal – it will happen. It is a year charted out as surely and – for me – as enticingly as a long voyage.

For the past ten years I have been living in a false paradise. I have learnt to live with the largest slug and snail population in the Western world. I cope with the mountains of soil that are excavated every day by my resident moles, although they have sorely tested my sense of humour. But I count myself lucky. It could be worse. As I drive down the lane rabbits scatter in every direction, and when I go for a walk with the dogs they pop up like a computer game. But despite my garden being surrounded by fields, I have never seen a single rabbit in it nor a trace of their activity. I had assumed that this was because on three sides we are surrounded by a flood plain which, for obvious reasons, is not a place where rabbits burrow. I had not reckoned that they have been spending the past ten years working out how to get at all the juicy rabbit food in this garden and have finally cracked it.

The first sighting of trouble was just after Christmas, when I noticed that half a dozen apple trees had been gnawed. I wrapped chicken wire around the trunks which, I thought, should deter them. But yesterday morning I went and opened the tunnel and found a whacking great burrow in the middle of one of the raised beds. The equivalent of a rabbit JCB had gone under the edge, picked the spot where he could do most damage and tried to set up home. To add insult to injury, he had not even deigned to nibble at my mibuna, corn salad or endive as he excavated. He will be back, no doubt, but every cloud has a silver lining because, dear bunny, I am not in the least bit squeamish and I love rabbit pie.

3 March 2002
Clematis

I have kept a garden journal for the past ten years or so. There are plenty of days when I have nothing to enter beyond the weather. But it is surprising how the record builds up, day by day like a huge jigsaw, describing the relationship between me and my garden. However, its main function is to record what comes into flower or fruit when, and to monitor what I sow and plant. You think you will remember these things but you never do. And whilst the garden journal might be banal, it does not lie.

Anyway, to my surprise I see that on 1 March 1998 I planted the *Clematis montana* in the coppice. I thought that it had been there for ages, but there it is in black ink before me: 'Planted *Clematis montana* "Liliaceae" in coppice to scramble through hawthorn.' (I also, it says, double-dug raised bed and moved ten gooseberry bushes, and weeded and dug greenhouse border *and* dug two beds in veg garden. But I was younger then.) In four years the clematis has not only become established to the point of swamping the hawthorn tree – which is large as hawthorns go – but has become even more established as a fixture in the garden. It feels as though it has always been there. The flowering of this particular clematis is one of the seasonal markers – just as is the wonderful spring blue of *Clematis alpina* 'Frances Rivis' in the spring garden, and the incredible mass of flowers on the two *C. viticella* 'Purpurea Plena Elegans' in the jewel garden. They make a clematis calendar. There are a dozen other such markers throughout the year. I suppose the real moral of this is that if you plant something in the right place and have just a little patience, it is amazing how quickly it becomes part of the landscape.

Just to show that I am both honest *and* lazy, the next day, exactly four years ago, reads, 'Mild. Grey. Only went outside to feed the chickens.'

The wind smashed four of the cold frames and some glass in the greenhouse. The cold frames are my fault because I ordered perspex, thinking that it was safer for the children, without realising how brittle it is. They were a breakage waiting to happen. I am hopeless at fixing that kind of thing. I look at the damage and am filled with an overwhelming sense of incompetence. I get exactly the same feeling when any of the garden machinery breaks down. I know Real Men can fix these kind of things, but I can't and I ain't. It will stay broken for weeks, whilst I promise myself that this time I will fix it, until I get someone else to do it for me. This ritual is constantly played out with most things that are not to do with plants, soil or wood in the garden. I can make things, but I cannot make things work.

4 March 2000
Repairs

We cut the grass for the first time the other day. It felt slightly premature – like opening Christmas presents on 23 December – but is such a mainline hit of pleasure. A couple of passes with the mower and you are through a door straight into spring. I even like the hot smell of the engine in the early March sun.

5 March 2001
Mowing

Looking down across the herb garden, box balls and vegetable garden. //

I have just counted twenty-seven cowslips in flower. Things are out of kilter, although I suppose it is us who are most out of synch, not the plants. They are merely responding to a potent cocktail of daylight and temperature whereas we refuse to make the tiny adjustment necessary to shift into spring mode a few weeks earlier, even though we have been watching the effects of global warming all around us for at least five years. My daughter has just walked in with a thick bunch of violets, smelling like love-hearts. (You don't know what love-hearts are? That betrays a deprived childhood.) The violets are flowering as profligately as bluebells. This seems to me as luxurious as champagne and caviar or linen sheets changed every day. These are not dog violets (*Viola riviniana*) but scented sweet violets (*V. odorata*), which like a slightly more open position. This, I suspect, is why they are so happy at the moment. When the hazels they are planted under grow bigger, they might find life slightly less perfect until we coppice the hazels back.

I moved about a dozen thalictrums from one part of the jewel garden to another, mainly because they had been planted too close to the edge. I had to take out a section of box hedging to do this and dig really deep to lever out all the bright yellow roots. These thalictrums are really a wetland wild flower, but they have established very happily in the border and are now planted in amongst the grasses of the slightly looser section of the jewel garden. Most of our work in there at the moment is rearranging furniture of this kind, and it is the perfect time of year to be doing it.

This morning I was getting dressed when I saw a ten-ton lorry parked patiently outside the house. It had the look of a lorry that had been there a while. Extraordinary how such a lump could creep silently down the lane without rousing the sleeping house. Maybe the cargo – ten tons of mushroom compost for mulching – softened the approach.

It was tipped alongside the previous load that came a few days ago, and a final delivery will take its place when we have made space by shifting this lot. Thirty tons of black, fungal-fragrant manure to lay as a blanket over the soil, every bit shovelled into a barrow, wheeled to the relevant spot in the garden and then spread, mostly shovel by shovel so as not to damage the emerging plants. The area covered is roughly half an acre of borders, of which two-thirds is occupied by plants. Let's call it eight hundred square yards spread with a layer two inches thick. This is approximately forty tons of mulch – four lorry-loads. It takes us about ten man-days of solid eight-hour graft to do it. Each load costs £205,

// The spring garden path was made from our building debris.

which works out at a little over a pound for every square yard mulched and probably as much again to handle it.

Why go to such expense and labour? Is it worth it? As far as one can measure these things (and I am not by nature a measurer – I like guesses and hunches and rules of thumb and eye – it is why most science is a mystery to me) I think it is probably the best single investment of time and money that anyone could put into their garden.

9 March 2003
Poison
. . . .

One of our walls and the hedge outside the kitchen window is filled with woody nightshade, or *Solanum dulcamara*. This sprawling cousin of the potato and tomato has rather pretty little purple flowers and scarlet berries which are extremely bitter. It is often called 'deadly nightshade' whereas in fact its intense bitterness is unpleasant rather than harmful. Not so the 'real' deadly nightshade (*Atropa bella-donna*), which is a less woody herbaceous perennial. It was spread round Britain by the Romans, who especially valued the cosmetic side-effects of its powerful poison. The plant synthesises atropine (hence its name) and even greater quantities of hyoscyamine, which are quickly absorbed into the bloodstream if ingested and, amongst other symptoms, make the pupils dilate, which is why Roman women made eyedrops of the stuff, in order that they might become big-eyed beautiful ladies. The danger, of course, was that you became big-eyed dead or very sick ladies.

We have clumps of hemlock (*Conium maculatum*) growing in our orchard, looking like clumps of huge cow parsley. It famously did for Socrates. Its most obvious quality, other than its stately size and the purple splodges on its stems, is that it smells as rank as a dirty mouse cage. Culpeper recommended a cold poultice of the leaves 'applied to the priveties' to cure lustful thoughts – presumably as an antidote to nightshade-soaked eyes.

You don't have to be remotely exotic or obscure to be exposed to the dangers of the garden. A hearty portion of spinach accompanied by an equal measure of chard followed by treble helpings of rhubarb would load you with so much oxalic acid that you would be very sorry for yourself indeed. The leaves of rhubarb have a much higher concentration than the stalks, which is why they, and not the rest of the plant, are regarded as poisonous. I once just brushed my bare stomach on a rue bush whilst I was bending over it and as a result had a line of really deep burns that caused blisters which took months to heal and scarring that lasted for over a year – even though I was only vaguely aware of the initial contact. Since then I have deported rue from the garden. I don't like the smell either.

I have just been on the best holiday I have ever had. The weather was fantastic, with blazing sun during the day – although never uncomfortably hot. Then at night the temperature dropped so we could sit by a huge wood fire with a drink after a good meal. The food, by the way, was exactly as I like it, home-cooked and organic with the best seasonal ingredients. Although it was very relaxed, there was masses to do and I took more exercise than I have done for months – all of it outdoors too. All in all I feel great, and everyone says that I look better than I have done for ages.

Where was this wonderful place? Well, it was about as exclusive as you can get, but it cost me nothing. Totally free. I took my holiday outside in the garden. I told everyone that I was going away and never once answered the phone or checked my email. Every morning I got up, took the children to school, had a leisurely breakfast, and then Sarah and I went outside and stayed outside until it got dark. Never less than eight hours' hard graft a day. By evening I could just about stagger to a bath. It was heaven. The weather was miraculous – the best March sun I can remember in nearly half a century. We got loads done – completely making and planting a new section of the garden and working round other jobs that press for attention at this time of year. I cut the grass, finished the pruning and the mulching, weeded, sowed seeds and pricked out seedlings.

It could be argued that this was the least imaginative choice of holiday possible – after all, I do this kind of thing all year round. But for fifty weeks of the year I am always in a hurry. There is always something that must be done that I don't get round to doing. Invariably the garden is the first to suffer under this regime. Things get put aside, abandoned or bodged. So to spend a week doing what I love best in the world – gardening – with the person I love most in the world – Sarah – in the place I love most in the world – my home – in my favourite season – spring – in the sunshine is the nearest I can get to pure happiness.

I was in the top greenhouse the other day, planting out rocket seedlings. The wind was rattling and shaking the glass, which had about half a dozen loose or cracked panes, but it was warm and calm inside. So when I heard a crack I did not immediately look up. When I did, I saw that a large diamond-shaped section of glass was sticking into the ground a couple of feet from where my bent head had just been. If it had happened a minute or two later it could have damaged one of the rocket seedlings...

As I write this the north wind is buffeting this hop kiln with extraordinary force, shaking the entire building and testing my sangfroid more than a fractured greenhouse. Light is blowing across the sky and these windows with extraordinary shifts of intensity, flurrying from a full glare to twilight sombreness. Everything, but everything, is moving. Outside, the garden is flexing and twisting in communal, orchestrated undulations yet seems remarkably untouched. But there is evidence that the wind's long-lasting effects will only become apparent in months, even years.

We only get north or east winds here perhaps two weeks of the year, around the end of March and early April. This is enough to send all the fruit trees on the edge of the orchard growing hysterically southwards, the branches permanently streaming away from the north as though frozen in a windy blast. You see this on cliff tops, of course, but somehow you expect it there. The reason for it is not that the branches are being blown into permanent posture by the force of the wind, but that the new growth is being effectively pruned by it. The soft tissue of the new growth simply stops growing, whereas the shelter of the tree itself, however small, is enough to protect the branches on the other side from being damaged and they grow away vigorously. Hence the lopsidedness is not a case of extra growth in one direction but of an absence of growth in the other. The winds of today will add to this and will be noticeable long after I have forgotten about them.

12 March 2005
Snow!
. . . .

The combination of a few lovely early spring days and global warming tends to make the British gardener cocky. Well, I speak for myself. I get overconfident and overexcited. The garden and a long spring beckon like a siren and I start sowing and planting like mad.

I am writing this wrapped in two jerseys and a scarf with a blizzard making the lovely view from my window into a white smudge. For the last couple of days we have been going through a blast of arctic weather with snow and shrivelling northerly winds.

Only someone totally out of love with life could not enjoy this to some extent. Snow is always beautiful, and it doesn't hurt to have the lesson rammed home that the weather can never be taken for granted. It is, I suppose, the greatest single temptation for the gardener to try and kick-start the garden into action as soon as possible in spring. But, as any old-timer will tell you with a knowing smile borne of hard experience, you cannot cheat the weather. What you lose in spring you will gain at the back end.

// *Yellow bamboo, Phyllostachys aurea, weighed down by snow.*

In Herefordshire, where the soil is mostly a rich clay loam, it can easily be the second week of May before anything can be sown outside because the ground is just not dry or warm enough before then. In my childhood in Hampshire we would always sow carrots, parsnips, radishes, spinach, peas and broad beans by mid-March, but here, a hundred miles north on sticky ground, you can add a month to that – if you are lucky. A couple of years ago I did not get my potatoes into the ground before the end of the first week in June, but I still got a decent crop from them by the beginning of October. The best crop of carrots that I have so far grown was the result of getting behind and not preparing the intended plot for them to grow in. I cleared my spring cabbage at the end of May and then it poured with rain and I got busy and the weeks slipped past. Eventually, in the second week of July I sowed the carrots. They never had a hint of fly and lasted in the ground perfectly happily until the following April. Just holding back a bit can often be the fastest way forward.

Shoulder

The low woven fences that surround the raised beds in the vegetable garden were inspired by the wattle and daub of the house and pictures of Tudor gardens. I made them myself and am proud of them and I like the way they look. However, now they need replacing and I have a problem. It is mainly to do with shoulders. My shoulder became almost completely useless a couple of years ago but has been patiently reassembled over the past months through a regime of intense exercise and physiotherapy. It now does me pretty well, but it knows its limitations, especially when it comes to the banging in of posts. I have bought a hundred chestnut posts, each four feet long, of which three feet have to be hammered into the ground at eighteen-inch intervals to form the uprights through which hazel rods are threaded to make the low fences. These are only a foot high but there is a tremendous strain put on the posts, and unless they are in the ground absolutely securely (and in a dead straight line) they bend or snap. Each post takes about ten blows with a twenty-pound sledgehammer at maximum effort. That is twenty thousand pounds of force borne by the shoulder of the hammerer.

In the past I have loved this job, relishing the way in which the whippy hazel, cut whilst green, binds to form such a rigid, strong structure in amongst the otherwise soft leafiness of the vegetables. But the absence of a post-worthy shoulder has forced my hand. Age has caught up with me. So I shall replace the fences with oak boards and box hedges. I have calculated that there are 175 metres of hedging to be grown,

Pots waiting to be washed outside the potting shed. //

which amounts to 525 plants to be raised. To buy them, even wholesale as year-old rooted cuttings, would cost the best part of £1,500, and if I were to get them retail as reasonably sized plants I could quadruple that. Six thousand quid! Actually if I had the money to spare I would consider it well spent, but I don't, so home-grown cuttings it will be.

19 March 2005
Coppice

I have always felt that the best gardens aspired to coppice and that the best woods have all the elements of the very best gardens. Certainly I would exchange my own garden for ten acres of hazel coppice, but as that is not currently on offer I have done the next best thing and made a miniature version on this plot. It is an area of about twenty metres by twenty which I have filled with hazel, a few ash, some alder, a couple of cherries and an old hawthorn that was the only plant growing on the spot when I started. The hazel has all been grown from self-sown seedlings from the big old tree growing just outside our back door. The squirrels take the nuts and drop them, and they pop up amongst the hellebores and pulmonarias. Hazel coppice is traditionally increased by layering, which it does very easily, but the seedlings were free so I potted them all up, let them grow a bit and then planted out seventy or so.

That was seven years ago. The pathetically small seedlings have now become fifteen tall thickets growing above a carpet of primroses, violets, wood anemones, narcissi and bluebells. Every night for the past month a song thrush has challenged the world in melody from the same perch right at its heart. It is private and beautiful and quite my favourite part of the garden.

So yesterday I started to cut it all down. Tom asked me if I was sad to see it all go, but I had waited nearly fifty years for the moment when I could cut my own coppice coup and it was every bit as good and rewarding as I had hoped. It was no more sad than cutting the long grass in the orchard is sad, or cutting asparagus sprues in May. It is a harvest, and I shall waste none of it. The straight lengths, or rods, will be used as bean sticks and supporting framework for the pleached limes and espaliered fruit trees (so much nicer than bamboo or wires), and the brushwood for pea sticks and supporting herbaceous plants. The odd knobble of wood will go on the fire in the house.

This cycle of harvest every seven years or so can continue without modification for at least five hundred years with the same plants. Working it is to play a tiny part in a river of time. Treating such woodland with anything other than respect is contemptible.

// *The first harvest of hazel bean sticks from the coppice.*

The process of cutting and preparing the wood was a treat. I experimented with various billhooks but found a small but very sharp axe to be best. I thought of using a chainsaw, and I guess if I had weeks and weeks of cutting to do I would but, in line with my resolution to use the minimum of mechanised kit, I stuck with the axe. It is work that is both easy and satisfyingly hot and tiring. It mocks the gym. It is quiet and yet the thwack of steel into wood is an important part of the experience. It is dramatic, generating surprising amounts of fallen wood, yet steady and contained. In short, it is one of those things that raises the quality of life.

20 March 2004
Dry border
. . . .

Over the past month we have been developing a new piece of the garden. For the past ten years it has been part of the yard in front of the barns and has been where all the building materials have been stored, where the mushroom compost gets delivered and where extra cars get parked. But slowly we have been clearing it and are left with a space with capabilities for horticultural improvement of perhaps seven metres wide and fifteen metres long. This was all covered with a layer of tarmac which was easy to lift with a pick and shovel. Then we put a brick-edged flag path through the middle leading from the courtyard, leaving a border three by fifteen metres backed by south- and west-facing walls and its mirror in front of north- and west-facing walls. Both were almost solid stone – some of which appeared to be the remnants of earlier buildings so were left untouched. There was no soil. These are hardly ideal growing conditions, but we added about three inches of topsoil and a couple of inches of compost was spread over that and mixed well in. The result is a layer just deep enough to bury the roots of most plants. Below that is not even subsoil but free-draining stone. So anything that we plant has to either have very shallow roots or thrive in poor soil.

One of the joys of a mature garden is that it is full of plants in the wrong place, doing OK-ish but longing to be moved to a situation where their talents might shine more brightly. Last autumn we lifted all our sedums because they were growing too floppy and spilling into anarchy before we were able to appreciate them. They had been heeled into our nursery beds without any real alternative home, so it was obvious that this was the ideal place for them. On poor soil they are short and strong and their flowers hold themselves upright. On our normal soil they grow until mid-May and then, top-heavy, keel over and have to be supported for the rest of the year.

We have various clumps of *Stachys byzantina* growing in our walled garden that, in truth, seem completely contented, but I did not let that get in the way of digging them up and transplanting them to the more spartan environment of the new garden. Their soft, silky leaves are designed to retain moisture, so this will be a chance for them to fulfil their evolutionary destiny – and be decorative in the process. I put in half a dozen white-flowering rosemarys near the edge of the path so that the trailing hand can brush their aromatic flanks, and some thyme at their feet to keep the Mediterranean theme going. I also planted a clump of lemon balm as an experiment. Elsewhere in the garden it is an invasive weed, but I figured that the conditions might restrict it sufficiently. We shall see.

We grow *Euphorbia griffithii* and *E. palustris* in our garden with ease, but *E. characias* has never thrived. Now is its chance. There were two *E. c.* subsp. *wulfenii* tucked away, and I transplanted them. They resented this and have flopped badly but will come good I hope. I will add *E. cyparissias* and move some *E. polychroma* and *E. amygdaloides* var. *robbiae*, both from the spring garden where they like the dry shade.

Bronze fennel seeds itself all over the place in this garden and I dug up a barrow-load of roots to transplant, although a dozen or so were enough. They actually do not transplant very readily, so I shall sow seeds as a backup. The giant fennel, *Ferula communis*, is growing well in the jewel garden and in theory would love this new rough, barren spot, but I think the taproot would have a job getting through the stone. Perhaps I will buy one small, plant it and let it try and take hold.

I moved a couple of melianthus that have struggled through our winters for years. They are now in full sun and my reasoning is that the sparseness of the soil will make them tougher and less sappy and therefore better able to cope with the cold. I suspect that this may be wishful thinking. The same brand of doubt accompanied the planting of the cardoons – not regarding their hardiness but because their great roots will need more space in which to grow. Never mind. It is an experiment, and we have more than enough cardoons to spare.

Finally I planted a fig against the sunny west-facing wall and a honeysuckle, *Lonicera caprifolium*, against the north wall in a pocket of soil amongst all the stone. I am wondering whether to grow a wisteria or rose against the south wall alongside the 'Conference' pear I put in last year. I think it might well be a white wisteria.

At this point I had filled up a surprising amount of the available space. I shall add cerinthe, gaura, nasturtiums, geraniums, eryngium and crambe and sprinkle various poppy seeds and still not have to order a single plant. Will it all be healthy? Will it look good?

21 March 1999
Equinox
....

Today is the best day of the year. There is no other calendar day that is such a cast-iron, sure-fire cert to raise the spirits. Christmas and birthdays pale into anticlimactic insignificance. It doesn't matter what the weather is like or what actually happens, the gift of an extra hour's light at the end of the day is a prize beyond price. Today stands like a see-saw in the calendar, balanced exactly on the fulcrum of night and day, and then tomorrow gently tips towards the light, spilling the days down into sunshine.

If you want to garden or just be outside (which for me is half the point of gardening) there is now a real chance to do it after work. Next week the clocks go back and there will be a man-made extra hour of daylight. But even without it, evening belongs to the day from now on, and the sensation of it expanding and unfolding over the coming months is exhilarating. In the garden evening light is usually the best of the day, and the range of pleasure to be had from colour, scent and particularly birdsong is dramatic.

And we have shifted a season. Plant growth is more likely to be triggered by light than heat, and research increasingly shows that many plants have amazingly accurate clocks or genetic memory of the calendar. It doesn't matter if there is snow outside your window, plants will be busily growing in response to the lengthening days. Amazing.

23 March 2003
Chicory
....

It certainly feels like spring, and is starting to look like spring too, with the hedges peeking new leaves daily and the spring flowers now at their early best. Despite all this, the vegetable garden is playing hard to get. In fact one of the common misconceptions about growing vegetables is that there is a spring harvest that runs parallel to the floral one and somehow matches it in abundance. There isn't. It doesn't.

It is too early for any new outdoor vegetables other than rhubarb and sorrel – neither of which really qualifies as a vegetable at all, the former playing the role of a fruit and the latter a herb, although in fact rhubarb stalks are as much a vegetable as celery, and sorrel, which adds such a sharp lemony edge to fresh spring eggs, is simply a herbaceous perennial.

The truth is that March, April and most of May are months of doing and waiting with almost nothing to show for it. At the moment we have lots of soil, some in weathered clods ready for the final cultivation before sowing, a few beds teased into a fine tilth but pummelled by rain, and an embarrassing number of my thirty-two separate vegetable beds unattended since the last crop was cleared. Yes, the garlic that I put in absurdly late (in February) is up, and yes, there are still leeks and cabbages and (rather unexpectedly) celeriac, but all struggling on beyond the call of duty. However, there is an astonishingly bright flare of colour and productivity from two beds where there are rows of red leaves bursting up as though they had been fired like rockets from way below the ground to explode out into the light. They come from the chicory 'Red Treviso' which, all winter, supplied us with crimson, slightly bitter leaves that perfectly complemented the rather blander tastes and textures of the various winter lettuces that I grow under cover.

We have had and are having quite a lot of cold weather. We have had perhaps a dozen nights below minus 5 and one when it dropped down to minus 14. Inevitably there is a gardening price to pay for this. We have lost a couple of bay trees, some artichokes, an agapanthus, four melianthus, and all our broccoli, cabbages and cavolo nero (but not the kale or Brussels sprouts) and no doubt more casualties will be revealed as the growing season unfolds.

24 March 2001
Clematis

Certainly the *Clematis cirrhosa* 'Freckles' is a goner. Maureen gave it to me for my birthday about five years ago and I treasured it. This was not just because it was a present and I thought of Maureen with pleasure every time I looked at it, which I did, but because it was so bloody difficult to get established. I planted it in the southern lee of a hawthorn with loads of compost, bone meal and good technique. It was a quarter-century of clematis planting gathered into flawless ritual. The clematis repaid this in the first year or so by merely not dying. It then grudgingly grew a foot or so before succumbing to the first spring frost (as ever, it is the frosts of March and April that do the damage). It did finally take off and grew up to the top of the hawthorn, covered in delicate bronzed leaves although it never produced a single flower. But last year it was covered in yellow flower-bells although I had to squint up into the sky to see most of them, tangled up in amongst the black spikes and incipient buds of the tree. And now it is as dead as last year's unpruned viticella, and all the squinting in the world will not conjure any flowers in the sky.

Is anything in gardening quite so satisfying as the first cut of the grass on a sudden, hot March day? It is like taking a tramp and giving them a bath, meal and clean clothes. The person remains the same but everybody feels better about it. That tired, stubbly shagginess of winter is instantly replaced by definition. And the scent of new-mown grass at this time of

25 March 2000
Hope

93

year is as intoxicating as the headiest lily. Bottle it and you would put all antidepressant merchants out of business overnight.

Some years ago Sarah and I were staying with the first of our friends to have a child. I suppose he must have been just over a year old. In the morning we heard this call from his bedroom: 'It's day! It's day!' Ever since then we have used it as a kind of mantra to remind ourselves of the wonder of a beautiful morning or a call to arms. The child in question is now a strapping man who worked for us on our farm last summer and, ironically, found it difficult to get up for an early start ...

Well, at this time of year I am chanting a constant, euphoric 'It's day! It's day!' Last Tuesday was the vernal equinox and this morning the clock acknowledged this tipping towards the light and gave us an extra hour of daylight in the evening. For all but the most resolutely matitudinal gardeners this makes all the difference in the world. It is, at last, day.

Hurray, Easter is here (and a fine pagan celebration is due if Christianity does not fit the bill). It was shockingly dark at 6.30 this morning, but it will be deliciously, luxuriously light at 6.30 this evening, and a spring and summer of long, light days stretch out ahead. The Continent has its café society and the evening *passeggiata*, Americans pile off to mountains and deserts, but we take to our gardens, private, utterly domestic and yet part of the outdoors that we all inevitably share. The back garden is our great outdoors.

I shall be finishing off the revamping of the fruit garden. Actually it is not so much revamping as recycling. The story is typical of the way that Sarah and I garden. Three years ago I made an overspill vegetable plot. This was a series of raised beds hedged by hawthorn. The idea was that it would free the main vegetable garden to be increasingly ornamental. But the hedges have grown fast and are now six feet tall all round and, however hard I trim them back, about three feet wide. You get spiked in the backside every time you stoop to cut a lettuce. Then we decided that we were growing far too many vegetables. Why have this overspill bit at all? Then, by the by, Sarah said that she wanted a wood between the raised beds and our boundary. Who wouldn't? Unfortunately the site is taken and, much as a wood would have been good, it is now all but impossible. It is where we grow our soft fruit and there is a greenhouse and the nursery bed and it is where the compost and leaf mould are made.

One of the three paths that run the complete length of the garden. //

You can guess the rest. We are making a wood. So the process of moving said soft fruit, compost, greenhouse, etc. has begun. The serendipity is that the raised beds are ideal for the fruit. Now that the bushes have all been moved (quite a job – some are six years old with roots like small trees) it makes a good *place* – the combinations of the small plot with thick, high hedges and the raised beds in their utilitarian orderliness with the bushes arrayed along them like flower arrangements on a show bench are very pleasing.

I have planted strawberries along the south-facing sides of the beds, but there is no room for the raspberries. They will have to remain where they are until they are engulfed by the circling woodland. Actually, brushing through the undergrowth to collect a basket of raspberries is a beautiful thought.

So the core of the new fruit garden is made up of red and white currants, gooseberries and blackcurrants. It is a woody dream of a summer pudding.

28 March 1999
Heaven

I pruned our pleached limes last week, cutting them right back to the three-tier framework and reducing the width to the thickness of the branches. I love this annual job because it is a real admission of spring. The brick path is knee deep in prunings by the time I finish, and the trees look as radically denuded as a clipped poodle, but I know that they will grow back with a vengeance.

The river overflowed again last week, washing into the garden and confirming to us that our intention of making a bog garden down at the boundary nearest the river is viable. Global warming is making us change our plans and we might as well use these warm, wet winters and springs to grow plants that like it. It also means that we shall have to drain the path near there. I have bought a long yellow coil of perforated pipe, so next week I shall dig a trench and put it in on a layer of hardcore. This will then drain out into the boggy bit, making it boggier yet.

I love these late spring evenings in the garden more than any other time of year. Work to do outside and the wherewithal to do it. Heaven.

April

I have noticed that outside is not where people work any more. It is where we play. I'm being disingenuous as ever, writing comfy and smug under the canopy of a hop kiln, the perfect paradigm of modern rural life – the writer hacking out words that can earn ten times what the grind of agri- or horticulture can ever generate from the same buildings or space.

Yet we should all get out more and relax less. Decent hurting labour involving weather and dirt and the odd ache and strain does more good than the same time in a bright, airless gym. Throw in something immeasurable like a flower raised from seed or a shaft of sunlight changing the whole world just as you have given up on it for the day and you get health *and* salvation.

It is Easter. It is always like this at Easter for gardeners. A bit battered but on the up. You take stock. And not before time. The truth is that it doesn't take much. There are little clumps of violets in the garden that fill all the spaces worn away by winter. A tree full of blossom is personal – a private audience. A cup of coffee outside in real sun while the thrush takes on all comers in song from the ash tree is better than any five-star food eaten indoors. Only a lover or the laughter of children can equal the warmth of thin April sunshine.

I went to a tree nursery the other day to buy some yew and hornbeam hedging. Britain has a wonderful network of small nurseries whose work is largely unsung and, I suspect, mostly undervalued by the general public. We have all become accustomed to shopping for plants at garden centres and whilst they can be enjoyable places to visit, they inevitably have a limited range and their prices are always higher than direct from any nursery. Nurserymen will also be able to advise you in much greater depth about their own plants than the best-informed sales assistant at a garden centre. Anyway, after I had got my few dozen hornbeams and yews and was nosing around, I was very taken with some purple-leafed hazels. They were big, well-structured shrubs – too big in fact to fit into the back of the Land Rover – but very reasonably priced, so I ordered four of them.

I know exactly where I want to plant them. We try and use various purple-leafed shrubs in our larger borders because they work as an excellent foil for richer-coloured flowers. I remember seeing a marvellous purple hazel at the back of a border at Kiftsgate Court in Gloucestershire that had been coppiced so the leaves were much larger than normal, and I realised that purple foliage could work in this way. So we planted purple hazel, *Corylus maxima* 'Purpurea', purple elder,

Sambucus nigra 'Guincho Purple' and the smoke bush, *Cotinus coggygria* 'Velvet Cloak'. But, mysteriously, they and subsequent replacements failed to thrive. Eventually we concluded that this was due to competition for light from the intensely vigorous annuals such as opium poppies and purple orache growing all around them. The young shrubs are intensely sensitive to low light levels and suffer badly. It is, of course, a vicious circle. Because they are not getting enough light they grow very slowly and because they are growing slowly they remain shaded out for longer. But when dug up and put somewhere sunny in a pot they recover quite quickly. I am hoping that the purple hazels I have ordered, which are already five feet tall with strong stems, should be vigorous enough to push out into the sun and provide the perfect backdrop for all the vivid reds, blues and oranges around them.

3 April 1999
Sweet peas

All the sweet peas are in the ground now, and the tripods that they are to climb up are all in position ready for them. This makes a huge difference to the way that the entire garden looks, adding height and rhythmic structure after the slow reduction of winter. My experience is that however carefully they are handled, they will stop growing for a few weeks whilst they get used to the move from the pots that they have been in all winter. Then they will start to grow strongly at about the end of the month.

4 April 2002
Growth

Every day the garden seems to be making itself anew. I remember that when I lived in London, I would rush home at the end of the day at this time of year just to see how much everything had changed. Most people thought I was barmy, but any gardener would understand this.

Now I work at home it is less dramatic, but not always. I have just taken a walk around the garden, fed the chickens, watered the tunnel, taken no less than six keel slugs away from the poor little *Angelica gigas* plants that are being eaten to death, and moved the *Cosmos bipinnatus* 'Purity' seedlings out of the sun, putting the sunflower 'Velvet Queen' in its place so that it can bask in the glass-amplified April heat. It is the sort of mid-afternoon round I do before writing anything to lock my mind into a proper horticultural shape. Nothing unusual about it at all, except that I swear that everything has grown an inch since this morning. The pear blossom – 'Black Worcester' in the orchard and espaliered 'Doyenné du Comice' in the vegetable garden – has opened since lunchtime, and the tulip 'Queen of Sheba' is now all fully out.

// *The jewel garden just about to explode into spring.*

5 April 1999
Shapes

I have completed planting all our soft fruit, with the currants the last to go in. Every year at this time I seem to be in this kind of rush to get things into the ground that should have been planted in autumn. I suppose that the rush is in my head and it really does not matter. I am inordinately proud of the new soft-fruit area and take myself down there at any opportunity to look at the shapes the bushes and cordoned fruit make. This business of shapes and the spaces between shapes and the shapes that spaces make increasingly delights. I am sure that it is the central secret of a good garden. A shape we must make is the fruit cage, which is sitting ready to go up before the birds take all the buds.

6 April 1998
'Taihaku'

I have just seen the most beautiful flowering tree in my life. It was a cherry, *Prunus* 'Taihaku', with a short trunk from which spread half a dozen strong branches growing out at forty-five degrees to span an area of perhaps thirty feet across. From these hung spindly branches sprung like kinetic sculpture, and on the end of each one was a bundle of huge white blossom, hanging like delicate explosions caught and

// The new leaves of the pleached limes hang like green raindrops.

frozen in mid-air. There was not a leaf on the tree, just thousands of white flowers set against a stony white sky. When I was a child we had a large Japanese cherry which, although I last saw it twenty years ago, I reckon must have been *Prunus* 'Kanzan'. I have not seen it in flower for over thirty-five years because I was sent away to school at seven, and it always flowered in early May, whilst I was away. But I can clearly remember the thick pink puffiness of the tree in full blossom, the flowers exactly the colour of Wall's strawberry ice cream. I can see it now, looking up through the branches at blue sky hustled with clouds and the first petals drifting to the ground. When I got home in mid-May each year, the yard would be littered with the brown remnants of flower and the tree reverted to modesty. No one thinks that children mind these things. They do.

Cherries are sky flowers really. The trees exist only to hold the blossoms up in the air, and to elaborate on their form is an unnecessary embellishment. Of course this imposes constraints on your life. To have the sublime pleasure of putting your head in the flower-clouds you must be around when they flower. The imperatives of work, school or other pleasures must come second and your life must be organised around their flowering calendar. How un-modern and un-businesslike! But how good.

Gardening is one of the few domestic activities that force you to work within the rhythm of the seasons and the natural annual cycle. In the main this means slowing down and being responsive to the actual pace of things rather than hustling about like a demented estate agent. It means being conversant with largely alien concepts such as the emergence of spring, weather, rainfall or the soil that you live on. I like the hippiedom of this and consider it like a dose of moral syrup of figs: it clears the crap.

But the other side of gardening that I also love is the way that, short of building a house, one can make something on a bigger scale than anywhere else. As well as a spiritual clean-out, the making is a game and, goddammit, such a good one. I always feel that this is an aspect of gardening that is never celebrated enough.

When starting out on a garden, all the conventionally sensible advice preaches patience and a steady accumulation of growth towards maturity over a period of years, if not decades.

There is certainly pleasure in seeing things grow and gradually assume the hints and forms of the objects we want them to become. But

7 April 1997
Trees

the emergence is only tolerated because of the reward of that anticipated end. The bits of my own garden that I like best are those that most nearly look finished. They look more real than the rest. It just so happens that all these bits feature trees that I bought already big four years ago. It was at a sale at this time of year, and they were all going so cheap that I couldn't resist them, even though it was late in the season for tree planting and I didn't really have the time to deal with them. But clearly it was worth it. Putting in a large tree is an event rather than one waiting to happen in the unimaginable future. It instantly transforms a garden in the way that a large statue does.

8 April 2005
Blossom

'Taihaku' is showing off, producing blossom to out-flower even the most floriferous plum and sweet cherry. The espaliered pears are competing hard if only by virtue of numbers. The bullace, having come into flower three weeks ago, is drifting gently to the ground, having all but done its stuff for the year. You cannot overdo the blossom. Here to a blossomy infinity would not be too far. When I was a child I remember seeing Samuel Palmer's paintings of blossom in Shoreham with the flowers like snow or an overflowing washing machine. I always felt that the magic of pear blossom was the most powerful. Apple blossom often feels as though it is about to happen or is going over, because the leaves are much more fully formed and can submerge the flowers. (Although Palmer's apple blossom is insanely, wonderfully bounteous. Horticulturally wrong but telling the exact truth about blossom as a perception.)

Like the damsons, bullaces and plums, pear blossom is always dainty. The flowers crowd into the branches but somehow politely so, not jostling but sharing the air. They are always pure white and carried whilst the leaves are only just beginning to open. In fact the first flowers arrive on completely bare branches, and the last are frilled with the green of the emerging leaves. Around this part of the world there are still a few perry orchards with huge pear trees, hundreds of years old and as big as beeches, and when they are in flower on a blue-skied day it is a marvel to rank with the best of the large magnolias, tulip trees or any flowering, growing thing on this earth. Mature orchards are being bulldozed daily to conform to CAP subsidy requirements. We should be subsidising blossom, not industrial food and poisoned landscapes. It is insane.

Quince flowers are the best, the very best of all blossom. The flowers, some varieties pure white, others the candiest of all pinks, do not appear

// 'Taihaku' blossom against blue sky. Worth waiting all year for.

until well into May, when the tree is fully clothed in leaf, with short stems so the petals appear to be sitting on top of the downy leaves like a bird on its nest. As the bud becomes flower, for a few days it unfurls in a stripy cone of emerging petals. I have four quince trees and love everything about them from tangle of branch to voluptuous fruits. If I were a farmer I would plant a whole field of quinces.

But gardeners can do their bit to set the world aright. Plant a fruit tree and subsidise happiness for all who harvest the blossom with their eyes. Even if you live in the heart of the unforgiving city, remember the earth. Be true to it. Pear blossom in a back street shines as bright as in an orchard on the side of the Malvern Hills.

9 April 2000
Rain

It is astonishing what a day of rain can do after weeks of drought. I came home having spent a showery day in London to find inches of growth on everything. There is a sense, at this time of year, of everything bunching beneath the soil, poised to grow, like horses at the gate. The weeds, of course, are bunched more tightly than anything else, and Gareth has been blitzing the nettles, docks and creeping buttercups. Every hour spent weeding thoroughly around this time can save days later on.

I planted out coriander and chervil seedlings, raised in plugs, and planted the last of the potatoes, broad beans and onion sets. The early lettuces sown in Jiffy 7's are three times the size of those sown directly into the soil of the tunnel and are resisting slug attack the better for it. I firmly believe that this system of sowing juicy crops like lettuce, spinach, chicory and brassicas in blocks, plugs or Jiffy 7's, and then transplanting when they are big enough, is the best way to outwit snails and slugs.

Sarah cleaned up the herb garden, weeding it, cutting back all the winter-worn leaves of marjoram, thyme and bay. We struggle to keep bay outside – it always gets frosted – but I would love a big tree of it. A few leaves on the rosemary go black and drop, and that is a sign that the whole plant will follow within a month or two. I have never got to the bottom of this, but certainly a combination of cold and wet makes it much worse. I brutalised the sage, hacking it right back beyond Sarah's level of acceptability because otherwise it sprawls indefinitely with diminishing leaf returns. I think that the answer is, as with most herbs, to keep propagating and replacing old plants with new. We have given up growing thyme in the herb garden as it will not tolerate any shade and for all the cutting back inevitably other plants sprawl over it. So now we are growing it in rows in the vegetable garden, along with the garlic, parsley, chives and sorrel.

// Lettuce seedlings in the slug-free safety of the greenhouse.

I am in the middle of an intensive burst of filming, so last week raced off on Saturday after spending the morning moving plants in the jewel garden and did not get back until late Friday night. Whilst I was away Sarah completely replanted the new borders made round a new lawn which in turn was made round the trampoline. We call this the bouncing garden. It has a framework of forty-odd roses, and the main foliage comes from cardoons, fennels, lovage and my favourite thistle, the onopordum. This latter becomes the biggest and best weed you can have, but can be controlled by digging up the seedlings in autumn, before they develop long taproots. I had intended there to be standard hollies all the way round the three sides of the lawn, but Sarah decided against it as she planted. She is right. It will be better with a looser structure. Also, being Sarah, she got Gareth to move a large box (*Buxus sempervirens* 'Handsworthiensis' – extraordinarily vigorous and great for tall hedges or large topiary) two feet to the right to square it up. I would never have bothered, but again, she is right.

Sarah also planted white foxgloves all the way down the lime walk. This is a stroke of genius, as a few years ago we planted it with *Nicotiana sylvestris*, which looked fabulous and smelt even better, but as the limes have grown the shade they now cast is too much for the tobacco plants, and last year they were a flop. The foxgloves will like the shade and not mind competing with the limes for food and water. They are underplanted with *Alchemilla mollis*.

10 April 1999
Foxgloves

I planted three quinces in what is to become the new cutting garden. I read the other day that they did better planted in spring rather than during the conventional winter months. Which is just as well, seeing that they were heeled in in November for 'a week'. I am afraid that really is the story of my gardening life, fighting on at least five fronts at once and often losing five battles simultaneously. But I obviously want it to be like that and would manufacture the sense of being happily overwhelmed wherever I was. It doesn't matter too much. It is only gardening.

11 April 1999
Five fronts

Round about the middle of March our spring garden assumes a very distinctive aroma. It is slightly rancid, slightly foxy, and I love it. I admit that it has taken a few years to reach this position, but now as the crown imperial fritillaries grow and emit their particular stink, I know that soon they will adorn the garden with their mad flowers like tribal headdresses. They are slow to get going, and although we

13 April 2005
Whiff

A nest uncovered by late pruning. I moved it to a less exposed place. //

planted about two dozen bulbs some four years ago, some have been lost, some are blind (so far), and the flowering ones have taken their time in getting stronger each year.

But it is worth the wait. They are the most exotic-looking thing that we grow, at this time of year at least, but are completely at home in the woodland conditions of a shrubby border. We have three types: the common one, which is orange or brick-coloured, the yellow 'Lutea' and the deep orange 'Rubra'. Well, I say that we have 'Rubra', but as I write this is still a bit theoretical. I planted a dozen bulbs in our jewel garden last year, but so far only three have shown themselves above ground and as yet without a hint of flower. But I have known them take a couple of years to bloom.

There is a legend that the crown imperial fritillary was the one flower that refused to bow as Jesus passed by on the hill of Calvary so has bowed its head in repentance ever since. Be that as it may (or may not), its bowed bells attract bumblebees and queen wasps like no other. It is an ancient garden plant, appearing in paintings hundreds of years ago and featuring in the very oldest books on gardening. The reason that they grow well, if a little slowly, for me is that they love heavy clay soil and never do so well in very sandy conditions, even though they originate, like so many bulbs, from rocky hillsides around Turkey and Afghanistan. The bulbs are whoppers and should be planted on their sides about nine inches deep and the plant lifted and replanted every few years to give it a renewed burst of energy, although I admit that I have not yet done this to any of mine. They are good at making offsets and a few bulbs will gradually spread into a stand of punk-haired imperial splendour.

14 April 2000
Pottering

Gardening at this time of year becomes a race. But when it is wet our clay soil becomes immediately out of bounds. Nothing can be planted or sown, grass cannot be cut, hardly any weeding can happen because the weeds come up all slicked with soil, filling the wheelbarrow with a congealed lump of earth that will sprout healthy weeds if dumped. This is when potting shed and greenhouses come into their own. Our potting shed is dry and reasonably warm, and I can happily spend all day there. I have the radio on (Radio 4, more afternoon plays please), frequent cups of tea and am completely absorbed. Pots have to be organised and washed and compost mixed for various purposes. This weekend I took cuttings from the applemint growing outside the back door, from salvias that I had taken as cuttings last September and from the dahlia tubers that we have forced in pots. I sowed lettuce ('Little Gem', 'Lobjoits',

// Imperial fritillaries in the spring garden smell deliciously of fox.

'Kendo', oak-leaf and 'Little Leprechaun'), cardoons, squashes, cucumbers, cabbages, spinach, tomatoes, cornflowers, lupins, grasses, sunflowers, *Cerinthe major* 'Purpurascens', euphorbias and love-in-the-mist.

Everything edible is sown in plugs, two seeds to a plug so that they can grow fast in a slug-free environment before transplanting outside, although it is a battle trying to keep the slimy little bastards out of the greenhouse. I had to completely reorganise the greenhouse to fit the new stuff and played in there happily for at least an hour, moving A to B and then outside to C, which is the cold frames. These were, of course, full up, so they had to be sorted too. I spent an hour watering in the cold greenhouse – with the rain pattering on the roof – and gave all the salad crops that now fill it a really good weed and thin. This would have felt like a dreadful intrusion into precious time if it had not been raining, but bad weather flicked the coin and made it all positive.

15 April 2006
Primroses

I love primroses, and am cheered by everything about them. For a few weeks the mass of them growing in the little coppice is a performance that I cannot get enough of. They are a flowery shore after a long voyage. This is a childhood thing. For me primroses and Easter Sunday grow out of the same soil, with a posy dibbed into the earth at the end of every grave in a little Hampshire churchyard. Religion seems to me to be one of humankind's less successful activities – though I am always deeply moved by humanity's attempts to celebrate and appease the gods. Easter produces displays of laceration, processions, fiestas and swirling ritual, but in the Home Counties we did it with little bunches of primroses. That has filtered into this garden in the shape of the two dogs' graves, which are planted completely with primroses. I guess all our gardens are filled with the flowers of our lost childhood.

I would argue that the wild primrose is perfect and that any attempt to 'improve' it is a profound misuse of time and energy. A primrose *cannot* be violet or apricot or magenta or worse and retain any sense of self. Not that this has stopped anyone. Some of these of course are unquestionably lovely, and all are loved by someone, but none are the real thing.

Last year I coppiced one half of our little wood, and this year the primroses there are twice as good for the injection of extra light that they received. Gradually, as the canopy grows over, they will lessen a little and then be recharged by another clearance in seven years' time. I love the slowness of that rhythm. I might appear to be wavering but speed up the picture and really I am dancing.

The primroses grow with extra vigour in the year after coppicing. //

16 April 2004
Easterly

My broad beans are already forming small pods. I confess that they are growing inside a tunnel – but without any extra heat, and the doors are thrown wide open all day except when it is actually freezing or on the rare occasions when we have an east wind blowing. It is a killer, that easterly. It only seems to blow in spring and every three or four years sets in for as long as a week. From a heated room the day can look fine and bright, but as soon as you step outside the wind slices you in half. The whole of one side of our house – which, being timber-framed, is extremely well ventilated – becomes arctic. However, this is mercifully rare, and the beans – and lettuces, rocket, mizuna, mibuna, endive, spinach and radicchio – are all very happy and at least a month ahead of their outdoor counterparts.

17 April 2004
Violets

Funny how some plants are modest. Of course size has something to do with it but not always. Daisies aren't modest, and neither are aconites or muscari. Of course the added coyness of hanging flower heads helps – think of hellebores and snakeshead fritillaries – but that is all false humility. Lift the flowers up and they shout their beauty at you.

But the sweet violet, *Viola odorata*, has a quietness that comes from an inner certainty. It is beautiful. That's a fact. There are people who might say a camellia or *Skimmia japonica* is beautiful, but that would be a case of not having yet learnt the error of their ways. Not so violets. Their beauty is unarguable and inviolate from opinion. They also grow naturally in places that, especially at this time of year, not only look beautiful but make us feel good. By bringing that into the garden or even a pot just outside the back door, you capture the essence of British woodland.

Yet look closely, and *bashful* or *modest* suddenly seem wholly inappropriate words. The tiny flowers are as exotic and precise as any iris or orchid. Nothing could be more expressly geared to enticing insects. Two arms of petals are flung wide – We are over here! Great to see you! – and enclosing the pollen are three more petals that begin costively wrapped about the stamens like a pouch and then open to provide directions like air-traffic controllers parking planes at an airport, two petals pointing straight forward – This way please, that's it, left a bit – and a landing bay like a lower lip.

Then there is the scent. It is the most elusive of all fragrances, instantly recognisable. I came into my workroom the other day having been away for a little while to find a posy of our first violets – perhaps

half a dozen tiny flowers – that Sarah had put by my keyboard. As I sat at the desk I was suffused with violet. For a few seconds my world *became* that fragrance, every cell willingly submitting to it.

The purple sprouting broccoli is now trying to make its yellow flowers faster than we can eat it. I love it best when the purple heads are very small – no bigger than a fingernail – and you can eat the leaves, stem and head all together. It makes for an incredibly delicate treat that is only available for perhaps four weeks in the year – quite unlike the muscular lumps of broccoli that are so ubiquitous in every restaurant and supermarket.

Increasingly I feel surfeited by the sheer availability of food. The anticipation and recollection of a pleasure is as important as the experience itself, and all that is blended into a bland smear by constant access. Tasteless broccoli in August? No thanks. Get a garden or an allotment and taste the real thing.

18 April 2004
Broccoli

Violets have spread through the coppice from a handful of plants. //

In these heady days of apple blossom, bluebells and jubilant cow parsley, it is a two-ton mechanical digger that has seduced me most completely. I, who have fumed at the march of the glib makeover, have been thoroughly made over.

It was not planned. We have been threatening to Do Something about the bonfire bit for years whilst steadily doing nothing, until the other day it was sprung upon us. 'Bonfire bit' is pathetic, but there you are, these names stick. It started out as the splayed end of a ditch that divided the garden. Initially there was only one bit narrow enough to jump across, but we made a couple of bridges from hardcore and excess soil from the soakaway and gradually, over perhaps two years, the ditch became a level strip covered with topsoil and eventually was planted as part of the coppice. But the end bit, the bonfire bit, the bit we never dealt with, became a dumping ground. The infill mindset was attached to the spot even though it had been filled in years ago. All the subsoil from our path-making, weeds that wouldn't compost, turf that was too raggedy to keep, was heaped up, barrow-load by barrow-load, around the bonfire that was at the centre of this area. It became a sprawling heap.

We thought of making a kind of land-art mount to pick up on the Tudor-house theme but felt that this was a bit pretentious; of making it the site for an environmentally friendly building made out of recycled and found materials, which was/is being seriously considered but is not something to be snatched at; and of making a pond, but we have a perfectly good river on our doorstep, often literally. Anyway, all these things depended upon a digger, and it was far too wet to get access.

Until this dry April. As day has followed desiccated day, we realised that there was unlikely to be a better chance to get a digger in and sort out this bit of the garden for a long while. So on Wednesday Sarah rang a local contractor who – almost perversely, the way things happen around here – turned up to give us a quote about an hour later, and at seven on Friday morning Des arrived with his digger. Sarah had gone to London for the day but left instructions, having organised things so (as Don democracy works) she had the final say. The hardcore and the worst of the weedy subsoil were to be buried in the centre and the rest worked into a metre-high platform with gently sloping banks. It was to be a mount after all. Sort of.

There was a horse chestnut at the back that I planted four years ago and wanted to keep but I realised that it did not fit in with the new scheme of things. So I asked Des if he would rip it out too. 'I'd much rather not,' he said. 'I spent three days last week ripping out forty acres

The last of the sun at the end of April. The end of a good day. //

of mature standard apples,' he explained. 'Broke my heart.' So we decided to keep the chestnut but move it.

There were two problems. The first was where to put the thing. I like horse chestnuts very much indeed. I think that the sticky buds make the best spring cut 'flowers', the leaves opening miraculously whilst they are in the vase. I think that the real flowers are wonderful and heavy with every association of sunny spring days. I think that the mature tree in full leaf is handsome, and the conkers in autumn never lose their wonder. But they are large trees, spreading almost as wide as they grow high.

The second problem is that wherever it was to go meant tons of tracked machinery working its destructive way through the garden. Even though the ground was dry and hard, it still made a hell of a mess. In the end we worked a route through the chickens and the orchard to the cricket pitch (only a cricket pitch for four months or so a year and it can be brought forward a few yards). The tree was planted exactly where the stumps normally go.

Once this distraction was completed, Des went back to making the earth platform. He carved out two new paths along the flanking hedges and then gently, gently shaped the soil into a miraculously level stage with slopes that look as though six gardeners with rakes had spent hours adjusting and fine-tuning them. By half past four he was done, the machine that ripped out trees and boulders without a judder having stroked the 'bonfire bit' into something entirely new.

<table>
<tr><td>

21 April 2002
Lunch
....

</td><td>

I have worked out that this is the first spring that I have spent in this garden. Every other year has been broken up and distracted by filming commitments which either crowded out my calendar or else all came together at precisely the times when I wanted to be at home. Ten years! Now I am trapped indoors by a book project and, OK, just a little indolence, so I might as well be cavorting in front of a film crew in Guadalajara or Guisborough. Not quite. Lunch outside again today. Couldn't have done that on the road. It would have been, 'Sorry, the kitchen closes after 1.45' or some revolting 'home-made, country-fayre' concoction out of a vat in Slough.

</td></tr>
</table>

We always eat in the walled garden. Before we moved here it *was* the garden. Everything else was farm. I have an old photograph of vegetables growing in anonymous rows, with cattle in the yard the other side of the wall. To be honest, it is a bit pretentious calling it the 'walled' garden, if not untrue. The wall curves around two sides only, west and north, but gives us a good south-facing stone suntrap. To the south is the rough hedge with overgrown damsons that screens us from the track in summer and around us the yew hedge I planted nine years ago, now a foursquare and ageless green wall.

Whilst the rest of the garden was still a field pretending to be a garden, it had identity. It belonged to the household in a way that a brand-new garden never can. I divided it into four square beds into which we planted the collection of old roses we had brought with us, accompanied by herbs. Roses and herbs always go well together, and there was enough vigour in both parties to complete the sense of maturity and permanence. Given that the house was a building site and the rest of the garden effectively a ploughed field, this gave a valuable sense of putting down roots. It was outdoor nest-building. We made a sort of terrace laid with sandstone flags and a table from planks and trestles. We eat out there as often as we can. In fact it is the only place in the garden where Sarah and I ever stop and not-garden. It is a place where sitting feels right.

The trampoline was the catalyst for change. We tried it down the end of the garden in the orchard, but the children wanted it included in this most domesticated bit of the garden, even though there was no room for it. So we dug everything up and Sarah replanted newly made borders around the edge of a lawn, in the centre of which was a large round trampoline. I had no problem with this. What it lost in conventional horticultural charm it gained in the quality of bouncing. The place came into its own. Most of my measures of real happiness have been established here, good food eaten outside, good company, good bouncing and good midsummer flowers.

The reality of establishing a largish new garden on a shoestring is made up of the rigmarole that has filled the last few days. It goes like this: Brian and his Bobcat were booked to clear away the huge pile of rubbish we dug up when making a new border, path and grassed area in front of the house. At the same time he was to bring in his lorry a load of topsoil to sow the grass seed into.

The day began bright and beautiful. I went off to London at dawn to earn the money to pay for this, leaving Sarah – frantically busy herself – to 'be around in case anything happened'. The problems began at once. In order to tip the topsoil, Brian had to move the rubbish. And to move the rubbish he had to put it in his lorry. And to put it into his lorry he had to tip the topsoil …

23 April 1995
Kerfuffle

My mobile rang on the train. Where should we dump the topsoil? In a neighbouring field. That would need permission from the farmer, and the farmer was not answering his phone – probably due to the more pressing demands of farming. I said that I would keep trying him, finally got him somewhere between Charlbury and Oxford, and got the go-ahead. I rang back to give Brian the tip-off.

Then I got another call, this time in a taxi. The people from the mushroom farm had just rung: they could deliver the twelve tons of mushroom compost we had ordered in an hour's time, was that OK? One of the beauties of gardening on a largish scale is that you can employ the economies of scale, so that things like mushroom compost can be bought in bulk at a fraction of its normal price. A thick mulch of this was exactly what we needed now that we had finished our spring weeding. Yes, of course it was OK, the timing was perfect. Sort of.

The sixteen-ton lorry apparently only just fitted down the lane but, having negotiated its narrowness, couldn't turn the corner into our yard where the compost was to go. Another phone call: Where should we put it? In the field. Would I ring the farmer, he knew me ... I would, I did, he said yes, by now bemused. I made a mental note to show material, liquid thanks.

When I came home I inspected the work by torchlight and saw that it was good. Half the topsoil was spread, all the rubbish was moved, and the field was well and truly carved up by the Bobcat's wheels. I went to bed wondering if the farmer had noticed.

Brian was back by 8 a.m. with another load of topsoil, which he dumped in situ this time. We decided to move the mushroom compost and tidy up as quickly as we could. The only place that the compost could reasonably go was where we park our cars and over the wall by the back door. This latter spot was occupied by a ton of firewood that Mike had delivered. Mike is the strongest man I know. When I was young that role was filled by Tommy Ball, with the mind of a child, sleeves rolled almost to his armpits and hands like shovels. He was a woodman as well. Tommy had a speech impediment and would come into the pub and order a pint o' cherry brandy in an almost incomprehensible Hampshire burr. Just you behave now, the landlord would say, or I'll tell your mum. Tommy must be an old man now. It is unthinkable.

Mike had tossed the oak in cord lengths from his truck, over the wall into the back yard as though they were bean sticks. I now had to move it to make room for the mushroom compost, and it made me squeal with effort. The rest was dumped in the car park, so the cars had to be moved, blocking the lane. At that point Eric Hyde came down with

his tractor to feed the lambs. He volunteered to walk the last quarter of a mile across the fields, and we watched him guiltily as he stumped off, half-hundred sack of nuts over one shoulder.

I then had a call from daytime telly asking me to do a live item on their show. I asked what they had in mind. Oh anything, they said, whatever it is that you would be doing in your garden now.

26 April 2003
Tulips

We await the first tulips with all the nervous anxiety of a father-to-be outside a delivery room. They take such a long time coming, gradually showing leaves, then bud, then stem and finally opening flowers at a time when in the borders there is precious little else going on.

But there is one tulip that is at its best in early April and which, last year at least, had finished its display by the time the main ranks had swept into colour, and that is *Tulipa sylvestris*. We have this planted right under a hornbeam hedge, in full baking sun and, I confess, shamefully set in a thick crop of chickweed. We put the first bulbs in four years ago and they have spread themselves steadily, so they obviously like it there,

The tulip 'West Point' in the spring garden. Note rampant goosegrass. //

despite being bounded between the hedge roots and a cobble path. I love the way that they mimic daffodils in their yellowness and the way the flower heads hang, although they are more graceful than any daff that I know. They are scented in a rather surprising, spicy way, and with the hot weather we have been having you catch a delicious whiff of it in the afternoon as you pass into the vegetable garden. This is the least cultivated or precious of all tulips, growing as a weed, especially of vineyards. It has an invasive stoloniferous habit and probably spread with vine stock. Some say that it was brought to this country by the Romans as a weed in their vines, but it has also escaped from gardens all over Europe and naturalised itself. I certainly do not want it to escape from this garden, but it can spread as far and wide as it chooses within our boundaries.

28 April 2000
Shelter

We have lifted a section of the terrace where we eat and moved the York stone to the new bit of the jewel garden. This gives us a place to sit there – in what was the chicken run only a couple of years ago – and increases the border in the walled garden. This is exciting on both counts. Any extra planting space is pounced upon, and this corner had been chosen for paving precisely because it was so sunny. As it turned out, it was too hot in the middle of the day (when we are most likely to eat outside), and the butter used to melt. I shall dig the soil, add plenty of compost and plant it up with roses, rosemary, lavender, verbascums, melianthus, poppies and, in the autumn, tulips for next spring.

The new site for the paving has got an experimental cover made from a post at each corner of the square and bean sticks nailed an inch apart over the top. I remember sitting under a similar shelter in Mexico and thinking that it was the business. But the experimental status is because it does rather spoil the view across the river to the church.

29 April 2005
Tulips

Sometimes you just want to say, Look – here we are again. Yes, I know it is exactly where we were last year, and yes, I know that these particular flowers or plants did pretty much exactly the same kind of thing then and every preceding year before that, but if that is not a miracle then I genuinely don't know what is. One of the joys of gardening is the process of doing the same thing year after year and even day after day. Instead of being boring, this constant and subtle repetition is actually the most fascinating part of it.

Five years ago when Sarah and I started to make our jewel garden, we realised that we were going to have to use tulips to create an early

splash of rich colour. For the next three years we planted thousands of bulbs each winter, building the tapestry of burgundies, rubies, oranges and purples with the silky petals of 'Abu Hassan', 'Queen of Sheba', 'Generaal de Wet', 'Rococo', 'Ballerina', 'Queen of Night' and the 'Black', 'Flaming', 'Blue' and 'Orange' Parrots. Each April, appearing in this flaming mix of brilliant colour, they astonish me anew.

But there is a piece of new tulip planting that we have done this year that is in one block of colour. This is in our herb garden, where we have planted the four beds with just 'Negrita', a voluptuous flower with a wonderful satiny plum-coloured skin-tight sheath of petal. We planted these at least a foot deep, using a crowbar for each bulb, so that we could plant herbs in and around them without disturbing the bulbs. They have responded by growing with exceptionally strong and straight stems. The massed effect, contained by clipped box hedges, is an exhilarating rush of colour at a time of year when the yellows and new greens are delicately appearing. There is nothing subtle or even gentle about it and yet at the same time there is nothing brash about it. For all their dramatic impact, these 'Negrita' are elegant and serene.

Tulip 'Ballerina' and rather bleached Stipa arundinacea. Often they recover. //

Sarah says that I am like an old dog plodding round the same beat morning and night, but for me the walk is measured with constant change. Routine can be rhythm.

My grandfather attributed his exceptionally long life to a routine devoid of variation. Living was grooved into place for a remarkably fit and healthy ninety-seven years. Meal times arriving like Swiss trains and he went to Harrods once a fortnight for a haircut and some ham. He argued with everyone, including the Inland Revenue, who, along with the lawyers, pretty much took all my inheritance (although in his will, in which he divided all his goods and chattels between my two brothers and myself, he stipulated that I should only receive my portion, subject to the whims of the trustees, after I 'attained the age of 30 or maturity, whichever came first'. He disinherited my father, his only child, in 1939 when my father joined the army, of which, for some obscure reason, my grandfather disapproved, despite the looming war. My brothers and I ended up with some gloomy paintings, about a dozen handmade suits each and a large collection of classical records. My grandfather couldn't abide Mozart – too twiddly – but was very strong on Brahms. He was an unpleasant man but undeniably formidable. My father, champion boxer, commando and the toughest man I have ever come across, was cowed to the end and only outlived him by a couple of years and that was that.

Both died at the back end of winter, the same people in dark coats at the same crematorium with black March branches and huddled daffodils. Then you wait a bit, all over the shop – it is never a good time when fathers die – and spring comes to the rescue. Fickle enough to be charming, like a cat going through a door, but grooved into the year with utter reliability. Thank you. Thank you.

May

My dog Red is a huge but deeply sensitive soul. Actually she is one of three dogs that we have, but the other two are Jack Russell terriers and, much as I love them, they do not have quite the same place in my affections. Red is a Blackdog. Blackdogs are formally known as St John's Water Dogs, but those of us who own and love them always call them Blackdogs. They are what Sarah calls 'expensive mongrels', being a cross between Newfoundlands, Labradors and Huskies, and Red is the third I have owned over the last twenty years. They are enormously strong, swim like fish, are dainty eaters and fiercely loyal. As I write this Red is lying on my feet and snoring loudly. She is wet from a swim in the river and consequently my trousers, which luckily I have not changed from a day in the garden, are sodden. Other than love and affection, three things in life excite her more than anything else: sticks, swimming in the river and – best of all – new, yellow tennis balls. No other colour will do. One will not do either. She walks around carrying two, and occasionally three, in her mouth with a look of total and utter bliss.

For the eleven and a half years that I have been in this garden I have always had at least one Blackdog within a few yards of me. Where I go they go. It is their garden as much as mine. Every morning, first thing, we walk round together, sniffing the air, opening the chickens and working the day out. Last thing at night we repeat the ritual by torchlight, although as this is followed by a biscuit, there is a slightly more excited tone to the proceedings. Chewed bits of stick are strategically deposited around the garden. At any one time at least half a dozen used yellow tennis balls are dotted under the hedges and in the borders. My last Blackdog, Red's uncle, is buried in the little coppice among the primroses and wood anemones. Red will be buried next to him, although not for ages yet I hope, and I would be more than happy to be planted next to them both when my time comes.

1 May 2004
Red

It always seems to me that May is like that desiccated paper confetti that you drop into a glass of water and watch grow out into a full, blossomy underwater bloom. Everything expands in May – light, day length, warmth and above all the sensation of being truly, richly alive. Spring grows up to become summer. The birds all come home – swallow, swift, martin, cuckoo and flycatcher all return to this garden, each one part of the summer household. But above all the world becomes that intense, luminous green that is suggested increasingly throughout April and lost to a steadier, heavier maturity by mid-June. But in May, everything shines from within.

2 May 2005
Hawthorn

And in May you have the incomparable combination of cow parsley and hawthorn blossom. Eat your heart out, white gardeners everywhere; May-time and May blossom do it better than you will ever know how. Hawthorn, or the May tree, only acquired that name towards the end of the sixteenth century and it celebrates the way that the tree bursts into flower on or around the first of the month. Well, as anybody remotely observant will tell you, it does no such thing. Even with global warming and an early season, hawthorn is unlikely to flower before the end of the first week of May, and it is at its best in my garden and the surrounding countryside during the third week of the month. I have seen it in full flower on Midsummer's Day (24 June) around Aberdeen. This calendar shift is, of course, due to the change from Julian to Gregorian mode in 1752, when eleven days were taken out to bring Britain in line with the rest of Europe. So what was May Day until 1751 became the modern 12 May – which fits in exactly with modern flowering. In fact one of the interesting side-effects of global warming is that we are shifting quite rapidly back to the same floral calendar as Shakespeare, Marvell and Pope.

I suspect that the lack of a vernacular name for hawthorn until relatively late is connected with the huge increase in enclosures in the sixteenth century. Hawthorn would have been the dominant hedging plant used to turn common land into bounded fields, and the increase in large-scale flowering (no flailing hedge-trimmers to smash the flowering buds back then) would have been a dramatic change to the countryside to coincide with May Day.

We have planted a whole load of hawthorn hedges this winter. It is certainly the easiest, least troublesome and fastest growing of all hedges. I don't know why more gardeners do not use it. It has much going for it. For a start it is probably the cheapest woody plant you can buy (hedging from a nursery works out at between ten and thirty pence per plant depending on the size). It grows fast in practically any soil or conditions, can be trimmed and shaped as you will, and yet responds by always growing back thicker and stronger. It has some of the loveliest blossom in the plant world, is probably the best cover for birds and insects, and is the ideal density to filter the wind. Its wonderfully vibrant spring-green foliage turns a brilliant autumnal red, and it carries masses of brilliant red berries ('haws') that are essential winter food for birds. It is also thorny so makes a protective barrier against uninvited visitors. I rest my case.

I think that its very usefulness is part of the reason that gardeners overlook hawthorn when deciding on a hedge. Since the sixteenth

// *Looking into the damp garden. A bit untended, but the nicer for it.*

century it has been the agricultural hedge of choice, and in the eighteenth and nineteenth centuries hundreds of thousands of miles of it were planted. So it has become associated with the ploughed fields and hedgerows of open countryside rather than the kind of neatly trimmed, decorative barriers that inhabit our predominantly suburban gardens.

Apple blossom

The apple trees are coming into harvest. I am, of course, talking about the blossom. These flowers, which range in my garden from the palest of pinks to a deep cherry, give me as much pleasure as the fruit will do in six months' time.

It is odd how flowering trees are so affected by their context. We marvel at the almost surreal voluptuousness of some of the magnolias, but what really marks them out as special is that they appear when there is not a single leaf on any tree and when the grass has hardly begun to grow. Their ideal backdrop is always a blue sky. Likewise rhododendrons and azaleas are mainly set in the context of the heavy green leaves that back them, so we focus in on the plant rather than putting them in the wider context of the garden or surrounding landscape (which, now I come to think of it, is why I cannot warm to them). But apple blossom is part of the incredible surge of joy that comes with May. You have to be deeply disconnected from the world about you not to feel that tingle in your veins throughout the first half of the month as the garden and countryside grow with astonishing zeal. The flowers that deck the apple branches are part of this overall picture.

In my orchard now the grass has made the transition from slightly shaggy winter growth to the straight-backed stems of spring. The hawthorns are heavy with leaf. Each apple tree is thinly flowered compared to the earlier blossom of damson, plum or pear, but the combined effect of over thirty apple trees, all with slightly different flowers, appearing like a rhythm between the end of April and mid-May, is as beautiful as the best summer border. Blue sky is good, but it will not make or break this scene. Greenness is at the heart of it; there is a green pulse running through these wonderful May days.

Damp garden

I get so bewitched by the sheer beauty of the surrounding countryside at this time of year that I overlook glaring faults in the garden that it is getting a little late to rectify. I am thinking of a piece of ground that we call (without much conviction) the damp garden. This is because it is the first bit to flood and the last to drain away, although the soil is actually no wetter than anywhere else. I have made two beds and planted them up with hostas, ligularias, royal ferns, fritillaries and teasels, with a good smattering of self-sown sweet rocket.

This year the self-sown rocket has been fabulous, with a particular deep mauve predominating. I passed a house the other day with a display of burgundy rocket that was stunning. I must go back and beg some seed. If this planting scheme sounds limited, it is, but that is the way I work. I try to get the basic idea of a border in the ground, live with it for a year or so, then gradually fill in, take bits out, divide and generally fine-tune. The idea remains constant, but its expression is constantly changing. I think that every area of planting needs a strong underlying theme or idea. It could be to do with colour, season, shape or plant type, but a general mishmash is much more difficult to sustain for more than a few glorious weeks.

This limited collection of moisture-loving plants has looked so vibrant, so exciting as they entered into high spring that I completely overlooked what had been nagging me all winter. The borders are the wrong shape and the wrong size. So I shall extend one of the borders by about another quarter and plant the four *Stipa gigantea* and three *Stipa arundinacea* that I have in pots. I have already put in a couple of bamboos, *Phyllostachys nigra* and *Phyllostachys aurea*, which will pick up the grassy theme. This will radically change the tone, but for the year-round shape, texture and balance of this bit of garden overall it is the best thing to do. Although for the next week or two, however clever we gardeners like to think we are with our colour schemes and planting plans, nature will be showing us just how it ought to be done.

5 May 2001
Exotica

I do not really approve of gardens that are dominated by tropical plants or other exotica. Nevertheless, a year ago I planted out about a dozen eremurus. Hardly indigenous – in fact they come from the steppes of Iran and Turkestan. But I have always admired the eremurus stands at Chelsea and wanted them as part of our walled pastel garden. It was the first time that I had grown them and I did it by the book, carefully overwintering them in pots outside in a very sharp compost and putting huge amounts of grit beneath them when I planted them out in May in our heavy soil. They didn't come to much and were generally disappointing. So much for my attempt at exotica, modest as it was.

Then came the autumn rains and a week of frost when it measured minus 14 one night and did not get above minus 5 for four days. I resigned myself to losing them. But they have come back much more vigorously than last year, along with the melianthus, tulips, alliums and all the Mediterranean plants in that area. Oops! There's my purist indigenous cover blown! But then, that is an exceptionally sheltered, sunny corner...

For the past couple of mornings I have been getting up as the light starts to lift, frost still sharp on the ground. Although frosts at this time of year can be very damaging, these have been curiously benign. Perhaps this is one of the advantages of everything being rather late.

6 May 2001
Frost

The pear blossom would usually be over by now but has yet to come out sufficiently to be affected. The damson blossom is at its best, and the 'Taihaku' cherry as full and fat as dollops of cream, but both are tough enough to shrug a little ice away. It is, of course, not the frost that does for things but the early-morning sun thawing the frozen cells too fast. So my gunnera sits under a cloche in a rather undignified way, like a starlet wearing a tea cosy, until mid-morning when the air has warmed everything up.

We have today just finished repairing the last of the flood damage from November. We put in a perforated pipe to try and channel away the water, digging a trench along the length of a grass path and filling the mud back in as best we could – which was not terribly well under the awful circumstances. This settled into a compacted rough surface.

7 May 2001
Sowing

So it has all been lifted with a fork, rotovated, mixed with sharp sand, levelled and re-sown with a tough, predominantly rye-grass mix. Sowing feels much better to me than turfing, more trusting. I quite like the wait for grass seed to wispily emerge as a faint green haze through squinted eyes.

Today, unable to concentrate on my writing, I walked round the garden, looking at it with fresher eyes than I have done for years. It looks and feels complete. It isn't, in fact, but probably only I see the unfulfilled potential. There is an awful lot going on, almost all of it rich and pleasing, and it needs a lot of tending to keep it going. I guess that this is where gardening arrives. It is a good example of the 'be careful what you wish for' homily. The garden that you plan and make will be, in the end, the garden that you get.

8 May 2005
Arrival

Overleaf. Looking across the lower part of the jewel garden. //

133

12 May 2002
Greening

As May slips in, there is the most astonishing greening of the world. It shouldn't surprise me – I've been here before nearly fifty times – but every year it shakes me to the core, scrambles the sediment that has silted up over winter and sends me spinning into a green space. It is like falling in love, like recovering one's sight. I suspect that all gardening, all life perhaps, is built up from just a few moments like these. Not many days in all, not a body of achievement. Just the few days each spring when you transcend your lumpen self. All lyric poetry, all mystical expression, all the most sublime music strains towards what every leaf does as carelessly each spring as it falls in autumn.

13 May 2006
Cuckoo

The first thing I heard this morning, as I opened my eyes to bright sunlight filtering through the river mist, was the cuckoo – the first since last summer. Saturday. Early May. Cuckoo. Sun. Six a.m. There is only one reasonable response to this and that is to slip out of bed, put on clothes that don't wake your sleeping partner and try not to creak the stairs too much as you go downstairs. Then outside, and instantly you are precisely, epicentrally, where it is at.

I swear the garden has never looked lovelier. There has never been more *point*. Some credit can go to those of us who have made and maintained it, but even the most blinkered, crepuscular duffer cannot have failed to notice the way that this spring has bloomed like no other. The end of April and the first half of May pulled together eight weeks of flower and conflated them into a few weeks of extraordinary, overlapping display. I have never known anything like it before. In this garden daffodils and bluebells flowered cheek by jowl beneath the apple blossom, and blackthorn, crab, pear and cherry jostled simultaneously for attention. Every tulip, from the earliest species to 'Queen of Night', always the last to arrive here, mingled like a coronation crowd. Behind it all, of course, there was the stained-glass window of iridescent green foliage that is normally more than enough to justify May-time ecstasy.

On a Saturday morning like this I go through the daily rituals with real pleasure. First I open the cold frames, which are in early May full to overflowing with plants that want to be planted outside into the soil but which would not cope with even a hint of frost – and frost is always a possibility. Experience shows that you risk all by planting out too early and absolutely nothing by being a few weeks late. So brugmansias, cannas, salvias, dahlias, pelargoniums, sunflowers, cosmos, squashes, cabbages, celery and climbing beans are squeezed in like a rush-hour Tube. It makes watering easy, though, and I do this next. If it is a hot day

// The allium 'Purple Sensation' and oriental poppy 'Beauty of Livermere'.

they will get watered again about an hour before closing the cold frame up for the night.

The propagating greenhouse is also watered, and vents are opened and watering cans refilled to take on the ambient temperature. Then on up to the top of the garden to the other greenhouse filled with rocket, endive and various lettuces. This indoor rocket is now bolting faster than it can be eaten, with hairy stems like a gangly teenager outgrowing its clothes. Just for a few weeks in April indoor rocket is the sweetest, least blemished, most peppery leaf possible, but once the bolt starts it cannot be recovered until next spring. All this will be dug up and replaced with tomatoes as soon as I have time. The same goes for the other greenhouse, which is filled with a winter mixture of parsley, lamb's lettuce (corn salad), mibuna, mizuna, 'Chicon de Charentes' lettuce (which is superb), Swiss chard, beetroot for its leaves, land cress and spinach, which was sown last August and has overwintered wonderfully well, becoming the biggest vegetable success of this spring – lovely raw but silkily delicious cooked.

In amongst this lot sit four trays of tomatoes, twenty three-inch pots each of 'Black Russian', 'Andine Cornue', 'Brandywine' and 'Costoluto Fiorentino'. They are getting leggy and need planting out, but before I can do that everything must be cleared from in here too. There is a pond here, fringed by nettles and dandelions and stocked with a bucket from the stream in the nearby field.

I feed the chickens, let them out into the orchard to eat grass and hunt out the grubs, remember that I left my tea down by the cold frames, and go back indoors and have some breakfast. It is not yet seven. So long the work, so short the time.

14 May 2000
Fine-tuning
....

I have just had the most perfect three days in the garden that I can remember for a very long time. As we sloshed into May it seemed we had never had better spring weather. The tulips were insanely perfect – I spent hours photographing and staring at them. There is something in the form and detail of tulips that manages to be decorously beautiful whilst being outrageously sexy. You cannot hide this in a cloak of horticulture or blind botany. The full curve of hip and buttock with the tuck of waist is drawn in satin petals. Tulips are our temple paintings, a celebration of beauty and sex growing in the safety of the garden.

Despite this infatuation, we got a lot done. Sarah and I weeded the jewel garden, kneeling on plywood squares and teasing the roots from the incredibly sticky soil. Terrible conditions to weed in, but it could not wait because after all of April's rain, in this heat and with our soil the weeds can grow inches every day and take over.

Sarah has spent long hours – days really – moving plants and thinking about it. She has a perfect memory for colour so can constantly fine-tune planting even when things are not in flower. This adds a range and subtlety to the garden that I arrive at only by accident. It is not just colour that gets shifted and shuffled. We have eight Irish yews in the jewel garden that are intended to give winter structure. They do it unsatisfactorily. It was hard to put a finger on what was wrong, and we were on the point of reluctantly losing them on the basis that the right thing in the wrong place is still wrong. But then Sarah, typically, suggested moving them all a metre or so to one side. This was (laboriously) done, and the result instantly clicked. One metre is the gap between uncomfortably wrong and unarguably right. This kind of fine-tuning seems to be a step up from the gung-ho efforts of setting a garden up and the really rewarding part of it, involving living with a space, considering it in different seasons, lights and moods – real gardening, in fact.

I planted out a couple of hundred rooted box cuttings that I took last September to make a pair of edging hedges and will take a few hundred more in a week or so. The yellow-green of the new growth on the box around the garden is fantastic at the moment. I let it grow shaggy until well into June before cutting just to make the most of the intensity of that colour. The same colour is dominating the spring garden, which is deliberately as yellow as possible until the end of May, when the cooler greens and greys take over. I moved half a dozen purple-stemmed cow parsley, *Anthriscus sylvestris* 'Ravenswing', into this yellow-fest. They had been in the jewel garden but, although the dark stems and leaves worked well, the white flowers were wrong. They are completely at home under the huge hazel. In the veg garden I sowed carrots, beetroot, chard, parsnips and peas, and planted out lettuce and spinach grown in soil blocks. And we had our first asparagus of the year. Life is sometimes very good indeed.

15 May 2006
Glory

I have learnt that gardens are like happiness. You cannot pursue it/them as an absolute thing or moment. You take and make them as they come, and every now and then there are fleeting glimpses that justify everything else – Vaughan's 'peeps into glory' – although at this time of year the opportunities for peeping are greater than ever and the glory all around. I had an email last year from a gardener wanting to know how to get rid of the cow parsley that was invading her borders. I wrote back

that I longed for that kind of invasive gift. Well, I have it now as the cow parsley spreads through the spring garden, muscling aside almost everything else. But a garden consisting only of cow parsley and hawthorn blossom would be glory enough for me.

It rained and it rained and it rained. I woke to heavy, fat rain on the roof, falling like a bag of nails on the tiles. I never left this seat all day but watched the puddles on the grass stretch and meet. I saw the news on the telly as I went to bed and, like everybody in such positions, vaguely realised that the place where the floods and disasters being shown were was in fact right here. Here on a screen but somehow not really us. The rain that woke me now lulled me to sleep.

The next morning I woke to find that the river Arrow, running a hundred yards from our back door, had burst its banks and that, peering out of the bedroom window, we were surrounded by water on three sides as far as the eye could see. It was lovely. Water flopped against one side of the house two feet deep, although it remained an inch or two below the step that would bring it into the back yard and from there into the kitchen. All the roads were flooded, and we spent the weekend house- and garden-bound, but none the worse for that.

The house remained dry, but the garden was half flooded. A corner of it floods each winter, but this time the water spread into the vegetable garden, so the broccoli grew out of a smooth brown mirror, and plastic cloches floated sweetly like toy boats. In places it was too deep for wellingtons, reaching the top bar of a five-bar gate leading to a field. It was all astonishingly beautiful and did not feel remotely like a disaster. In fact it drew a new map of the territory, like those satellite pictures of the world that started appearing some years ago showing human density in terms of colour-coded heat. Looking down from the attic I saw the garden with new, aquatic eyes. The only bad thing the water left in its wake was the extraordinary amount of rubbish it swept in, but even that, this being the countryside, was of the straw and stick variety and not used condoms, crisp packets and pork-pie wrappers.

This big flood is, we are told, the sort of thing that happens once in a lifetime. But we get one or two little floods into the garden every winter, or did until the past two years, which have been so dry. Clearly this little flooding has happened for centuries, because, unlike the heavy clay loam elsewhere in the garden, on this slightly sunken, marginal section the soil is a rich black silt two feet deep that must have gradually been washed in over the years.

Emergency drainage left a strip of concrete and an invaluable dry path. //

17 May 2001
JCB
....

There is nothing like a JCB for exposing the finer details of your garden. Thanks to last autumn's flooding we have had to install a new septic tank and drainage system, which has meant digging a huge hole right by the propagating greenhouse to put the tank into and nearly a hundred yards of drains three feet down. I had carefully routed the drains so that they did the least damage, but it still meant digging right through the herb garden, down a brick path, round the greenhouse, turning left down a long path (which was grass and is now lumpy mud), turning right round the oak that I planted ten years ago from an acorn, and straightening out up the orchard (which meant digging up and moving four five-year-old apple trees). It was not the trench that did the damage, of course, but the JCB and dumper truck that ferried in the twenty tons of stone necessary for proper drainage. Just to get these huge machines into a semi-mature, heavily planted garden is like taking a friendly elephant through the house.

It has all been put underground, earth pulled back and levelled over, but beneath this façade is a hard pan of compacted soil that leaves stagnant puddles after a light shower. The only solution will be to dig it all up and start again. And I am talking about an area roughly the size of the average back garden. But this exercise in horticultural pillage has opened up various opportunities. The first is that in order for the JCB to get into the orchard, we had to move the tunnel. Tunnels are surprisingly heavy when it comes to picking them up, but nine of us did just that, walking it to a different orientation. It is a huge improvement. Did I mention that half the soft fruit had to be moved to make room for this new spot? I lose track. But even that is an improvement, although the cropping will be down. And there are those finer details. As the trench snaked through the herb garden, exposing a lovely cross-section of the extent of the root run of the box hedge around it and the size of the lovage roots, I suddenly realised that the herb garden is all wrong. It needs redesigning and replanting. Suddenly a whole range of possibilities for creating a new sitting area that will catch the best of the evening sun has revealed itself.

So my advice to anyone wrestling with a design problem in the garden is this: Let a JCB loose for a day or two.

18 May 2005
Hurdles
....

The other day I had a lorry-load of fencing hurdles delivered. This was, to me, as exciting as taking delivery of a new car. They represent months of saving and yet are worth every penny. They are by no means the first that I have bought, but my love of them as beautiful objects and my respect and admiration for the hurdle makers who craft them increases

every time. Each is six square feet of flexible but enormously strong panel made from split hazel bound as tight as a drum skin and yet without a single nail or screw to hold it together.

When I first came to this garden it was an open field. So in the first year I made woven fences along all the lines where I wanted to plant hedges, marking out the structure of the garden with thousands of hazel 'rods' woven between hundreds of chestnut poles. Then I planted my hedging plants in the lee of the fences so that they had some protection from the wind. This made a huge difference – in the few places where there was no protection from the wind, the plants grew half as fast.

Both fencing materials, hazel rods and chestnut posts, come from coppice woodland, where the hazel and chestnut are cut every seven to twelve years for their flush of straight growth. In the case of chestnut this makes some of the best fencing stakes because it is very slow to rot in wet ground, is very strong and yet can be split easily with a wedge – which meant that I could double the number of my posts. But whereas hazel grows best in slightly alkaline soil, chestnut definitely prefers acidic conditions.

A stack of newly delivered hazel hurdles from Hampshire. //

My home-made fences were very amateurish because I used whole hazel stems, whereas a hurdle is made from stems split with a billhook. This is the real skill of them. An expert hurdle maker can take a ten-foot stem and slice his billhook in at an angle near the top and work the blade down so that it splits neatly in two whilst chatting. Try it. I have, many times, and it is desperately difficult.

The essence of hurdles is that they are light and portable and yet the perfect screen against the wind and unwanted eyes. There was a time, a hundred years or so ago, when they were made by the tens of thousand wherever there was coppice woodland, and used mainly for folding sheep on open downland, but the craft is now in the hands of a dangerously small number of highly skilled craftsmen and nearly all hurdles are made for garden use. I suppose that the pleasure that they give me – allied to their unsurpassed functional capacities – is the direct connection to an ancient skill practised in this country in the same manner with exactly the same materials since Iron Age times and the lovely woodland that they come from. Every hurdle represents a world of primroses, violets, wood anemones, ragged robin, bluebells, sweet

// The unfurling fronds of Osmunda regalis in the damp garden.

cicely, nightingales and butterflies that is intimately managed and respected by man. It is a kind of ideal halfway house between the garden and countryside at large, and one that we can all support and share in.

19 May 1999
Badminton

The best recent addition to the garden has been four badminton rackets and a shuttlecock. They have turned the new lawn in the walled garden, seeded last November, from an idea into a good place to be. The children now possess it, which was the sole reason for digging up the four borders that were splendidly there this time last year. A fair swap.

20 May 1999
Snails

Last year we were plagued by slugs, which ate all emerging seedlings. This year snails seem to have the ascendancy. At night I go and collect them up by the hundred and leave them in a bucket of salt water. I suspect that it is a cruel death. And, although I shall not stop waging war on them, they seem melancholy, calm creatures, and I rather like the way that they cling to the leeks in the torchlight.

21 May 2004
Blight

We have tulip-fire blight. This is the worst disaster to hit the garden. It means that all six thousand bulbs must be dug up and burnt. I noticed in March that the early 'Queen of Sheba' were spotted with blisters on their petals, which I took to be insect or scorch damage. I didn't take much notice to be honest – I was too excited by the flowers' existence to worry about the details of their appearance. Then a line of tulips in the jewel garden – all planted above an old path with much more stone in the soil than anywhere else – rotted and died. Over the first week of May every single tulip showed signs of spotting or actual rot. We could have wept. It has taken five years to bring our tulip stock up to its current level, and before the blight kicked in they looked amazing. Just stunning. Luckily there was that weekend at the end of April when the sun shone and we lived in a completely false sense of satisfaction and delight.

I discover that tulip fire is caused by a fungus called *Botrytis tulipae* which overwinters both in the bulbs and in the soil. It is spread above ground by spores on the foliage and petals both in the air and by water splashing from plant to plant. In other words, once you have it in the garden it is almost impossible to isolate it from the rest of your tulips. The spotting of the petals is caused by a hypersensitive reaction to the fungal spores. In the warm wet weather of early May the fungus grew

Overleaf. A snatch of the jangle of the jewel garden in spring. //

fast so that whole flower heads became covered in grey mould and collapsed on themselves.

The only answer, after digging them all up and burning them, is to keep the ground clear of tulips and fritillaries for at least three years before replanting. Ideally one would not plant tulips in the same ground for two consecutive years to avoid a build-up of the fungus. This will radically alter our garden for the next few years. But then everything changes. It will make us think afresh, even perhaps be radical about the jewel garden. It might be a good thing. But for the moment I can only mourn the loss of those weeks of outrageous display.

22 May 1998
Umbellifers

Sometimes England strikes you round the head like a cheap religious experience or a jolt of lust. Just now the cow parsley spins and spills along these border lanes under the shade of the May blossom like a good dream and I am riding it with the careless rapture of the dreamer. These greedy eyes that cannot look enough are me as a child wading chest high in cow parsley and calling out in joy, the feathery leaves delicately brushing my lips and eyelids and white coronets of tiny flowers smelling mustily familiar of something much older than me. Colour is reduced to just white clouds held by the hawthorn branches and a million white flowers gathered in one glance along a line of cow parsley with everything else in this piece of world a hundred tones of damp, glowing green. I do not believe that there is a more beautiful sight on the planet. But only a ghost of this can be stored, which is why every spring these moments expand so astonishingly, catch our knowing weariness so completely by surprise.

Why bother to garden when the countryside can do these things so much better than we can? Why fuss and primp when just sitting quietly and *looking* would reveal Eden better than anything we might make in our neat, officious little worlds? This is not a counsel of despair. That comes when the Council sends out tractors to flail the verges for neatness's sake in an act of ignorant bureaucratic vandalism. In a way the futility of recreating nature or competing with it is the key to gardening.

The vogue for cottage gardening – pursued most ardently by gardeners in town and suburbs, and bypassing the original spirit of cottage gardens that were made from poverty, using every inch of space for food, with a few flowers for the soul – is not just a cynical garden vogue but a real desire for the Arcadian softness of cow parsley. It is as though our Britishness manifests itself in a need for cow parsley as a symbol of all that is well with this country, and our gardens struggle to

// The flowering stem of the giant fennel Ferula communis grows to fifteen feet.

reinvent it all year long in the curious, muddled horticultural idioms that we have contrived out of the past few hundred years.

The contradiction is that the British countryside in May is simplified down in a way that only the most rigorously formal or minimal gardens ever are. 'Cottage' gardens are crammed, foot by square foot, with colours and species and textures that can never be found beyond the garden fence. The lessons are to keep it simple, to mass plants together however tiny your plot, and to use the power of repetition to provide a visual effect quite different from the individual plant. All except the most retentive gardeners do this by accident. For instance the forget-me-nots have been spectacular this year, a vague powder-blue haze with a tiny hint of pink at the centre of each minuscule flower. They are doing no more or less than the cow parsley but on a much smaller scale.

If it is so special, why don't we grow cow parsley in the garden as a prized seasonal trophy? You can buy it horticulturally dignified as *Anthriscus sylvestris*, but predictably it is much easier to get hold of the cultivated variety that has purplish leaves and stems and is called 'Ravenswing'. It is not in itself a bad thing and works very well in the context of a border. But the song that sung it into being is lost. A wild and haunting tune has been turned into a singalong melody. The cow parsley-ness of it is gone, replaced by something interesting, possibly beautiful, but not the thing itself.

The essence of a swathe of umbellifers along miles of country lanes is so removed from the general spirit of the back garden as to be simply confusing unless you look inside yourself and use your instinctive reaction to these flowers and bring that to the garden. This is what makes gardening the most fascinating of all activities: a garden is not just an arrangement of plants, but it is also a truthful portrait of the human spirit.

23 May 2003
Green

When I die I shall go to May. It will be green. Not environmentally correct green, for things will just be, without measurement or judgement, but actually the colour green in all its thousand shining faces. Every day will feel like Christmas Eve when I was ten. Every green leaf will be perfection exactly as it is and yet will grow and change every time I turn my eyes to it. Every moment will be like the arc of a diver breaking the waters of a green lake. I know this because this is what May is like here and now. Almost unbearable really. It does not hold for half an hour. Yet in the shifting, growing hymn of light and colour and leaf is the still, simple reason that I garden.

A mown path curving between field maples, leading to the orchard. //

Fred has fixed the cold frames at last. Over the past six months, one by one, the hinges have all broken, which is fine when they are shut at night but means that when open the lids balance on the bits of batten that prop them ajar as though on tiptoe. There is a reccurring theme to this kind of thing. At any one time there is always something broken. More often than not it seems as if everything is broken a bit, the whole garden acting as a kind of cipher for my life: perfectly OK, but not quite fixed. Because it is the garden, where I can pretty much do most things, it is even less likely to get done than if it were the car or the electrics of the house, where I reach for the phone at the first hint of trouble.

It is not as though the brokenness ever amounts to much. Often it is just a particularly weedy bit or a tree tie that needs replacing or a flap on the mower that catches every time you empty the grass. It is all do-able. But once I get in the garden I have a wall eye and don't see what I don't want to. This is why I take pictures of it obsessively – so that I can see it with anything like objectivity. Even then I can bluff my way through mistakes by blaming the inadequacies of my photographic skills. But when a professional does the job I am cornered. No way out.

What prompted all this self-flagellation is the condition of the spring garden. Now, at the very point where spring tips over into summer, its lushness has toppled into abandon. This is not a case of plants as weeds but of weeds as weeds. Goosegrass traces through the hellebore leaves like hysterical strands of spray string after a children's party. Nettles swagger amongst the dying snowdrop leaves. The lesser celandine, done with flowering, has retreated into itself but is fooling no one. It is merely regrouping. The chickweed is trying to climb the hazel. Rosebay willow herb is popping up all over the place, pretending to be small. Leave all this much longer and the spring garden will become a series of green hummocks, weed fighting weed for supremacy. I know because this is what happened last year, and only a radical clear-out in July salvaged the day.

But none of this can diminish the extraordinary vibrancy and freshness of the euphorbias, roses, May blossom, aquilegias and geraniums. The euphorbias are *E. palustris* and the smaller *E. polychroma*, and the roses *R. hugonis* and *R.* 'Cantabrigiensis'. In fact these are pretty indistinguishable to the untutored eye, both being bushes covered with small, cupped primrose-yellow flowers with delicate fern-like foliage. Both are lovely, real celebrations of high spring. I cannot help but think of roses as belonging to summer, and this is not yet summer. Real, weedy, slightly crocked life normally waits a week or two for the full blooming of its roses, and I cherish these two soft-flowered bushes especially for cheating the season.

// *The engine room. Cold frames and hardening-off frame. Invaluable.*

So I wander down the narrow path relishing the colours and don't mind that the green foil mostly belongs to weeds. As a rule I reckon you need an absolute minimum of fifty per cent green – whatever other colours are involved. Green is to the garden what white is to the page.

This spring, almost unbelievably, considering how essential and basic the plants are in most gardens, I have been learning about tulips and alliums. I suppose what I mean is that this is the first year that we have planted either flower in any quantity or range of variety with any real intent to transform the garden and our perception of it.

Tulip season is now gone but only just, and the main thing I learnt from our tulip blitz was that you can still plant tulips in February and get good flowering in May. By the time the tulips were on the fade the alliums were swinging in. I only really turned on to alliums at Chelsea last year. It is odd how you can be acquainted with a plant for years and not really get it at all and then suddenly see one and bing! A light goes on and you are ravished. I realised that alliums could add a whole idiosyncratic texture and dimension to a border, with their bulky basal leaves but flowers held aloft and taking up remarkably little space for such dramatic plants. But that is too clinical an analysis, and done with hindsight – what really happened was that I realised that they are lovely.

So we ordered a bunch of bulbs and planted alliums *aflatunense*, *cristophii*, *giganteum*, *siculum*, 'Purple Sensation', *ursinum*, *schubertii* and *sphaerocephalon* in our borders over the winter. In fact we ordered what seemed to be a huge amount, and they sat for weeks and even months in the potting shed under fleece to stop them freezing whilst we wondered what the bloody hell we were going to do with them all. But six months later I wish we had ordered twice as many.

The first out were the tall drumsticks of *Allium aflatunense*. These are about two to three feet tall with lilac flowers fringed with a silvery halo. There is apparently a white form too. As they emerge, the colour showing through the thin tissue of sheath, they look like flat-topped thistles but then open out to a cylinder. The leaves hang slightly dejected with a kink in the middle and – on ours – burnt tips as though touched by frost or fire. The same is true of the leaves of their offspring, *A.* 'Purple Sensation'. But the leaves are not what these are about. The colour of the umbels is a fabulously rich purple tinged with burgundy, the individual florets of each flower forcing out rather than hanging together within an invisible globe. We have them in the jewel garden backed by cardoons and interspersed with *Cerinthe major* 'Purpurascens'

Alliums seed themselves all over the garden. This is 'Purple Sensation'. //

that survived the winter, and they are pitched perfectly against the grey foliage of both plants. For the first few days that they came into flower, the tulip 'Queen of Sheba' was sprawling in the throes of a regal death, contributing richly to the intensity of the scene.

Just a few yards round the corner, but miles away in style and form, are clumps of *Allium schubertii* either side of a path. This has a whopping great flower ball and great fat, wavy leaves. At the moment it is a dumpy, bull-necked thing. For all that it has the delicate appearance of a front-row forward, it is not fully hardy, and I must remember to protect it with a mulch of straw before the first frosts.

In the artichoke walk the *Allium giganteum* are not yet out. To set the scene: The walk is a narrow path, some thirty yards long and just two feet wide. There is a five-foot bed flanking either side filled with artichokes and cardoons and, all spring, by the wallflower *Erysimum cheiri* 'Blood Red' now all but over and fading to a russet just like dried blood. Behind the beds are hornbeam hedges and above them pleached limes. The allium stems are fully four feet tall and will grow to six feet or more, topped by tight, pointed minarets and rising with straight and glabrous stems. They have the most wonderful leaves (hence my sniffiness about the leaves of *cristophii* and 'Purple Sensation') arching out in great glaucous, smoky straps from the centre. It would be enough to grow them for their leaves.

Back in the walled garden *Allium cristophii* is also poised but as yet unopened. Unlike the *A. aflatunense* on the other side of the same small bit of garden, these withhold their colour, revealing nothing yet other than a certain intensity of tone. The leaves have little hairs along the edge: a curiously delicate feature on such a robustly constructed plant. *Cristophii* is more open than many other alliums, more dandelion-like and tenuous in flower structure, although the purple stems of the florets within the umbel give it an intensity that glows from within the flower.

And the *Allium siculum*? I am ashamed to say that we never got round to planting them.

26 May 2000
Sewage

I may have spent last week at Chelsea Flower Show swanning around in linen suits, but the week before was devoid of any hint of glamour. In between filming and various journalistic commitments, my own gardening has been a bit curtailed. I did, however, manufacture a few hours the other evening, which was intended to set me up with a dose of horticultural reality to tide me over the lip-glossed fantasy of Chelsea.

Whilst wondering whether to start by planting out the climbing 'Blue Lake' beans that were beginning to outgrow their pots or to weed the spring garden, I thought I might check the drains because there was a bubbling from the loo when the bath was emptied, which is always worrying. So I lifted a manhole to find – well, you know exactly what I found. Another hour and the manhole would have floated away without my help. It hadn't rained for fifteen days – which in this part of the world amounts to a full-on drought – so it seemed unlikely that the problem was connected to our recent floods. I put on my waders and some rather fetching black elbow-length rubber gloves and delved into regions murkier than most. Unfathomable depths of yuck. We have some old bamboo drain rods so I spent the next two hours rodding the entire drainage system, the tributaries of which collect in the spring garden, which has the septic tank tucked into it. The spring garden is at its peak, all primroses, roses, Solomon's seal, forget-me-nots, aquilegias, euphorbias, the tulip 'West Point' which has gone on for ages, fat hostas ('Snowden' is already enormous) and the dappled shade of the hazel. But to solve the drainage problem I had to trample over half of its visual and olfactory fragrance, sloshing out buckets of ... of content.

This May has been a yardstick to measure Mays by.

But perhaps this has been a garden thing rather than a weather thing. It has certainly been drier than usual and sunnier and hotter – all easy enough to feel good about – but it is not just the weather. The best was the way that the blossom and all flowering plants came late and then stayed much longer than usual, all the while sustaining an almost bursting fullness and internal glow. I cannot think of any flowering plant that has suffered, and yet every season is inevitably a trade-off. You know the scene: the roses don't like the wet, but the hostas thrive in it. The tomatoes and basil ripen beautifully in the sun, but the lawn looks parched and brown. We have had none of that this time round.

We gardeners have had the best of the weather, seeing the fruits of it in a way that hardly anyone else can have noticed. We had a friend to stay the other day and she was saying how she hardly even notices the weather in London, let alone the seasons. I was filming in Dorset the other week and neither of the crew, both bright men in their early thirties, had ever worn wellingtons or seen cow parsley before. I cannot imagine a life that is dry-shod and devoid of billowing joy. Perhaps a garden is the only way to these bits of life nowadays. It makes them desperately important, as if they were not always so.

28 May 2001
Firstborn
....

This Bank Holiday is always special for me because it is my eldest son's birthday. Fifteen years ago I was handed this tiny person who opened one eye, took stock of this strange man and has had a pretty good measure of me since. All my children are loved without comparison or degree, but nothing can compare with the mixture of terror and elation when your first child is born. It is a door that can only be passed through once. I had been warned about the work and the fears, but no one had told me of the overwhelming love. You fall deeply in love with this brand-new person. The next morning, before going to the hospital, I went out to pick him a bunch of flowers. Lots of people had sent Sarah flowers, but I wanted to take him some for his own from the garden.

Unlike this year, spring '86 was fine, and by the end of May the garden was spilling with growth, but for all the abundance there was not a lot of choice – and, if I am honest, I was a much more limited gardener back then. I recall a spray of honeysuckle, a couple of tall violet-blue flowers of *Iris germanica*, the white, heart-shaped drops of *Dicentra spectabilis* 'Alba', probably some *Alchemilla mollis* – we had masses in that garden – and a few aquilegias. I do remember, slightly shamefully, being aware of the loss of these best specimens to the garden. I also picked some clematis – our two *Clematis montana*, one white and the other *C. montana* 'Elizabeth', which blushed a slightly unnecessary pink, were at their frothy peak. There was also the spiky purply-blue of *C. macropetala*, although thinking back, it must have been almost over. I put this mismatched posy next to the cot, a long strand of the white *montana* spilling down to the floor.

And now he is a strapping young man who sees a garden as a waste of a potential bike track, but – to his inevitable embarrassment – I shall go out tomorrow morning and pick him a bunch of flowers for his birthday nevertheless.

29 May 2004
Hurdles
....

Forty beautiful six-foot hazel hurdles were delivered the other day. These were made in Hampshire from woods that I know well and grew up amongst. Well-made hazel hurdles are created with an artistry that makes a mockery of cheap, imported imposters. They sustain managed coppice woodland that has survived with a minutely delicate ecosystem for hundreds of years. They filter the wind. They look lovely. They smell and feel of moments of almost unbearable happiness.

The man who made them pointed out that the darker wood was from a particular coppice we both knew. The acres of hazel and oak run like a thread through each fencing panel. How often can you get

// *Clematis montana 'Elizabeth' spilling over from our neighbour's garden.*

that exactness of provenance? How often can you bring back the same living plant that you played amongst forty years before and a hundred miles away without in any way damaging it? I find this thrilling and hauntingly beautiful.

When I was a child in Hampshire there was an old woman who forecast the weather by the piece of seaweed hanging outside her door. Her name was Dolly, and she renewed the seaweed every July on her annual day out on Hayling Island. She took my sister and me with her once, and we sat by the sea freezing in our bathing suits and she with sand on her thick flesh-coloured stockings. She said, 'Oak before ash, in for a splash, ash before oak, in for a soak.' This used to worry me. Was goodness involved? Was I tipping this balance, along with so many others, with my behaviour? And what sort of splash? How much of a soak?

A quick rain check now shows an oak across the fields heavy with leaf, whereas the half-dozen hedgerow ashes are only just changing from their winter upswept gauntness. But it would make little difference if it was the other way round, because the oak always comes into leaf before the ash, which is one of the last to arrive and amongst the first to fall in autumn. The leaves are brief. For some this is damnation enough – a tree that doesn't give enough of itself in full fig to justify inclusion in ever-smaller gardens. But there is more to ashes than mere summer dress, and it is too utilitarian and philistine to measure beauty in terms of longevity. Certainly a mature ash tree in midsummer is a lovely living thing. The pinnate leaves cast a particularly delicate shade, so there is always a feathery light filtering through.

Before they come into leaf the knobbly tips of the branches carry matt black buds, curiously inanimate and almost crustacean before they open out. The male flowers come next, frizzy and strange, like party streamers caught on the end of a stick, and then finally, after the rest of the arboreal world has had leaves out for weeks, the leaves emerge, floppy fronds that might be considered exotic on another, less determinedly common tree. Ashes are in fact part of the olive family and cousin to lilac and jasmine, so their exoticness is not entirely fanciful.

I have planted perhaps a dozen ashes in this garden more out of a kind of loyalty than anything else. They are not really a garden tree, but they are beautiful and very much my sort of tree so must be in any garden of mine. The outline of a common ash in a field is of a huge, blowsy tree with generously sweeping branches. As a young tree, though, it does not mimic its maturity, starting out spindly and only

Dawn sunlight makes stained-glass patterns on the nave of a path. //

slowly developing its promise. This, I think, is why it has never really been taken into the gardening lexicon. Gardens are growing smaller all the time, homes change hands more frequently than ever, and gardening has become a branch of home decorating. This all conspires to make the planting of a scrawny tree that will only be appreciated by someone else's children's children increasingly unlikely.

31 May 2003
Terracotta

I am not the world's best container gardener. It is not through lack of will – we have hundreds of lovely terracotta pots of all sizes, and at any one time there are dozens of them filled with plants. But I will confess that they come a lowly second to the rest of the garden rooted in the ground. Watering them all seems like the chore that breaks the camel's back, and I have learnt to position them as much for their proximity to a tap as for the ideal amount of sun or shade.

The most important pot that I own never has a plant in it. In fact it is really the ghost of a pot. Sarah and I spent Christmas 1985 in the south of France. We heard that there was a place that sold wonderful pots, but no one seemed to know where it was. Eventually we found an ex-pat Englishman who told us to 'bat on down to Biot and you'll see them in a field'. So we batted down to Biot and, sure enough, found a field full of wonderful pots. We ended up buying a huge one for £100 – by far the most money I had spent on any kind of garden object or plant. But it was a lovely thing, with exquisite lines. It just fitted in the back seat of our car, and we drove it home to our Hackney garden, where it took pride of place at the end of a path.

But in the great storm of October '87 it got smashed. We collected the pieces and eventually found someone to mend it who told us, by the by, that he thought that it was probably five hundred years old and worth £800 or £1,000. When we moved to this house, just over ten years ago, it came too, in its patched-up state. Then, about seven years ago, when I was filming in Thailand, I got a phone call. Disaster. The cat had pushed against it, toppling it over, and it had smashed again. We collected the pieces, and Sarah found someone to copy it from the resulting jigsaw. This proved to be tricky, not so much because it was in fifty pieces, but the potter said that it was technically impossible to make – the clay was so thin that he did not see how it had held its shape. So the copy is much cruder than the original but at least reminds us of what it was like and now stands, empty save for three large stones weighing it down, at the centre of the garden. And stuffed away in a corner of the shed are the impossibly thin pieces of the pot we bought nearly twenty years ago.

June

There is a point in the year when the walled garden is as perfect as any garden could be. This is no boast, just a recognition, like a perfect cup of tea or a chanced-upon moment of unalloyed happiness. You do not own these things, but merely bask in their grace. It is probably no coincidence that this particular bit of the garden receives the least horticultural attention. The rose bushes rise up to ten feet above sweet rocket, fennel, lovage, sage flowering lawlessly, the tough but wonderful geraniums *phaeum, pratense* and 'Ann Folkard', the spidery flowers of knapweed, *Centaurea montana* and overgrown curry plant with a splash of chalky yellow, and even the weeds like tansy and lemon balm look good at this early stage of summer.

The roses I love are all fulsome shrubs, spilling over with flower and leaf and a prickly tangle of bare stem against the sky in winter. Above all there is a sense of profligacy, of beauty so abundant that it can be utterly careless without any sense of waste.

This does not mean that all the flowers must be multi-petalled like the incredible cabbage roses (*Rosa × centifolia*). This year the simple, four- and five-petalled species roses have been exceptionally beautiful. But now, in our neglected, swamped-by-roses garden, the ruffled, bouffanted complexity of albas, gallicas, centifolias, damasks, mosses, hybrid perpetuals and Bourbons holds sway. This is their time and they are masters of all who survey them. Lord knows it is short enough. Within six weeks they will be going into decline. They are as seasonal as asparagus or snow.

We are entering the last of the yellow phase. The garden sets yellow against green with yellow roses 'Cantabrigiensis', *hugonis, foetida*, 'Frühlingsgold' and 'Canary Bird', yellow flags (*Iris pseudacorus*), yellow fire (*Euphorbia polychroma*), dandelions by the yellow million and, best of all, buttercups in the orchard grass, better than anything planted or conceived in the solemn ritual of design.

The orchard buttercups are *Ranunculus acris*, the meadow buttercup, the one we have all held under our chin to see if the reflection proves whether we like butter or not. They like a damp soil in grassland, and are a plant of hay meadows but are easily grazed out of existence. This is why they are so common in the long grass of orchards and dominant in carefully contrived garden 'wildflower meadows'.

We also have the creeping buttercup, *Ranunculus repens*, which is threatening to become a seriously intrusive weed in the increasingly wet soil. It has roots that take tenacious grip hard in by the roots of other, precious plants, and only by tucking your fingers right under the base of the plants and pulling hard will it come away to reveal their distinctive trailing white tentacles. The flowers are poor compensation.

Our other buttercup weed – getting worse every year – is the lesser celandine that has taken up residence in the spring garden. Digging it out just scatters it more. I have tried mulching it into submission, but that doesn't seem to have had much effect. Pretty though.

3 June 2005
Time

Above the doorway to the kitchen garden at Bryan's Ground, the superb garden made over the past ten years or so by David Wheeler and Simon Dorrell right on the border of England and Wales near Presteigne, is the inscription 'The time so short and work so long'. It is, of course, meant to be a reminder to crack on with things and not to waste a second of precious time, but I suspect that few gardeners will need reminding of this. I can hardly remember a time in the past twenty years when I did not feel that there was more work to be done – important, timely work – than I could possibly achieve in the time available to me. On a good day this means that I am energised and highly productive and I work fast and hard. On a bad day I can feel the wind falling out of my sails before I even begin, crushed by the magnitude of what I cannot hope to achieve.

There are obviously things I could do to make this situation better. The first thing I could do would be to simplify the garden so that it does not take around forty hours a week just to maintain it in the manner to which it has become accustomed. I don't *have* to have two acres of highly labour-intensive garden, the vast majority of which is cultivated, broken into twenty quite separate gardens all divided by more than a mile of hedging. As I write these words, I can hear my mother's voice – she was an extremely hard worker herself and had little time for what she regarded as 'idleness' – saying, 'You've made your bed and now you must lie in it.' But clearly I want this kind of garden. I could put half of it to grass and cut it once a week with a ride-on mower, but that would give me no pleasure. I love plants and caring for them, whether as a feast for the eye or for the table. That, for me, is what gardening is all about. I do have invaluable help two or three days a week, and I could get more, but it seems bonkers to pay someone to do what you love. What is the point of having a garden tended by others that you just look at?

But there is another solution, and as I get older and just a tiny bit wiser I am learning to avail myself of it more and more. It is not to try so hard. Just to let things happen. Although all my instincts are to crack on and get as much done as possible, I am trying to sit more and just look at things without minding if the first things I notice are jobs undone. At this time of year, as we enter summer proper, it is crazy not to relish every last second. I will always be a workaholic and probably always feel guilty when I am not working at something because, after all, the time is so short. But I am learning that just sometimes you have to stop and let the garden come to you as it is, to be relished with all its flaws and failings as well as its stunning beauty.

4 June 2000
Peas

My pea failure nags away at me. I like a pea. Everyone likes peas. Every garden with any veg in it at all has to have at least one row of peas, as much as a symbol of freshness and twining productivity as for any practical contribution to the table. Fresh peas, shovelled from the pod straight into your mouth, are a rolling green absolute. You measure other pleasures by it. If I live to be a hundred I shall not forget the sight of my daughter, seen from the bathroom window, her long auburn hair curling in tendrils, pea-like, quietly munching her way along a row of peas at seven o'clock on a sunny July morning.

It seems that the luxury of growing them just to shell and eat straight away only developed in the sixteenth century. Before that they were always grown for storing dried and eating as pottage. What we would call mushy peas, I suppose. But I do like peas in June, and I do not have any ready yet. Reading Cobbett in *The English Gardener* I see that this means that I am either an incompetent or just thoroughly unmanly. He writes, '[E]ver since I became a man, I can recollect that it was always deemed rather a sign of bad gardening if there were not green peas in the garden fit to gather on the fourth of June.' Here I am on the fourth of June and not a single green pea fit to gather in the garden.

5 June 2004
'Mrs Perry'

The oriental poppies are in their prime in the jewel garden. For the last week of May and the first week of June they dominate this large space with their incandescent range of colours from the deep crimson of 'Beauty of Livermere' to the pure white of 'Perry's White'. I love the story of how 'Perry's White' came into being. Until 1903 perennial poppies were all shades of red. But the nurseryman Amos Perry noticed a rich salmon pink form amongst his seedlings. Being the dutiful husband that he was, he named it 'Mrs Perry' and tried to breed a white form from it but without any success. Nine years later, he had an angry letter from a customer complaining that the supposedly pink 'Mrs Perry' that

Overleaf. The box balls at dawn, and later the same afternoon. //

he had bought in good faith had in fact turned out to have white flowers, so could he have his money back? Amos Perry rushed down to the customer, refunded his money with interest and took away the offending white-flowering poppy. And so 'Perry's White', the white oriental poppy with a splodge of crimson at the base of each petal, came into being. Nowadays it is prone to fading to pink, but I like it for all that.

The Pizzicato Group are short and good flowerers but with no one colour. The orange is fabulous, but we cut off the paler pink, mauve or even white flowers as they open because they would clash with the colour scheme. Sacrilegious? Not at all. It makes the orange flowers grow stronger and anyway, in our walled garden, where the colours are all soft, we cut off the orange flowers so it all balances out.

The first to flower for us is always 'Ladybird' although others follow hard on its heels if the sun shines in mid-May, which it most certainly did this year. As soon as the last one has flowered – not long now – I have to steel myself to cut all that lovely furry foliage right down to the ground and add barrow-loads of it to the compost heap. This leaves a horrible gap for a week or so, but the resulting light and air soon work their magic and new foliage grows back with a second flush of more modest flowers later in the year.

7 June 2003
Frost

This really is tempting fate, but I am prepared to say that the risk of frost is now safely past. In my landlocked, low-lying garden, frost haunts the month of May like a spectre at the feast. Just when you think you are safe it can rear its ugly head.

The worst instance I have had so far was on 6 June 1999. That year I was pushing the envelope when it came to planting out our veg, working to filming schedules rather than using experience and instinct which would have told me to take my time. The upshot was that I planted out masses of squashes and pumpkins in a brand-new pair of beds cut out of old meadow, each fifty feet long. The plan was to have a kind of grand pumpkin avenue. In fact that is how it did turn out, but it was a close-run thing. Because 5 June that year was an exceptionally lovely day, hot, bright and with a cloudless blue sky. I remember taking the dogs out as dusk fell around ten at night and thinking that the stars were exceptionally clear and that it was delightfully cool after the heat of the day. The next morning, while I was away filming, Sarah rang me to say that someone had sabotaged our squashes – it looked as though they had been sprayed with weedkiller. When I got home I immediately went to see. They looked as though a flame-thrower had passed over them, but

// Allium cristophii in the walled garden.

I realised what had happened. There had been a touch of ground frost, which had been just enough to burn three-quarters of the plants. The clear night skies had caused the temperature to plummet and – this was where the real damage was done – the clear morning sky had been lit by a hot sun, which had scorched the chilled, tender foliage. I have since learnt that these two beds are the first to get a hint of frost – which I had not noticed when they were still rough grass. Tender plants, a very localised frost pocket, late frost and burning June sunshine all combined to do for my poor pumpkins.

I drove through the Vale of Evesham the other day, where the fields are either orchards with the best plums in the world or planted with a patchwork of onions, cabbages, leeks and asparagus. We stopped to buy some of the first asparagus of the year, freshly cut from the field. Until twenty years ago the best asparagus came from this small region, cut at dawn and sent by train to the market the same day so that it could be in your local greengrocers the next morning. Now the supermarkets import it by the ton from Europe, and Evesham asparagus growers are a dying breed.

A friend's parents had an asparagus bed and the penile shoots that poked up through the chalky soil each spring were fascinating in a reptilian way, but they did not seem to have much to do with food. When I began growing vegetables myself, I was put off growing the stuff by the photographs in the 1961 edition of *The Vegetable Garden Displayed* – which for years was my vegetable bible. This showed the required planting trench as having the profile of a 'W', so that the bottom of the trench had a ridge running along its length. It was done with such terrifying crispness that I didn't dare try to dig it – let alone plant the asparagus roots along its ridge and wait three years before cutting shoots (for precisely six weeks the first year and eight weeks the second ... brilliant expertise or unnecessary bullshit?). Not only did it look difficult, it also was dauntingly long-term. The great attraction of vegetable growing is that, in the main, it is fast. Seed can be sown, grown and eaten in a matter of months. If it does not work you can try the whole procedure again next year, and this year's failure is next year's experience. But asparagus might sit there like a threat for years without ever either providing a good crop or giving you the chance to experiment. All in all it was best left to the Evesham growers.

However, when we stopped this time to get some asparagus for supper, I also bought four dozen F1 plants, persuaded by the grower that

The path leading through the orchard to the water meadows. //

they could just be planted 'normally' in any good soil and that I would be harvesting a few good spears from each plant in a year's time. He did add, slightly ominously, that I must keep them well watered 'if they are to take'. 'Taking' always implies a breathless period when the plant balances on a tightrope of living or dying. It is a time for crossed fingers and Emergency Care.

Whenever I get a plant I have never grown before I look it up in all the various reference books I have. (If nothing else, this process illustrates how much is slavishly copied from book to book.) In the case of asparagus, all agreed on the need for really good drainage, although the degree ranged from the cautionary to the severe, with one instructing to 'incorporate much old rubble, grit and bonfire soil. On top of this, and above the level of the surrounding soil, place a layer of very sandy, gritty soil; a load of sandy aggregate from a seaside quarry is ideal ... This aggregate mixed with leafmould, peat or fine compost and bonfire soil is the planting mixture ...' Phew! You need a builder's yard, not a garden, to do this. In the end I dug my new asparagus patch deeply and shovelled twelve inches of topsoil from two bordering paths to double the height of the soil. I planted them in a block at twelve-inch spacing, watered them well, kept them watered and have spent the past month watching them not taking. I haven't really worked out why, although I suppose I might have overdone the watering or that there is not enough sandy aggregate from a seaside quarry. It is too early to give up on them, but that corner of the vegetable garden has a quiet air of disaster about it.

9 June 2002
Teasels

I was thinking about the old lady and the lawnmower as I pulled teasels, blood sliding with water down my arms. Teasels are extraordinary plants. They got into the garden via the riverbank a few years ago and in certain places – especially the herb garden – have become the main weed, growing through the gentle dryness of sage, rosemary and marjoram like shining green eels. Like angelica they do not spread very far, dropping rather than scattering their seeds, and like angelica they do best on wet, fat soil. Other than that, they are not like angelica at all, except that I have an abundance of both where I don't want them and none in the spot that would serve us best. The really annoying thing is that I have been pulling up hundreds of teasels over the past couple of days and would willingly have transplanted some but, like angelica, they have a long taproot and once that has established itself cannot be shifted. The time to move them is in October or very early spring, before the taproot gets delving parsnip-fashion. For about three weeks in April

and early May they are the best thing in the garden, the leaves upturned and streamlined as though the plant has just been shot like an arrow and landed in the ground. When the light is behind them the young, thin-fletched leaves glow like stained glass. Age coarsens them and by the end of May the sun is sucked into the green, all delicacy replaced by vigour.

Weeding teasels is a wet, painful business. As you pull the plant up, water – by now there are three or four tiers of leaves with the accumulated reservoir of a teapotful – spills over your sleeves and trousers. Within minutes you are sopping. Added to this, the stalks and the spines of the long leaves are armed with short, very sharp thorns that graze your wet skin, and within minutes the water is mingled pink with blood.

The old lady and the lawnmower. I was told the story by a farmer friend whose smile got broader and more disbelieving as he told it. Apparently her husband, aged eighty-odd, was due to come out of hospital where he had been for a month with a dodgy heart, so she, aged eighty-one, decided to mow the grass for him. 'And I don't know how she did it,' the farmer said with his soft Herefordshire voice and widening grin, 'but the silly old thing cut her thumb and three fingers of one hand clean off.' I smiled idiotically back. 'Three fingers and a thumb! Doesn't bear thinking about, does it?' We both thought about it. 'Do you know, I asked her if she had got rid of the mower, and she said, Oh no, it is a real good'un and we still need a mower ...'

10 June 1995
Roses

. . . .

Why do men like roses so much? I guess that it is this measuring thing that men slip into, especially when they go a-gardening. Roses have convoluted enough pedigrees for the most ardent measurer, and their cultivation has for years been metronomic, with a certain spiky harshness that seems to be all man-made. But I think that the main reason that men like roses is because they are lovely, and under the cover of manly affairs, they allow us rough, tough chaps some conventionally acceptable softness and gentleness. It is what I am increasingly learning: to get the most out of gardening, you must let yourself be as feminine as possible.

Anyway, I love roses. It has been a fairly recent conversion. I used to think that they were boring plants with good flowers – in the same category as lilacs or *Lonicera fragrantissima* – and should be obscured in some way both before and after doing their floral bit. But about six years ago I ordered a couple of roses from a nursery for my mother-in-law's birthday. It just happened that this nursery – Acton Beauchamp Roses – specialised in old roses. I started by picking names from a rose catalogue simply because I liked the sound of them. The catalogue was handwritten and the names danced with romance, rolling from the tongue like a tumbling litany: 'Tuscany Superb', 'Alba Semiplena', 'Cardinal de Richelieu', 'Chapeau de Napoléon', 'Général Kléber', 'Pompon de Bourgogne', 'Souvenir du Docteur Jamain', 'Madame Plantier', 'Madame Legras de Saint Germain', 'Cuisse de Nymphe', *centifolia*, 'Fantin-Latour'. I was seduced by the sounds of them before I had any idea what they looked like. This was my first real connection with a nursery, with roses and with the glamour of plants. Up until then I'd seen them as bricks in the construction that made a garden.

I ordered more than fifty different roses from the list, all shrubs, mostly old. As the following summer unfolded I learnt to love many of them and to lust after many I had not yet planted. I never had time to pamper and fuss over greenfly, blackspot, rust or even pruning. Roses grow quite well without human interference. A little help does not go amiss, but it is not essential.

I bought more, including lots of rugosas and ramblers for the wood, and planted them all out, the shrubs in groups of three in large holes loaded with manure, each hole taking perhaps twenty minutes to

// *The gallica 'Cardinal de Richelieu' in the walled garden.*

excavate. The roses were poised all that winter, waiting for my future. There was none. The business went, the house went and the garden too. For a month before moving, the ground was frozen hard and I managed to salvage only a dozen roses from nearly two hundred. Half of them had never flowered for me.

I became very sad and could not bring myself to garden for over a year – the first gap for perhaps twenty years. The salvaged roses sat in pots in front of our rented house and flowered. Sarah would put a small vase with flowers from 'Rose de Rescht', 'Tuscany Superb', 'Charles de Mills', 'Alba Semiplena' and 'Chapeau de Napoléon' by our bed, and on the many sunny days that summer when I lay in that room, unable to get up, they shone deep into my particular darkness.

Then things, as they do, perked up. I planted these refugees in our new garden outside our new house, made them the fixed points of the herb garden, and within six months herbs and roses were flourishing. I got a job lot from a tree sale that just said 'Roses: mixed'. I had a fair idea that they were a mixture of 'Nevada' and the Frühling family, and at fifty pence each for the four dozen I was prepared to risk it. Half were 'Nevada'. I have a soft spot for this bruiser of a rose. The shoots are alizarin and the flowers – they are amongst the first to come and keep popping back almost to Christmas – are white with almost orange stamens. 'Frühlingsgold' and 'Frühlingsanfang' made up the rest of 'Roses: mixed', the former yellow and the latter white, and both tough and good.

I have picked a selection of roses and have them in a granite bowl before me. The colours range from the idiosyncratic slatey crimson of the gallica 'Cardinal de Richelieu', via the velvet red of 'Tuscany Superb' with its yellow core, through the extraordinary delicate pink of 'Cuisse de Nymphe' (Maiden's Blush), which illuminates the petals exactly – but exactly – like folds of richest silk, to the clear white of 'Alba Semiplena'. Fragrance rises up from them like dawn light.

The box psyllids have gone berserk this year. They are evident by the white, sticky dust that they exude and which puffs out of the box when you brush against it. Around the base of each of my box pebbles there is a ring of pale-grey powder as though someone has dusted themselves with talc and stepped away. *Psylla buxi* is an aphid that lays its eggs in box in late summer. These overwinter and the nymphs hatch out in early spring and feed off the juicy new growth. The white stuff is their poo. The nymphs, suitably nourished, then turn into winged adults and fly away, returning in midsummer, but they do not eat the box at this stage. The plant will put on new growth in April and then stop with some leaves curling up, cabbage fashion, and the tops of the hedge or bush often looking a bit bare. But no real damage is sustained, and after the nymphs have gone the box often has a growth spurt around the end of July. The upshot is that I have not had to trim any of my box before August for the past few years. Not good if you are trying to establish a hedge but very good if you already have one the size you want. I do nothing about them although I have heard that a weekly spray of dilute seaweed solution sufficiently strengthens the plant to resist the aphid.

Aphids have been as bad this year as I have known them for a long while. I cannot say I really mind. Gardeners should not get obsessed by the particular. It is the big picture that matters, especially at this time of year. Spring has been as lovely as it could possibly be, and an excess of aphids has not diminished my enjoyment of it in any way. In fact I have probably not been as behind or lax in general gardening terms for years – too much work and no help – and this has not dented my enjoyment or enthusiasm either. Which means that I am learning something new that I like either about gardening or about myself.

| 12 June 2005 'Patty's Plum' | The tulips were a disappointment this year, many blind, many showing all the signs of tulip fire, many not appearing at all, and those that did going over with unseemly haste. So we didn't get our proper fix of intense, outrageous late April/early May colour. But it is like any craving. Sweat it out and it passes. The green, all those fathoms deep of spring green, takes over and eases the pangs of colour denied. But not for long. Because pow! The oriental poppies slip from their sheaths with silky petals so saturated in colour that the entire garden suddenly spins around their intense axis. It is the moment when spring begins to evolve into summer. |

Sarah bought some new poppies from Hereford market the other day: the oriental poppy 'Patty's Plum'. These were not new to us or our garden – we first planted them three gardens ago in Hackney in the mid-'80s – but what was shockingly, wonderfully new was the colour. Only one was in flower, and it was a real, rich burgundy. All our other 'Patty's Plums' have been a much paler, rather mauve colour. It was one of those plants that you had to be told was beautiful and unusual. Your head admired it more than your belly. Well, the real thing is worth hunting down and you will know it when you see it. Anything less than voluptuous intensity in its satin petals is not as good as it can get.

// *'Patty's Plum' is an elusive colour. This one has faded in the sun.*

**13 June 1999
Return**

One of the best things about going away – and I have been away too much over the past few months – is the shock of change that greets your return. As the garden matures, the changes get faster and more dramatic. It is not just that I forget what the garden *does* at certain times of year – although I do – but that it is actually doing *different* things each year. As roots get stronger, top growth gets increasingly vigorous, and shapes and outlines start to appear that I had only dreamed of or, in some cases, never thought of. It is as though the future is suddenly funnelled into this private space, revealing itself dressed in flowers and leaves.

**14 June 1999
Sweet peas**

The other day we had friends to lunch with their various small children. Sarah picked the first bunch of sweet peas of the year for the table – which happened to be 'Painted Lady', pink and vanilla and as old-fashioned and conventionally pretty a flower as a 1940s starlet – and gave them to an eight-year-old girl sitting on her mother's knee. She smelt them and, looking around, I saw all the adults watching her with anticipation. This, I realised, was an initiation, for more than any other

// Allium cristophii and an oriental poppy hatching from its bud.

flower, the first scent of a bunch of sweet peas is a key that will thereafter always open a particular memory's door. The scent has a warmth and soft richness quite unlike anything else, with none of the slightly foetid tang that makes a perfume sexy, but it also holds unfathomable depths of gentle sensuousness. Wood pigeons at dawn. The silken shift of green barley in the breeze. It is a fragrance that enlarges awareness rather than sharpening it. If this fabulous depth of fragrance is available without any extra horticultural talent needed to produce it, it seems extraordinary that plant breeders should have deliberately developed a range of sweet peas that have no scent at all. In fact the majority of sweet peas from garden centres are all vacuously pretty, their fragrance genetically wiped away. Mad.

'Painted Lady' was one of the very earliest sweet pea varieties, being recognised as such as long ago as 1726, around a quarter of a century after the first sweet pea, *Lathyrus odoratus*, arrived in England via one Father Cupani. The first British sweet pea flowered in 1699 and is likely to have been what we now call 'Cupani'. So smelling 'Painted Lady' – developed a quarter of a century on from the first cultivated sweet pea – is a bit like hearing a Bach concerto on original instruments. It is not necessarily better or worse – just closer to the essence of the thing and the nearest we can ever get to time travel.

15 June 2002
Storm

The wind is sending the laburnum flowers shooting out at right angles. The last of the May blossom is scurrying around the back yard like dirty confetti. A storm is approaching. I can't say that we were not warned, and a combination of radio, television and internet weather reporting is all pretty accurate nowadays, but when bad weather does kick in at this time of year it is still a bit shocking. The main problem is that all the new foliage gets saturated with water so that the tender stems simply bend and buckle under its weight. Even the hedges are collapsing. Give it a month or so and the new growth will be sturdy enough to take the odd buffeting, but this storm has come at exactly the worst moment for the garden.

So last night I was staking and supporting plants until ten o'clock, by which time I figured that I was doing more harm blundering around in the gloom than anything the wind might achieve. For years I used canes and twine for supports and still do for my broad beans, but a few years ago Sarah devised a form of home-made supports made from steel wire like the stuff used to reinforce concrete. This is available from any steel merchant. Under her direction we cut these into lengths between

five and ten feet so that they made mini goalposts. Then, and this is the clever bit, we bent them around a large, smooth log so that the cross-bar section of the hoop was bowed. Once formed they hold their shape. We made hundreds of these, which are perfect for supporting herbaceous plants. The legs – which we cut to varying lengths but which are longer than anything of this type that you can buy – push easily into the ground and yet are rigid and will take the weight of a sodden cardoon in full summer majesty, whilst the curved cross bar wraps gently around it. The steel quickly rusted and is all but invisible, and in winter they stack neatly away.

Three or four of these home-made supports costing perhaps fifty pence each, all in, will completely corset the floppiest, sappiest plants such as oriental poppies like an Edwardian beauty in full evening dress, windblown garlands in her hair and dress billowing out from the cinched waist – underpinned by yards and yards of British steel.

It has rained for twelve days now. Occasionally it stops, regroups, tries to soften you with a blast of hot sunshine, waits until bits of clothing are scattered irretrievably around the garden, before hitting you with another sudden downpour. The grass paths ooze a thin brown bile beneath every step. We have got used to the piled density of the sky, although the winds have meant that at least the clouds shift and break occasionally, and the heavily veiled light means that the superabundance of greenness is saturated with a wet heaviness. Heavy Green – sounds like an eco-thrash band. But work has continued outside, despite the wet. This is partly because, as far as plants and gardens go, this is not *bad* weather – just wetter than normal, which means that growing is faster and easier. When the soil has been dry enough to dig and tread upon, it has been fantastic planting weather. But the other reason is that we have people coming to stay and, try and resist it as I might, I cannot deny an overriding desire to impress.

This is not the same as good hospitality, the completely honourable wish to make things as nice and welcoming as possible for one's guests. This is a much baser instinct. I want them to think well of me and the garden. So I have been going round tidying and titivating. But we benefit too, and you need an excuse to get a grip of things and make an effort.

I began by pulling up all the wallflowers. These were well past their sell-by date, but inevitably one clings to the shreds and tatters of flowers, infilling the gaps present to the eye with the memory of them at their best – which was the beginning of last month. The wallflowers were an

Sudden summer rain shines and cleans even as it falls. //

experiment, to see if the artichoke walk – more than forty metres long – would take just the one colour. It did, effortlessly.

So the artichoke walk became the wallflower walk, which, however successful the flowers, is a bloody silly name and must change. My eldest son suggested that we label the paths and avenues with numbers like roads as it wouldn't sound any more pretentious. The truth is that parts of gardens need names, both to identify them and to make the link between place and person. When you name something you possess a piece of it. However, by any name the wallflowers still smelt sweet, and you did not need a road map to find them because as you crossed the path to go to the end of the garden, you dipped into a warm pool of their honey-sweet fragrance.

There are already sweet peas planted up tripods (late – if I had done them on time they would almost be in flower by now) and squashes and pumpkins planted between the tripods. I really don't know if this is going to work, but I like the idea of a long, narrow path through the chaotic foliage of squashes punctuated by sweet peas, even though they are not an obvious conjunction. There may not be enough light and they may sprawl too much given the narrowness of the walk. We shall see.

There was not time to trim the hedges properly so we did the edges trick – trimming all the openings and angles of the hedges – which always gives a much bigger impression of sharpness than the actual work that goes into doing it. Suddenly one of the hawthorn hedges that was planted four years ago by George leapt out into maturity almost from nowhere. One minute it was a hedge-to-be, a hedge growing well that would one day look good, and then, without warning in the rain, it had arrived.

George died last winter, but his presence is in every corner of this garden. His widow came over the other day. It was their wedding anniversary, and she said that she knew that George would be here as much as anywhere.

17 June 2000
Vignettes

There are fresh vignettes every day in the jewel garden: a red peony half smothered by the lime yellow of the *Rubus thibetanus* and made twice as red as its fellow flowers by the comparison; the poppy 'Patty's Plum' finally hitting its stride after three years, growing six feet tall and bearing half a dozen wonderful rich, smoky flowers; the geums, especially 'Mrs J. Bradshaw', bounding back like old friends; the amazing alliums still going strong, with *Allium schubertii* mind-bogglingly strange. One sits in a brass test tube in front of me now, a flower driven to extremes.

The roses are at last spilling free, although there has been a lot of balling what with all the wet weather we have had. One of the most successful combinations is the geranium 'Ann Folkard' with its lime-green leaves and magenta flowers, and the new stems of the rose 'Scharlachglut', which are a deep purple and rise up to rich crimson flowers growing on last year's woody framework. These flowers fade in open sun to something hinting at pink, so we deadhead pretty ruthlessly, especially in sunny weather. This not only eases the aesthetic agonies but also prolongs flowering for weeks.

One of the most curious roses that we have is *Rosa sericea pteracantha* (try saying that after a drink or two), which has the most stunning ruby-red, translucent thorns, great spiked flanges growing off from the side of the stems. In fact we grow the rose for these alone. But this year, because of my lack of pruning, we were presented with a full flush of small white flowers in very early May. The first roses in the garden in fact. I realise that for the past five years or so that I have grown this rose,

18 June 2004
Pteracantha

We grow Rosa sericea pteracantha solely for its beautiful thorns. //

I have pruned off much of the old wood and so removed most of the flowers. The thorns look best on new wood, so I was not unhappy, but having seen how floriferous the bush can be, I'm tempted to hold back again next year. The moral of the story, of course, is that in the garden at least, you learn much more from your mistakes than you ever do from your successes.

19 June 2005
Hens

The months of April and May can be surprisingly lean in the vegetable and fruit garden, with the winter crops coming to an end and the spring and summer ones not really beginning. Although the very cold start to May did have the one small advantage of delaying the sudden spurt of growth that usually causes the broccoli and all winter salad crops to bolt almost overnight. But since March we have had a glut of one crop – eggs. We are now getting an average of nine eggs a day from our fourteen hens, which – despite assiduous application in the kitchen by all of us to the making of cakes, custards, sponge cakes, tortillas and every possible variation of dishes that involve eggs over and above our normal healthy consumption of fried, boiled, poached, scrambled and omeletted eggs – leaves a daily surplus. This accumulates, and at the moment there must be two or three dozen eggs sitting in a bowl on the kitchen windowsill.

But may this be the most of our problems. Too many delicious, fresh, organic eggs is hardly a crisis. I am a firm believer in the benefit of chickens in almost any garden that is big enough to accommodate a small coop or run that can be moved around a patch of grass. To my mind they are very much part of the gardener's armoury and yet too many people see them as a luxury for those of us lucky enough to live in the country. Just a couple of hens will lay an egg a day between them, keep the grass well nibbled thus saving on time, fuel and wasteful energy use, eat up troublesome grubs and insects as well as the animal and cooked waste that you cannot compost, and provide manure to add to the compost heap and company for all but the hardest-hearted person.

My own hens run in a fenced-off area along the boundary of the garden where they love to get in amongst an overgrown hawthorn hedge and bath in the dust that is too prevalent in this very dry year. I would like to have them running free around the garden and we have done this over the years, but they are terrible destroyers of lettuces and seed beds as well as being partial to tomato when they wander into the greenhouse and peck away at all the lower trusses of ripening fruit. Also we have a real problem with foxes. The other night, coming home late from an evening out, we encountered a pair of young cubs dancing and frisking in front of the car along the country lane. I knew that the little buggers or their distant cousins would sooner or later be paying a visit to my hens for a chicken dinner. Over the years I have lost at least half of my birds, including guinea fowl, ducks and countless chickens, to foxes. So I fence the birds in and the foxes out. But despite the need for all that fencing and constant vigilance and the overflowing bowl of eggs, I would not dream of having a garden without some hens.

I am on my knees. The earth is slightly damp and the thin blue cloth of my trousers is pressing an earthy clamminess, imprinting my skin with a fine cotton mesh of dirt. Down here I am hidden, surrounded by eremurus, *Angelica gigas*, a canna, a big (increasing) clump of thalictrum, and the rose with shark-fin thorns, *Rosa sericea pteracantha*, waiting to impale my ear should I tilt in its direction. It has happened before.

20 June 2005
Weeds

But I am completely happy, bending down to the under-layer of plants all about six inches tall carpeting the ground beneath me. In the vegetable garden a hoe does ninety per cent of the weeding, and I run it through the soil every few days in dry weather, but in a border a hoe, however finely honed, is too blunt an instrument. It knows no discrimination. Hand-weeding is the only answer. This is a process of constant sifting and selection, pulling away the plants that must go and carefully working around those that you want to remain and flourish. Inevitably all are jumbled together in a weedy mass of growth and you have to concentrate carefully and work with clever fingers so as not to pull out a tiny treasure. It is lovely work, completely satisfying in itself and a vital part of caring for a garden.

We all know the rather glib remark that 'a weed is a plant in the wrong place'. I have lots of plants in the 'wrong' place in as much as I might well move them to where their qualities can be enjoyed to better effect, but I would never consider them weeds. Most weeds are plants that you do not want. They also tend to be plants that are particularly well suited to growing in certain places, so thrive at the expense of neighbouring plants that you have carefully grown or expensively purchased. Some plants become weeds simply by virtue of their success. You merely want less of them. Beneath my crouching body there is a thicket of bronze fennel, purple orache, milk thistles, onopordums, nasturtiums and marigolds. Other than the milk thistles, all of these have been deliberately introduced into the garden and all are welcome. But not there. Not like that.

Overleaf. The stems of Stipa gigantea are lit like flares in the evening sun. //

Orache can become a thuggish weed, but for a few weeks at the end of May and beginning of June, whilst the plum-coloured leaves are still tender, it is a delicious component in any salad. So we try and weed it from the border almost straight to the plate. The bronze fennel has always seeded itself with abandon because we have encouraged it to do so – the seed heads are bejewelled coronets on an autumnal frosty morning and the best thing in the garden. The birds like the seeds (and so do I). But it has never become unreasonably intrusive before. This year it is growing like a zany thing. Looking down on to it, tucked into the border on my hands and knees, it looks almost like fluffy grass.

The reason for this explosion of growth is that this is the first year that we have not mulched. It was a big decision. Normally we mulch all the borders with a couple of inches of organic material, and the net effect is to suppress weeds, retain moisture and enrich the soil. But the last function, normally seen as such a virtue, was becoming a problem.

Everyone who comes to this garden comments on its extraordinary fecundity and vigour. Almost all of that is a result of the nature of this earth rather than anything that Sarah or I have done. It means that we are blessed with conditions which are continuously encouraging and rewarding. But it has gone too far. By adding all those tons and tons of compost every year we were gradually improving the fertility rather than just replacing what the plants were taking out.

The upshot was that all our flowering plants were starting to become impossibly leafy at the expense of the flowers. They were all growing at least fifty per cent taller than any reference to them said they would and toppling all over the place. Aphids, slugs and fungus latched on to all this soft, sappy growth like the bonanza that it certainly was. All that vigour and lushness was creating problems rather than health.

A healthy plant is one that adapts best to the situation in which it finds itself. There is no objective measure of this. It may well be that a smaller, later-flowering or -fruiting plant is much 'healthier' than another that is apparently outperforming it in every obvious respect because the less showy version can sustain that performance whereas the other has literally outgrown its resources.

So, this year we decided to try and reduce the fertility of the borders, and the jewel garden in particular, by not adding the customary blanket of weed-suppressing goodness. Hence the explosion of weeds of every kidney as for the first time in ten years sunlight is getting to the soil in spring and summer.

// *Looking across the herb garden from the house to the box balls.*

Today, on the summer solstice, the sun apparently reaches its furthest distance from the equator at 7 p.m. I will be raising a glass or two to that, outside in the garden, rain or shine. That, of course, is the nub of the matter. So often, solstices, eclipses, full or new moons, comets, displays of shooting stars or other celestial displays are dependent upon the vagaries of the weather. However, nothing will dampen or cloud my own private celebrations of the longest day. It is the pivot of my year upon which I slowly rise and, I fear, fall. This is because it is the peak of everything that we gardeners aspire to. For sure there is still much to come and summer has only just really kicked in, but this great, shining expanse of day is the horticultural ideal, regardless of what is actually growing outside. Enough has grown to celebrate the fullness of high summer, but there is time enough remaining to sow and grow almost anything. It might technically be downhill all the way from here to 21 December, but for a few weeks the days stretch out for ever and the amount of daylight available is almost – almost – enough to satisfy the need to garden.

I was having a discussion about this the other day with a friend. His view was that the greatest gift a garden can offer is that moment of reflection and tranquillity – usually on a long summer's evening – when you can sit back with a drink and bask in the reflected glory of your labours. I suspect that most people share that view. But for me the greatest pleasure a garden has to offer is to be out there doing. ('Come on,' my mother used to say, 'let's be up and doing.') If I sit for more than a minute or two I always see something that needs doing, and the seat becomes a whole lot less inviting than the simple pleasure of actually *gardening* rather than just looking at the garden. My idea of horticultural heaven is to be weeding or planting as the light gently falls around me and to be able to continue until after 10 p.m. There is always the tendency to go on too long until it gets so dark that the weeds get planted and the precious seedlings weeded, but the pleasure is never diminished.

I increasingly feel that the secret of a good garden is to choose your spreaders carefully so that you are swamped by loveliness. I know that this goes against the grain of many gardeners' buttock-clenching desire to control every flicker of colour and millimetre of growth but there are no transcendental moments to be had down that route. The garden must teeter on the edge of anarchy to unfold fully, and disaster and joyous success will therefore be separated by a few days or a few square feet of accidental combinations. The best gardeners hold the centre together by stealth and coercion rather than by strutting their horticultural stuff.

My dawn walks with a camera are always accompanied by a hungry cat. //

In my case this is true by default. I want to control the garden, but it cocks a snook at my busiest attempts. For the last week in May and the first week of June the roughest, least tended bit of the garden was the most majestic. Nothing else matched the chaotic glory of the patch where I had had compost heaps for three years. Out of sight from the house and therefore un-minded, it became a jungle of angelica, sweet rocket and especially onopordums rising above the chest-high grasses, milk thistles and docks. The four large compost heaps were effectively a mulch five feet deep for two years, and even though we moved them with a bulldozer, the goodness clearly worked into the soil to produce such vigorous growth. It also showed onopordums' irrepressible ability to seed themselves in ineradicable quantities.

We got our first onopordums from chalky Hampshire soil, roughly dug up and wrapped in a twist of wet newspaper by a friend who laughed at our eagerness to plant them in our little London garden, saying that we were barmy to introduce such a weed. That was fifteen years ago. Seed from those same plants is thriving in this garden, three moves down the line. Long may they spread. I love them. Huge – ten feet high – the palest, milkiest blue possible and with papery, brittle leaves edged with hurting spines, they are as exotic and awesome as anything in a botanic garden.

23 June 2001
Maturity

Midsummer has arrived with a fullness that I have rarely known before. So far spring and early summer have been astonishingly good for this garden and, by implication, for us gardeners. The garden has astonished us by doing pretty much all that has been asked of it and a whole lot more. It was only eight years ago that this plot was a bare field. It had been left as set-aside for a few years before I took it over and it took me a year to clear the brambles, tussocky grass and great swathes of nettles. From spring '93 I planted the bones of the garden – the trees and hedges – and began to lay out the borders and various sections of my grand plan.

For at least the first three years any visitor had to take it on trust as practically nothing was more than four feet tall and was growing slowly on this windswept site. I remember visiting Sir Roy Strong, whose garden is a few miles down the road from here, and him telling me that no garden looks like anything for three years and not like very much for five, but then it suddenly turns a corner. After seven years it gains maturity, and after twelve it has a patina of age that is hard to measure. We seem to have reached that point a few years early. This is now a mature garden. It is like finding that your little child is grown up and behaving as an adult. Not unpleasant but very surprising.

// *Oriental poppy flowers brim with sunlight in the jewel garden.*

26 June 2004
Eremurus
. . . .

As the year turns, the foxtail lilies seem to be the plants that best sum up this time for me. I say that the year has turned because the days are technically getting shorter, but for the moment the hours of daylight are marvellously long. On the basis that I need around six hours of sleep, it means that it is light for every waking hour.

The eremurus look at their best in the morning. We have *E. himalaicus*, which is white, and *E. bungei*, which is yellow and rather shorter, planted in our walled garden. Although a yew hedge blocks the sun's rays at dawn, as it rises it starts to slant down into the borders. Then a miracle happens and the eremurus, which by now are standing tall and in full flower, become suffused with light and seem to burn and glow like flaming torches. It is a fabulous sight but only lasts from about 7.10 to 7.45. It is a precise thing, you see, and there are probably only a couple of days in the year when I am there at that time in the morning and when there is a cloudless sky and when the eremurus are sufficiently tall to catch the sun as it peeps over the hedge. But I treasure those days every year and make an appointment with that special combination of plant, sun and cup of tea.

// Eremurus bungei in the jewel garden.

The purpose of the orchard is to house the thirty-seven different varieties of apple that I grow. It does that very well but, if I am honest, it is not much of an ask. Apple trees do not often go walkabout. They stay put, grow a little, bear some fruit and generally hang around, and I love them for it.

But the orchard, as a place, is much more than the sum of its apples. For a start it is very grassy. At this time of year it becomes less a crop of apples than a good crop of hay with a few small apple trees dotted in amongst it. And what hay! For the past month the buttercups have grown a metre tall and glistened with a fabulous golden sheen. It has had crocuses, narcissi and cowslips in turn, and underneath the grass are creeping buttercup, normal buttercups, red clover, meadow geraniums, plantains, sorrel, dandelions and daisies, all wild flowers or weeds according to your inclination.

It will be twenty-five years before the apple trees make the canopy that I envisage. But the grass beneath them changes dramatically from week to week throughout the year. It is unglamorous and ordinary but I adore it. There are a few narrow paths cut through it and an open area that serves for cricket in summer and football in winter. The cricket wicket is recognisably a lawn, albeit one whose uneven surface hugely exaggerates my rather anodyne leg-breaks.

I went out and tried to pick one of each of the grasses that occur naturally in this orchard. The common bent (*Agrostis castellana*) has loose fronds of widely spaced seed heads, each seed visible within its transparent casing. Next to it is a bent stem with the seeds dispersed, husk-like and wrecked like a broken spider's web. There is the violet plume of Yorkshire fog (*Holcus lanatus*), which is dominating the orchard at the moment. Mixed in is red fescue (*Festuca rubra*), much more delicate but equally pink; the whole field shimmers with this pink haze that sits a couple of feet above the ground, balanced on the end of stalks, billowing pollen at the slightest touch.

Then there is a slender head of crested dog's tail (*Cynosurus cristatus*) looking like a foxtail (not to be confused with foxtail grasses, although trying not to confuse any grass with another is terribly difficult, as almost all are nearly identical to at least a couple of others). Cocksfoot (*Dactylis glomerata*) is more apparently visible and when picked and standing in a vase is wonderfully constructed, with widely spaced 'branches' looking as though they are soldered on to the main stem and carrying tufts of flower heads. Smooth meadow-grass (*Poa pratensis*) has a tucked-in neatness to it despite its tufty heads. It is orderly stuff, made to be mown.

The thing that amazes me is that the great swathe of hay is exactly the same stuff as our home-made cricket square. None of it was sown or man-made in any way. It has been a grazed paddock for at least the last century, and our repeated mowing has merely made the short bits more grassy and lawn-like.

This weekend I shall cut and rake it all.

30 June 2002
Roses

This is high season for roses – in this garden at least – but the roses are having a hard time of it. They are good, of course – wonderful even – in the way that roses cannot help but be, but it is clearly a struggle, and they are not doing as well as they might. I realise that in writing this I am falling into the trap of categorising all roses into one petally lump, whereas they make distinct groups, each one doing and achieving different things. There you go – another trap I have fallen into. Roses don't achieve or do. They toil not neither do they spin. They just *be*. And whilst just being they manage to define subtlety, sensuality, fragrance, delicacy and power. It's a good trick.

Since I have been gardening there has been a noticeable shift away from hybrid teas and floribundas to old, or classic, roses, but these are still in a minority, even though they are superior in almost every way. One of the problems with hybrid teas has been that they are easy to hybridise and therefore so easy to make ugly. One of life's lesser ironies is that flowers – one of the best and most beautiful things on this planet – are invented daily by people who have the aesthetic judgement of the average town planner on an off day. And one of the confusing aspects of gardening is that enthusiasm for horticulture can evince itself in fanatical love of a plant, with lives literally devoted to its cultivation, amassing extraordinary depth of knowledge and yet without any development of aesthetic judgement. It is as though after forty years a great art historian were unable to tell the difference between a Bayswater Road daub and a Matisse and yet knew everything about the provenance of both.

I think that is why I always return to writing about this garden. In the end every judgement and decision is subjective and bound up inextricably with taste and preferences. To abstract any garden plant from the garden where it has most meaning to you is to diminish it. Context is everything.

July

It is odd how little changes strike one starkly. For example, the cracks in the paving are filled this year with couch grass growing flat like that coarse grass you get in the tropics. Why now? It is no great problem – the flamethrower deals with it and any excuse is good enough, but it is a new development. And there are hedges that are hedges-to-be for years until literally from one month to another they become proper finished things. There are a couple of hawthorn hedges flanking paths that have done that since May, yet the growth can only be measured in inches.

Now here's a funny thing. We breed slugs and snails in this garden at an absurd rate, and in previous years all our attempts at delphinium-growing have foundered on the smacking of slug lips. Yet this year we have perfect delphiniums, uneaten, maculate towers of shimmering azure blue, violet and purple. Monkland church spire can only echo them hazily across the fields beyond the river.

In the thin, chalky soil of north Hampshire where I grew up, delphiniums marked hot summer days like pillars of flowering righteousness. They were as reliably present in the summer herbaceous border as church was on Sundays. I would return from school in early July to find them there unheralded and confident on a summer's day thick with heat and the uncountable days ahead. The memory of this makes me very sad. The thing I resent and regret most about being sent away to boarding school was that the seasons of my subsequent childhood were lost. You would say goodbye to home in mid-spring and return in high summer with all the shifting movement and subtlety of growing things discarded. May and June were glimpsed as though from a train, beyond all reach save memory. I cannot remember any flowers at school. Just mown grass and the smell of linseed oil and the horrible rhododendrons. You can take the child away from home, but you cannot take home from inside the child. The longing festers. You learn to hold it inside and it hangs on there, gardens, fields and whole parishes tucked away as a survival kit.

Years later, in the mid-'80s, Sarah and I were driving down to Kent at about this time of year. We went round a corner and the barley, still green, suddenly billowed and rippled like silk on the downland. I felt exactly the same acute pang of homesickness then as I did as a child, allowed out for a day, seeing the beech tree fill with leaf and the hedges smoky with cow parsley. Spring was drifting into summer without me. It was then that I knew London was an exile and probably then that I mentally pulled out of our business and started screwing up that patch of our lives.

Now we have delphiniums of our own, in our own grown-up lives, growing here in Herefordshire, a hundred miles from Hampshire and so many miles of water under the bridge. I can't think that we have done anything particularly out of the ordinary this year that has made the flowers grow so tall and unpalatable to the slugs and snails. I am talking of *Delphinium elatum* hybrids, by far the most common and easiest to grow. We have two types, Black Knight, which is a dark indigo with a black eye that makes the whole flower verge into navy, and King Arthur, which is inky blue with a white eye. White is officially banned from the jewel garden but keeps sneaking in under some guise or other. It passes the colour police in this instance because the combined effect is not white and blue but a violet made softer and paler. We bought these as young plants and planted them in April of last year, and they have grown this spring without hesitation, flowering since the third week of May.

We have 'Faust' on order – saw it at Chelsea and loved its shimmering Rothko-like intensity of purple. The hybrids come in colours ranging from deep purple to white via blue, mauve and pink. But I want my delphiniums to be essentially blue. This partly to reclaim lost emotional territory, but also because blues don't come cheap in the garden and should be encouraged and nurtured at every possible opportunity. Delphiniums don't just turn out willingly in indigos, navys, cobalts, aquamarines and icy sapphires, but do so with the volume turned up. They make a big blue sound and, despite my own maudlin memories and the connotation of the blues, it is a joyous noise.

3 July 2004
Drought

Normally I celebrate drought, smugly relishing the water retention of our clay soil whilst other parts of the country bake. But even we are suffering now. I suppose that this is global warming insomuch as it is a trend that is gradually extending rather than a freak.

The upshot is that we are revising our water use and capacity. Last week we rigged up a pump to the enormous tank that collects all the rainwater from three or four of the roofs of our barns. For years this has seemed a half-good thing. At least we collected the water even if we hardly ever got round to using it beyond dipping the occasional bucket in. Once I tried siphoning it out, but the dead rat floating on the surface rather put me off that first mouthful. So now the water both runs to a smaller dipping tank by the greenhouse and cold frames and also can be pumped to the vegetable garden. The flower gardens must fend for themselves. In fact we have never watered them in ten years. Everything gets a good soak when planted and then must survive on the rain. The

// *Stimpy, the one of the identical cat twins with mad eyes, posing.*

real problem at this time of year is that there is so much foliage for the rain to negotiate before it reaches the ground that you can have quite prolonged showers without a single drop touching the soil. The leaves get sodden and weigh the plants down, but it all evaporates, and the combination of dry roots and wet leaves sets up ideal conditions for fungae to develop.

Four years ago we bought the farm buildings attached to this house. Included were a pair of brick hop kilns which would form a wonderfully tall, rich orangey-pink backdrop for a green garden. But beneath the mass of nettles growing in a baked layer of decades-old manure was stone. Digging was out of the question. We could have paved it, but we would never have used it for eating or sitting in because it is north-facing. So we decided to dig out pockets in the stone and plant them each with a box bush, as much because we had a spare twenty-odd plants that we had moved from our previous garden as anything else.

In the end I dug sixty-four holes, which took more than a month, on and off, and which became one of those good ideas you rather regret having. I cleared barrow-load after barrow-load of cobbles from my excavations; these we used to surface the grid between the planting holes. The irregular smoothness of the cobbles softens the grid, and the box are all clipped into rough pebble shapes rather than perfect circles, which, given my ineptitude in being accurate about anything, would be a disaster anyway. I want them to grow big enough so that they almost touch, and there is a temptation to leave them untrimmed (they have put on as much as a foot already this year). But that would be a mistake as we would lose the density that is so vital to their shape. So each year I cut back hard, and slowly, very slowly, they will inflate like cobbly balloons.

I took two days off this last week to clip them and to cut the other box hedges around the garden. Like all annual jobs, I look forward to this as a seasonal marker rather than as a chore to get out the way. The transference from exuberant shagginess to tightly cropped cool is a celebration of both states and a mark of transition from spring to summer. Mind you, clearing up the barrow-loads of clippings from the cobbles is as much fun as clearing up after a party.

As well as the box hedges, we have also given the hornbeam hedges a light trim. Normally we do this just once, in August, and that too involves mammoth clearing up. But this year, as an experiment, we are going to do two light cuts with half the clearing in each case plus more

The box balls, all grown from cuttings, are clipped once a year. //

clipped outlines. The whole point of clipped hedges is to provide a container and a foil for the uncontained and unclipped stuff going on within and around them. So the tighter they are controlled, the more untrammelled everything else seems.

5 July 2003
Figs

Last night as I was having my supper outside – as we do every night at this time of year unless it is raining or blowing a gale – I glanced up and saw that the fig tree silhouetted against the evening sky was dotted with figs. Dozens and dozens of them. You could be forgiven for thinking that this was in itself not that remarkable – after all, where do figs come from if not from fig trees? It should be even less extraordinary when you take into account that this particular fig is just one of six growing against the south-facing interior wall of our walled garden, and the other five have been producing figs, to a greater or lesser degree, without fail for the past six years. But this one plant, which has grown with twice the vigour of the others, has never raised so much as a fruiting bud. Not a dicky bird. Then – on a sultry midsummer evening – bingo!

// *We grow our figs for decoration. The fruit are a delicious bonus.*

I have grown figs for the past twenty years with a success that I have always put down to their willingness to grow and fruit without much help from me other than a prune every spring with another cut-back of leaves in August to expose the fruit to as much sunshine as possible. I always grow 'Brown Turkey' as it is the only one guaranteed to ripen, although were I to garden again in London or on the south coast I might try 'Brunswick' or 'White Ischia'. Figs are as exotic a fruit as I grow, as I am not one for growing anything that would not normally thrive – let alone survive – in the climate of my garden. This means that I have stopped growing peaches, apricots, nectarines and grapes – all of which need a sheltered, south-facing wall to have any chance here. But my figs do OK, all losing some tips to cold winds and frost but regrowing happily enough.

I have nine plants in all, all bought on the same day eight years ago. A couple that are in pots have remained pretty small, while the one that had not fruited until this year has got exceptionally big. I now realise that it is planted on the site of an old earth closet. This means that its roots have developed in hundreds of years of finest Herefordshire night soil, and therein lies its lack of fruit. Give a fig too much legroom for its roots and too rich a soil and it will put all its energy into growing branches and leaves rather than fruit. What I suspect has happened is that it has finally outgrown its root run and is now feeling constricted – which is exactly what you want it to feel to get maximum fruit.

6 July 2003
Blues

I've got the summer blues. No, not yet another parade of my misery, just a revel in the lovely blueness of the season. Blue is a rare commodity at any time of year. Blue never takes over in the way that yellow, red or even purple does. Even in a bluebell wood at its peak, the colour shimmers elusively. Certainly this garden hasn't got enough of it, and I suppose there is nothing to blame but my own failure to plant more blue plants. But even at the ordering stage, blue seems to slip away. It is like clutching at the sky.

One of the biggest successes for us this year is the *Baptisia australis*, which has lovely pea-like indigo flowers spaced evenly against beautifully balanced pale foliage through which the magenta geranium 'Ann Folkard' peeks. The baptisia has been growing in the garden for three years without being remotely convincing but has now come good in a spectacular way, so is a plant really worth persevering with. And, unlike lupins or delphiniums, it is completely slug-proof.

Anchusa azurea 'Loddon Royalist' is becoming one of those gardening clichés that results from the combination of good looks and toughness. It is pretty well a must for a mixed border. Other than its long-lasting blue flowers, it has the great virtue of supporting itself well, which is a rare thing in a tall herbaceous perennial.

The monkshoods are later to come into flower but tough, long-lasting, a rich blue (although never exactly clear) and very poisonous. *Aconitum* 'Bressingham Spire' is one of the first to flower here, and *A. carmichaelii* adds a powerful dash of deathly blue to the softer tones of October.

It need not all be intense. Nigella is both icy and softly cushioned by its thread-thin foliage and drifts through the borders having self-seeded itself year after year. Cornflowers (*Centaurea cyanus*) are more reluctant in this garden, though in our last garden we broadcast them over rough, freshly cultivated ground made up mainly of thick clods of brick-like subsoil and they came up tall, proud and as blue as Robert Johnson at the crossroads.

8 July 2000
Forty-five

I am forty-five today and it is time to take stock. It astonishes me that I have been gardening for more than thirty years. This is not so much on account of the length of time as because I still seem to know so little. Here I am, having reached what must optimistically be half a lifetime, and I feel that I need another forty-five years to know anything about anything.

But I am happily unlearning some things I can do without. I have nourished a bundle of prejudices over the past ten or twenty years and am delighted when I suddenly find that they are no longer applicable. I used to announce proudly that I hated all rhododendrons. Then I visited the wonderful Crarae Garden near Loch Fyne in western Scotland and was staggered at the beauty of the wonderful mix of rhododendrons, azaleas and nothofagus planted alongside the burn that tumbles down the steep hillside. Magical. This spring I was filming down in Cornwall in the gardens of Penjerrick and Glendurgan, and the rhododendrons were extraordinary – this time set off by fantastic tree ferns, *Dicksonia antarctica*. But I think that it will take another forty-five years to learn to love camellias.

Still, a day working in my own garden, a lovely evening with a meal outside and a bottle of champagne will be all the celebration I need.

Everything is always in a state of flux here. Everything that is right seems to be so as much by luck as by judgement and the wrong just part of the process towards rightness.

We have finally planted the last ten metres of a yew hedge begun about six years ago. Each year we have threatened to complete the job and each year fifty things have seemed more urgent. As ever, we are kicking ourselves that we didn't get on with it because it would have been well established by now. I cannot help but love a hedge, even like this when it is a series of small plants at thirty-inch centres that will not join to make anything resembling a proper hedge for a few years yet. I love these lines in time and space.

Last year we sowed a lot of white foxgloves, missed the planting time in autumn and had trays of the damn things hanging around all winter. About half of them are out now, making wonderful white turrets of flower where we finally planted them along either side of the brick path lined with hornbeam hedges and pleached limes. But the other half show no sign of producing more than leaves. At least, if not overflowing, our path is half full.

It is a shirt thing. I instinctively tuck my shirt in. My twelve-year-old son Adam, all his friends and every living soul that he admires wear their shirts outside their trousers. Tucked-in shirts are sad. Shirt flaps are our badge of status, and I know that to casually pull the offending lengths of cloth from my waistband and flaunt them flapping Liam-like in front of Adam and his friends would be saddest of all. Yet I like this. This is where we begin. I like the way that he is sailing off so blithely, shirts ahoy. I am like a tug, cumbersome and unlovely but there to pull him off the rocks if needed. It is a good scene.

Twelve is a fine age for a boy, an age when sex is not yet a blanket of miserable yet irresistible fog and, short of being able to drive, there is liberty enough to do most of the things you want. We live in the country and Adam is a country boy. His idea of happiness is days riding his mountain bike in the fields and woods with friends. Always with friends. He does things alone solely in order to be better at doing them when he sees his friends again. As his nearest one lives five miles away, this means he can only see them if I drive him or their parents drive them. The greatest service I can offer this holiday is to be a cross between a twenty-four-hour taxi service and a chauffeur with access to unlimited petty cash and chocolate. Actually the cash side of things gets not so petty as soon as mountain bikes enter the equation, so a chauffeur brilliantly working the futures market from the seat of the waiting vehicle, equipped with a fridge for the chocolate, would be best.

Whilst mountain bikes are a long-term passion, cricket has become important this summer. What Adam loves more than anything is for me to bowl at him. This is the first thing that we both enjoy equally. Everything in the past has been a matter of me playing his games, of enacting the father. I never played any sort of game with my own father, and it moves me profoundly that Adam is able to do this with me. I never learnt to play games for fun. You either won or were beaten, and practice was directed only at improving the chances of winning. In our cricket on the lawn we are completely equal, two boys playing a game together for the fun of it. The best thing I can do that will make both of us happy over the coming eight weeks will be to tear myself away from the computer screen more often, tell my editors to stuff it and bowl some more overs. I know that in a year or so the innocence will be gone and the countryside boring, so I should treasure this last summer of childhood. I also know that however unplayable my leg-breaks might be, Adam will never rate them that highly because they are all bowled with my shirt tucked firmly in.

12 July 2003
Poppies

The poppy invasion is just coming to an end. It happens every June, but it never fails to surprise me just how thoroughly they engulf our garden. We have oriental poppies (*Papaver orientale*) that are big – enormous even – but not engulfing. We have delicate shirley poppies, bright-red field poppies (*Papaver rhoeas*), orange California poppies (*Eschscholzia californica*) and plume poppies (*Macleaya cordata*), but the poppy that has taken most freely to my garden is the opium poppy, *Papaver somniferum*. What began as a packet or two of seed shaken into the borders has become an annual appearance of thousands of these beautiful flowers in a whole range of colours and forms – almost all of which have crossed themselves.

Sometimes this has thrown up some extraordinary surprises. For instance, this year we have a handful of pure white ones in our jewel garden. They must be the offspring of some of the many shades of pink and purple that are the most common. Some are blood red and a few the most staggeringly intense shade of burgundy or plum. When one of these self-hybrids produces a gem, we wait until the last petal has fallen and then put a paper bag over it and pull the whole plant up, roots and all, to keep in the potting shed hanging upside down. The seeds ripen and fall into the bag, which then gets stored in the fridge until the

// Opium poppies, Papaver somniferum, self-sow right across the garden.

following spring. Mind you, before now I have earmarked a particular poppy, meaning to bag it the next day, only to go out and find every petal gone and the seed head indistinguishable from the thousands around it. So now we tie a piece of twine around the stem as soon as it flowers to mark it. And we thin out hundreds each year because they can crowd out and block all light from the later perennials they grow up through, reaching six feet in our rich soil. When the last one has finished flowering we thin even harder but keep quite a few well into autumn for their fabulous seed heads – which, of course, is why so many seed themselves everywhere.

Ignorance is freedom. For years salvias have left me to roam through the untrammelled (and vast) spaces of my own unknowing. Until a year or so ago salvia was the fancy name for the sage that I grew in its green (*S. officinalis*), purple (*S.* 'Purpurascens') and variegated (*S.* 'Tricolor') forms. As well as the normal broad-leafed sage, we have the narrow-leafed version (*S. lavandulifolia*), which is really much better for culinary use and grows just as easily. Which is to say that once planted you can hardly stop it performing year after year. At the end of a cold winter it might look like a straggly refugee, but cut back hard in March it soon sprouts new leaves of exuberant freshness. Then here come the flowers, a mass of violet and purple spikes sprouting the typically salvian lowered bottom petal with its hood arched above it. Even if you cannot abide the taste or smell of the plant, the flowers make its place in the garden essential. I love the taste myself, and the oily, instantly distinctive scent, and writing this makes me hungry for potatoes cooked in a hot oven with oil, parmesan and lots of sage.

Now new sages have come into my blinkered life. I've realised that *Salvia sclarea*, or clary sage, has been around the garden for the past five years, husbanded by Sarah, without me ever bothering to engage with it, even by asking what it was. Should I admit that level of disconnection? I like its vernacular names Sweaty Betty and Hot Housemaid. Poor Betty, labouring into an unaromatic lather for a pittance. But her flowers are lovely in the right place, great spikes of creamy lilac and big, floppy leaves.

Someone gave us *Salvia guaranitica* last summer, and we potted it up to overwinter in the cool greenhouse. It flowered in early March before being put out in April. That first flush of flowers has gone, but it has grown strongly to about four feet and is about to have another go, which is great because it is an exquisitely intense bluey-purple.

Ligularias 'The Rocket' and 'Desdemona' in the damp garden. //

14 July 2000
Tobacco
· ·

It may be a God-awful summer, but there has still been the odd evening when one could sit outside, fed enough, tired enough, drunk enough just to let the night crawl in quietly like the tide submerging day. To properly relish the gloaming it has to smell good, and gardeners should create mixtures of scent as carefully and deliberately as any perfumer. Perhaps it is due to the absence of competition from visual stimuli, but scent always seems to be stronger in the evening, particularly on a still day.

Thinking along these lines, I planted out the tobacco plants. *The* tobacco plants? Are they obligatory? Well, yes, they do seem to be. At least the marvellous *Nicotiana sylvestris* are. Summer is not right without the six-foot spikes with white tubes of flower falling off them like floral dreadlocks, the whole thing rising up from great, fleshy, surprisingly sticky leaves. The warm flush of tobacco-plant scent just as the sun is slipping below the tree line is as much a measure of summer as sweet peas, dry grass or tomatoes. The season could exist without these things. But it wouldn't exist *enough*.

// Tobacco plants, Nicotiana sylvestris, bedded out in the herb garden.

The roses are billowing and astonishing, which is no more than I expected, but there are odd spurts of growth that seem to have accelerated – like the apples that were marble-sized when I went away and are now green golf balls on the trees. The limes have become entirely shaggy, the orchard grass tired and sere. Finally, the strawberries had developed into a fantastic crop – the best we have ever had. Sarah and I picked them at ten o'clock at night, the horizon blazing with turquoise, then ate them outside in the warm dark. I know that I am shamelessly sentimental, nostalgic and soft as a ripe berry, but dear God of Gardens, this is a hard fact: if I die tomorrow at least I have known the best that this life has to offer.

I am writing this with the rain beating down on the skylight and my hair dripping on to the keyboard. Such joys! The drumming and splashes are music to my ears. This is the first proper rain that we have had in this corner of the country for weeks, and whilst the weather has been lovely, the ground is parched. I never find it too hot in this country. The sunnier it is the happier I am, and I am quite content to trade a few over-hot, sleepless nights for days of glorious sunshine. But the poor garden needs weeks of steady rain just to get back to a reasonable starting point.

Over the past fifteen years a drought has simply meant that the ground will be dry enough to work easily. Being heavy soil, when it gets properly wet it can take weeks to dry out. As a rule, if it rains at any time during the day it will prohibit mowing or working the soil for at least the remainder of that day. So we learn to be very responsive to the state of the soil and do the necessary work when the time is right – regardless of whether it is convenient for us. Of course the other disadvantage of this very heavy ground is that when it does dry out it forms concrete-hard lumps that need a mallet to break up – literally.

Well, this summer it has needed a pickaxe to break the soil to plant into. Great cracks zigzag across the lawns and borders, and quite a few hedgerow trees have already died. But the extraordinary thing is not what damage has been done but just how untroubled much of the garden seems to be. In the vegetable garden all the beet crops – spinach, chard, beetroot – are looking better than ever. My lettuces have been superb. The root crops and peas have not done well, but I put that down to the cold in May as much as to drought.

Plants like brugmansia, canna, ginger and ligularia – all pretty good indicators of drought – are so far so happy. The plant that seems to be suffering most in my borders is *Lysimachia ciliata* 'Firecracker', but it

Overleaf. I love the musty smell of summer rain on dusty earth. //

will do no harm to curtail its rampant spread. The box and yew hedges are fine, and so far only the field maple seems to be suffering from the deciduous hedges. But they will show the effects of drought more clearly in a month or so. I think things are – so far – bearing up for two reasons. The first is that because I never water anything, the roots have to go deep for their sustenance. This makes them stronger and less prone to drying out. The second is that I have added hundreds of tons of compost and manure to this garden so that the soil is open enough for the roots to grow fully and yet able to retain as much water as possible. In other words I am reaping the dividend of all the hours of backbreaking work of digging and spreading the stuff.

22 July 2001
'ad 'er
....

I remember being given a lift a few years ago into a little market town near here by a neighbouring farmer, a ruddy, broad-beamed man with an unconvincing moustache pelmetting a perpetual grin. We talked hops and cattle prices on the way. As we drove down the street we passed a woman with pushchair and toddler, and he smiled and waved. 'I've 'ad 'er,' he said. We passed another, younger girl at a bus stop. Another wave. 'I've 'ad 'er too,' he said.

I saunter round the garden at this time of year counting the triumphs without tallying any to myself. I've 'ad roses, alliums, lilies and poppies. I've had delphiniums, acanthus, crambe and clematis too. But I've had them like I've had sun on my head or lungs full of air. This is midsummer proper, the middle of what we experience as summer rather than a notional dateline you cross at midnight like a map mark in the middle of the ocean. The baby buzzards flop around the sky, mewling and whistling for help, as gawky as dancing chickens. Their parents soar elegantly in attendance over the garden, used to being taken for granted here in the buzzard-rich west. A storm sits on the horizon like a plank, undecided. In the vegetable garden there is a row of bolting 'Lobjoits' lettuces standing like a reproach, although I swear that they have all shot like this overnight. The ligularias, massed all together in this garden for the first time, having spent years dotted about the borders, blaze furiously, with *dentata* surprisingly orange and *przewalskii* black-stemmed, lemon-yellow and only half there at any one time. The orchard is cut and bleached, unused to the exposure. The apples take over the space after a couple of months as almost incidental ornament to the grass.

The odd thing about this time of year is that it is so solid and assured. Up until the end of June everything seems fragile in its freshness, everything changing daily, usually for the better. You go

// Only one corner of the yard, packed with pots, gets good sun.

away for a couple of days and the world is a different place. As the years go by I increasingly regret and resent having to go away from here between April and August. The sense of missing the party gets worse all the time.

25 July 1999
Meaning

The most common criticism that I have of many publicly acclaimed gardens is that the whole is less than the sum of the parts. You can find something to like in most gardens. But I like gardens that are a piece of work, a recognisable entity, albeit made up of many different areas or even styles. I like to see the hand that made them evident everywhere. Good gardens must always be more than the sum of their plants.

I like this garden more than any other garden in the world, and I probably would do even if I thought it was no good, which I don't. I think that it is fantastic. It makes me very happy every time I step out into it. The point is that unless you love the garden that you are making, I don't think that you can properly appreciate other gardens. Unless you are engaged in the day-to-day struggle to realise this huge outdoor work

// *Fennel in the herb garden is grown as much for its seed as its leaves.*

of art, you will not see beyond the surface of what other people are trying to achieve – or have achieved – in their gardens.

Everything here has been made by Sarah and me, working in complete harmony, largely with our own hands. It is still very much work in progress. I like the great long alleyways cutting out into the countryside with the boxy areas going off them, and I like the way that it is all so ambitious and crammed. There is no doubt that after a certain age one puts into the garden the hopes and aspirations that youth put into the wider world. Modesty is an underrated virtue, and in your garden you can be both modest and ambitious without one compromising the other.

I love the intimacy that one has with a garden, the way that each plant as it grows is utterly familiar in every cast of light and change of weather. It is a personal place in the way that no one else's garden could ever be. This is not the objective analysis of a botanical drawing – a genre, incidentally, which has always left me cold – but the subjective relationship of the self with something beyond and bigger than you. Every square yard is heavy with meaning.

This, I think, is the essence of a lovely garden, otherwise it is all surface glamour, just like a Chelsea show garden waiting for the judges. That besuited, solemn gang would not get far here before tripping on something. I love the way that the paths are strewn with children's bikes and toys. I like the dog's punctured footballs wedged in the bottom of the hedge and my fork standing in the leeks, not put away since I used it there a week ago. All this domestic paraphernalia is as important as the first tithonia flowering this morning or the way that the difficult, awkward jewel garden is coming together, or the alchemilla spilling all the way along both sides of my fortieth-birthday forty-yard path, or the *Acanthus mollis* with better flower spikes this year than ever, or the spring garden at its April best.

Sarah called me from a country-house sale, the escalating bark of an auctioneer behind her. Would I like to come over and meet her there? Not really. I was doing something else. This one was special, she said, I would find it really interesting. There were some fascinating old gardening tools I should see. I was persuaded. Oh, she added as I was about to put the phone down, bring the trailer and the chainsaw.

It turned out that Sarah had bid for 'The contents of a potting shed'. The bidding was blind because no one knew what the contents consisted of since the door was jammed shut and the window blocked. So Sarah

26 July 1995
Treasure
....

stuck her finger up at fifty quid, no one else bid, and it was knocked down to her. Everyone thought she was mad. The door was jammed because a large ash tree had fallen on the shed and smashed the roof. It was not unreasonable to suppose that whatever was inside was smashed as well. Nevertheless Sarah was as fiercely jaunty as I was unchivalrously gloomy, muttering bitterly about fifty-pound notes and drains as I started the saw.

The tree was cleared and the door broached. We both peeked inside. There, despite the pierced roof and imploded tiles, we saw row upon row of clay pots of all sizes, all undamaged. Treasure! There were more than eight hundred in all, averaging out at just over a halfpenny each, and at least half were nine-inch pots or over. All eight hundred had to be carried down a long path to the trailer, loaded up carefully and unloaded into a less derelict potting shed at the other end. It took two twenty-mile round trips travelling gently to minimise breakages, but six hours later all were moved.

And what riches! Forget the cost of buying them – the market price that day was fifty quid after all – just the frank delight of possessing them made one feel a lottery winner, and we basked in their dull orange glow as they were stacked on their sides in ranks within the gloom of the potting shed that had been hitherto potless. This happened four years ago, just after we had bought the house and before any gardening had started, and although we have been profligate and careless with pots, they still remain in their hundreds.

27 July 2003
Hedges

It is the hedge-cutting season. Well, it feels like a season here because it takes weeks to do them, what with my absenteeism and the part-time, if heroic, assistance from Norman and Jayne. Because this garden is so lush, we try hard to keep the things that are meant to be trim as crisp as possible. This means cutting the hedges two or even three times a year. It is not hard to know when to do it. The hornbeams go from plump like a well-feathered hen to shaggy almost overnight around midsummer.

We have something like half a mile of hornbeam to cut if you include both faces. The outsides, flanking paths, are easiest, although the temptation to sweep the hedge-cutter upwards and thus create a bulging profile, thinnest at the bottom, has to be constantly resisted. The insides not only mean negotiating over-full borders but also getting the trimmings out without making the garden look like a combine harvester has trundled round. Then there are the tops to be cut, which needs the Henchman, a kind of platform on wheels. It also needs me because no

one else associated with this household will do heights. I love it up there, am happy to go as high as the platform will take me, looking at my garden with a swallow's eye. And then it all has to be cleared up. On the paths the cuttings get mown in situ and taken straight to the compost heap, where they are ideal as a mixer for grass. Elsewhere it is just a matter of laborious raking, gathering and removal.

So why all the bother? This is expensive work using expensive kit and time that I just don't have to spare. The truth is that cutting the hedges is as important to my garden as mowing the grass or growing vegetables. A hedge is as much topiary as your cone or box ball. Their crispness is the rest of the garden's licence to frolic and spill.

All change. It is the summer holidays, and Tom has celebrated this by shaving his head and cutting the orchard on the same day. It is a combination that satisfies everyone because the hair business is strictly forbidden by school, so satisfyingly rebellious, and cutting the grass earns major brownie points from me.

28 July 2002
Holidays

Late summer hedge cutting redefines and tightens the whole garden. //

228

Both field and child are blinking slightly in the unaccustomed exposure. The change in both is shockingly dramatic. But it is a significant milepost in the motion of the year, the cutting of the long grass and, unlike Tom's hair, which will regrow soon enough, it changes everything. You would think that it would be tinged with sadness, the passing of the orchard's lushness, but it feels entirely positive – a harvest rather than clearing up after the event. The grass had got tired and flat and all its fluffy beauty was reduced to railway-siding scruffiness measured out in thistles and docks. When it was all gathered and shipped to its own separate compost heap the orchard stood raw and exposed, the spaces between the trees a sudden sharpness of bleached grass. The chickens love this new open space and rummage between the fruit trees excitedly, the cockerel quite beside himself trying to be in four different places at once.

And the apple trees themselves are suddenly cast in a new light. Between blossom time and now they are mostly just shapes against the sky, defining elements in the landscape but without much individual identity. Now, made approachable by the big grass cut, they become important by their differences. The apples have done their June drop unnoticed into the long grass and those that remain are ripening for the fall. Again, this is not cause for regret at time passing but exciting. Something new is beginning to happen.

There is an interesting case study in my damp garden. Most of our hostas are grown there with the exception of some 'Blue Seer' in the jewel garden. This means that there are around sixty different hostas all growing together, in amongst ligularias, the regal fern, lysimachia, lovage and a range of other moisture-loving plants. They are divided into two beds either side of a narrow path. One of these beds is deeply shaded by a tall hornbeam hedge, only getting sun after midday. The shade happens to fall almost exactly along the middle of the path. As a consequence of this division, the hostas, which were growing exceptionally well at that time, responded very differently to the succession of sharp frosts that we had in May. Although the temperature was exactly the same across the whole of this section of garden, the piece shaded from the morning sun showed no sign of frost damage at all, whereas the hostas on the other side, identical in growth, variety and soil, were badly burnt.

There was nothing that we could do about this so we left them to get on with their lives, which, to all intents and purposes, they have been

30 July 2005
Hostas

Clematis grow well for us. This is 'Lasurstern' in the jewel garden. //

229

doing. But a few weeks ago Sarah and I were walking round the garden at about 10 p.m., relishing the lovely late light of midsummer, when we noticed that some of the hostas were laden with snails. Dozens of the things, slowly munching through the leaves of 'Snowden' and *sieboldiana* var. *elegans*, both of which constitute a substantial mouthful. On the other side of the path, no more than three feet away, exactly the same hostas were untouched, totally slug- and snail-free.

This just goes to show that predators will always attack weak or damaged plants first. A healthy plant will both be less appealing to most predators and better able to recover from any attack. Slugs and snails, of course, like rotting vegetation best, and the frost-damaged leaves of the hostas were perfect fodder. Likewise, hostas grown in pots or against a wall, and which are therefore likely to be too dry, are more stressed and desirable to a passing snail than one grown in rich, moist soil.

I notice this daily at this time of year with my lettuces. I cut at least two good-sized lettuces every day. These are, to all outward appearances, without blemish. They taste fantastic. But I have to wash them very carefully to remove the slugs. Last night I counted the slugs washed out. It came to twenty-three, although I will admit that some of these were very small indeed – although big enough to know if you were chewing on them. Was this a sign of how 'bad' my slug situation is or a tribute to the robust health of my lettuces? I, of course, think that the latter is the case.

August

Our dry garden has been put to the test this hot, dry summer. Our office has a large window that looks straight on to the back of the border so you look out through spires of *Acanthus mollis* flowers and the oaten heads of *Stipa gigantea* on to the verbena beyond. It is like looking into an aquarium.

We planted up the dry garden using just spares that we had around the place. We started with our sedums as these had been the prime instigators of the whole pick-and-shovelling process. The truth is that our 'normal' soil is fare far too rich for any sedum. Sure enough, having moved them to their new quarters they have stood short and firm and without any need of staking.

It all went so well that we had two more goes at expanding the area last summer and autumn, adding borders across the rest of the yard that back on to the curved stone wall of the walled garden. The dry garden is now bounded by brick and stone with a large fig softening this by overhanging and creating just a touch of summer shade. A builder's yard is now a flower yard. The extra planting space proved to be even more hostile territory than the first bed because as we began to dig we uncovered the footings of the original early-fourteenth-century hall house on the site. This meant that we had to be very careful and not remove anything that might possibly damage it. After about six weeks of careful excavation, photographing every stage, we were left with a depth of a couple of inches which we duly backfilled with loam before tentatively starting to plant.

We planted lots of *Verbena bonariensis* that I had overwintered in pots as seedlings, and I also took lots of cuttings in the spring from their new growth – all of which have prospered. They are now all standing seven foot tall, with scarcely any foliage but strong straight stems. Teasels – which every book will tell you grow best in damp conditions – are also straight and tall. Evening primrose has seeded itself and flourished. I put in a white *Cistus* 'Thrive' named after the excellent charity of the same name. We have some grasses – *Stipa arundinacea* and *gigantea* – which are both less lusty than their counterparts elsewhere in the garden but perfectly healthy. There are a couple of clumps of *Miscanthus sinensis* 'Gracillimus' that have so far retained a fresh green amidst all the parched stems and foliage. The alliums loved it, as did the tulips and opium poppies, although all are now ghosts with rattling seeds. We planted *Achillea* 'Moonlight' with its powdery grey foliage in honour of the late Alan Bloom, and foxgloves, feverfew and mulleins because we had them to hand. Rosemary, lavender and oregano have finally found a home they feel comfortable in. In the first bed, with its extra three inches of soil, the gaura are flopping and flowering in a delightfully louche manner. In the shallower soil it grows upright and half the size but still with the pretty white butterfly flowers that keep reappearing well into autumn. We planted both *Acanthus mollis* and *Acanthus spinosus* and the *A. mollis* is doing much the better of the two.

There is a theme emerging here. On this sun-baked, thin soil plants have to be tough to survive. Foliage suffers. The blue and grey foliage does much better, and plants draw into themselves to minimise evaporation and demands upon their roots. But the flowers are fine, and the ratio of foliage to flower much lower than anywhere else in the garden. Although I am a firm advocate of having lots of foliage to flower – it is the essential rice to the curry – there is something wonderful about the tall sparseness of this piece of garden. Nothing is extravagant, nothing wasted, yet the overall display is powerful and dramatic. It was never intended to be more than an experiment but already, one year on, I love its stately airiness and confidence. It can certainly be improved, but these gardens we make and live in have no need for that kind of objective measurement. Delight is the only meaningful prize.

3 August 1999
Blackcurrants
....

I feel quite evangelical about blackcurrants because this is the first year that I have ever grown them properly. In the past we have had the odd bush, usually in the wrong place and not looked after, so last winter we set about making a 'proper' soft-fruit area, with raspberries, gooseberries, and red-, white and blackcurrants, all inside a fruit cage. It felt a very stolidly grown-up thing to do, but it's been great and the blackcurrants greatest of all. Once they are in the ground and heavily mulched you can pretty much forget about them until you harvest the great mass of glossy black berries, like caviar on steroids, attached to their strigs (the bit that the berries – any berries – are all attached to).

Blackcurrant ice cream knows no peers. Hot blackcurrant sauce with meringues. Try it. Nothing will ever be quite the same again. And, perhaps most convincingly of all, there is Summer Pudding which, if halfway decent, is the best of all puddings. Ever. It is a particularly British thing, and that musty tartness is part of our cultural taste, like drinking tea and eating marmalade for breakfast. Perhaps when the Pilgrim Fathers went to America they found strawberries, blueberries, hackberries, chokeberries but no currants, and they pined for them: 'Currence' were ordered from London agents by the Massachusetts colonists in 1628 as a matter of urgency.

We had friends staying the other day from Papua New Guinea. Their idea of English heaven was to go up to the top of the garden to where the three rows of raspberries grow and pick colanders full of the fruit, popping one into their mouths for each one that was collected. And we were all there too, eight of us standing in the narrow corridors between the dense rows of canes, a solid wall of raspberries reaching above our heads, slipping the soft, knobbly fruits from their cones, dividing them evenly just so – one for the mouth and one for the kitchen. A raspberry party.

Oh, but it has been a year for the fruit! Strawberries so sweet and honey-warm till we were sick of the sight of them, gooseberries like opals and as winey rich as the most revered grape, redcurrants and blackcurrants and slinky white currants by the bucket – and freezer – full. All the months of weather accumulated and conspired to make the perfect conditions, a warm, dry early spring so the new growth ripened and the flowers set, enough rain for the young fruit to swell, and then dry weather when they were nearing ripeness so the sugars slowly accumulated to give an intensity of taste rarely found in an English summer. But best of all have been the raspberries.

I have always adored them but I used to be terrified of picking raspberries. When I was a boy they were grown in a permanent fruit cage that was irresistible in summer to blackbirds, which seemed to get in easily enough but to be incapable of making their own way out. At any one time there would be two or three trapped in there. Collecting fruit meant braving birds fluttering in the confined space of the netting and I hated – was petrified – of this. For a couple of years after I planted my own adult raspberries I grew them in a fruit cage, and sure enough every day there were trapped and frantic blackbirds and thrushes hurling themselves at the netting that had to be negotiated in order to pick a bowl of fruit. A few years ago I realised that I did not have to do this. I was a grown-up. It was my garden, my fruit, my fruit cage. Freedom – a real liberation – meant not caging the raspberries.

Now the birds have lots, we have lots, sometimes our friends have lots, and there seems to be plenty for everyone and everything. And no more raspberry terror.

The blackbirds shriek a warning from hidden branches as the cats saunter down the paths, and one sings an ecstatic evensong every dusk on the dead branch of an alder at the edge of the garden. But they scatter the mulch on the borders like chickens in a barnyard, steal the raspberries and redcurrants, and peck great holes in the strawberries. I love them

7 August 2003
Raspberries

8 August 2004
Birds

for it. I would put out bowls of fruit at each corner and renew the mulch each morning like strewing herbs if I thought that was what it took to make them stay.

To notice birds you have to watch them. This takes no more than your eyes and the desire to look, but I have fallen miserably short recently. It has been a year mostly seen from the window of a car, looking into the blind lens of a camera or gazing out of the window of this room. It is no way to carry on. I have snatched at perfection like glimpses from a train. Birds have been in every frame.

I love sitting with a mug of tea, hands dirty, back aching, watching the birds watching me. In the winter I am inevitably accompanied by a robin, all head-cocked aggression, or more timidly by a wren, flitting like a mouse along the bottom of the hedges. These are not birds that will bring the twitchers driving through the night, yet how many other wild animals do we have the opportunity to observe so closely? Who else but gardeners are so regularly in such a good position to watch and share this glimpse of life?

We share our garden with two kinds of birds. The first are those that dip in and out of our sky. Sometimes, like the swallows, they are predictable and a measure of a season. Swallows in summer, fieldfares in autumn and curlews heralding spring. Others, like the occasional heart-stopping peregrine, grace us with a rare visit. The swifts, swallows and house martins are my favourites, and when they go they leave an empty space much bigger than the scimitar span of their wings. It is a real loss. Because we live next to a river and water meadows, we have ducks, geese, curlews, heron and the oddly misplaced but common shag. We have ravens, crows, rooks and magpies but practically no jays, very few wood pigeons but loads of doves. Sparrowhawks are more common here than kestrels. Buzzards much more common than both. The tawny owls too-wit and kee-wick to each other half the night, although I heard on the radio this morning that numbers are 'dangerously down'. Last spring a barn owl flew across the corner of the garden at the same time of day for weeks on end. Each time we feared it might be the last. One day it was. The numbers *are* dangerously down.

Then there are the birds that occupy the body of the garden itself. A garden like this, lush, saturated with growth and all the attendant seed, fruit, berry and leaf, plus the unknowable numbers of insects, caterpillars, and crawling creeping beings – all of which get bundled stupidly under the banner of 'pests' – provides the perfect home for song and small woodland birds of almost every type. Finches, tits, flycatchers, blackbirds, thrushes, robins, sparrows, starlings (although far fewer of

// Light plays a vital role in the jewel garden as the sun sits lower.

these nowadays) and wrens (have you heard a wren's song slowed to 16 rpm? It is the music of an oboe or a cello...) inhabit the garden just as much as we or the plants do. They provide the soundtrack, they provide the extras filling the scene.

I suppose that there is a third category that is completely borrowed. Whereas the birds that occupy 'our' sky feel as much a part of the garden as the clouds, for the next five months the fields around us will have flocks of visiting redwings and fieldfares that scatter into the orchard and hedgerows but on the whole try and avoid us. Both are thrushes visiting from the north to escape the worst of Arctic winters but whereas the redwings are shy and flighty, the fieldfares are the most truculent of birds, strutting and looking for a fight like a pack of football fans in a foreign city. Pheasants stray into the garden and last year raised a brood in the jewel garden. In summer we have the cuckoo or, more accurately, its call. Often distant sound falls into the garden and, as long as it lasts, out-blooms any plant. The song and call of skylark, cuckoo and curlew are all sounds we hear much more often than we see the birds that make them.

9 August 2003
Ducks

Sarah gave me six ducks for my birthday. I have always had a soft spot for ducks. We did keep a few some years ago, but three flew away to the river and were never seen again, and the other four were eaten by the fox. I did not have the heart to replace them simply to serve as fox-fodder, so we have been duckless for a while. Ducks are the most charming of all fowl but also, as an organic gardener, I am very keen on having them around as slug-catchers and like the idea of a posse of them working through the garden on a daily de-slugging mission. So I was thrilled when I was handed a cardboard box that was tied with a big bow and which cheeped when I took it. Inside were three pairs of tiny ducklings. When I asked what breed they were I was told 'white-ish, piebald and blackish'. It would do. In the end most ducks are variations on a mallard, and these were very attractive regardless of their anonymous pedigree.

For the first few days we kept them in a broody coop to get used to the place and made them a round pond. I have made lots of ponds on telly, but this was the first for my own garden. It was perfectly round, two good paces in diameter and rather inviting. But when the ducks were let out and pointed at the water they studiously ignored it. We tried herding them into it, but they scooted round the outside squawking in alarm. We even picked them up and put them in the water, on the basis that nature might kick in and their genetic disposition to up tail and

dabble would take over. Not a bit of it. It was like putting a cat in a bath. Total horror and as quick an exit as possible. After five days of this pond-phobia I was getting worried. They seemed to regard me as their new parent, so would I have to get in, quack invitingly and dip my head under water? Given the heatwave it was not an unattractive prospect. Finally one evening, following another abortive water-induction ceremony, one of them calmly walked up to the pond and sailed into it. The others followed serenely. Since then you can hardly get them off it.

Which just shows that you can take a duck to water, but they will swim when they damn well choose to.

10 August 1997
Poppies

The poppies have been amazing this year, in field and in garden. Driving through Suffolk the other day I passed field after blood-red field. It is impossible for anyone remotely sensible of twentieth-century history not to be profoundly moved by this as well as delighted. The field poppy (*Papaver rhoeas*) has always been a symbol of death and rebirth, and no other flower combines exquisite delicacy of tissue with

A birthday present from Sarah. Every one was eaten by a fox. //

such a vibrant blaze of colour. After the flat fields of Flanders were shelled into a nightmare of mud, flesh and bone, the poppies grew as never before, dormant seed stimulated by obscene disturbance and fertilised by the rotting flesh of young men. That the flowers should be so brightly sanguine and yet so fragile merely confirmed the aptness of their flowering.

Everywhere where the ground is disturbed, be it by shells or the plough, poppies will grow. It is only the blanket spraying of crops with herbicides that stops this. It seems that until the Second World War and its immediate aftermath, when food production intensified and to that end sprays of every kind were encouraged, poppies were not really regarded as a flower, just a weedy inflorescence. Only in their absence have our hearts grown fonder. But poppy seeds are incredibly patient. Each flower will produce around 17,000 seeds of which around 3,000 will remain viable and dormant in untilled ground for at least a century before bursting into flower when the ground is disturbed and the seeds are exposed to light. This year, because of the BSE scare, many farmers have cultivated grassland that has been unploughed since the war. Hence the rash of red in the fields for the first time in half a century. Likewise when a garden is cleared for the first time for years poppies will grow seemingly from nowhere, the ghosts of abandoned borders.

Stasis

I have been spending a lot of time in the vegetable garden, changing the vegetables over rather in the way that one changes the bed linen. It has taken me days spread over weeks, although, because of the drought, it has been accompanied by a curious *Mary Celeste* stasis, with the barrow half full and the tools where I left them and the peas and beans stuck at an age when change means decline. This lack of urgency is nonsense, of course, a kind of dry-soil-induced indolence that will be washed away with the first storm. There is *so* much to do and so little time.

But we are plugging away, which is the real secret of gardening. Sarah and I spent all weekend in the veg garden, working hard and long together for the first time since she broke her wrist at the end of April. It was hot, dirty, tiring and entirely happy. The early potatoes ('Premiere' and 'Charlotte') got blight and have been cleared, dug and stored. 'Premiere' is sold as being particularly blight-resistant, ho ho. I shall not grow it again.

We harvested the onions. It is not a great crop this year but will do. Not enough water at the right time. The garlic was not great either.

Newly clipped box in the hop kiln yard. //

We pulled the early broad beans and peas ('Aquadulce' and 'Red Epicure' for the beans, the peas were 'Douce Provence' and 'Carouby de Maussane'). They were very good this year. Too good really as we could not eat, or even process for freezing, at the same pace as beans and peas were being produced, even though the children love to descend on the peas and stand, quietly busy, plucking them from the vine and shovelling them from pod to mouth.

12 August 2000
Garlic

We had the best-ever garlic harvest this year. Every little clove has translated into a great fat bulb, reeking wonderfully of the Mediterranean.

I adore garlic and regard it as a miracle food, making most things taste better and wonderful for your health. It also seems to be good for the soil as anything growing in the same ground immediately following the garlic crop always does very well, so I followed it with cabbages (Savoy), purple sprouting broccoli and calabrese. I don't know why I grow the latter, because no one in the household really likes it – but every year I feel as though we should try to make something genuinely delicious from it. I am sure that the brassicas will not taste even slightly of garlic, although I wouldn't mind if they did and would be more than happy if that in turn kept the horrible cabbage whites at bay.

I regard these as a major pest even though they are a pretty butterfly. One year I offered the children ten pence for the carcass of each one they caught – thinking that this would keep them quiet for hours and only cost me about fifty pence – but within an hour I had forked out nearly five quid. I know I should net against them, but I hate nets in the veg garden for both practical and aesthetic reasons. I like to be able to get in and poke and prod at what I grow. Mind you, I didn't net the blackcurrants, and almost overnight the blackbirds and thrushes ate every last one. Perhaps I should plant garlic with those as well.

13 August 2001
Onions

It is a measure of the turning year when the onions are all harvested. This year's are all in, and they are not a bad crop, although in truth I am not really sure at which point an onion harvest becomes good or bad. Most have been grown from sets, with 'Sturon', 'Turbo' and 'Setton' very successful. I grew 'Red Baron' from seed, and they have done fine, although the 'Brunswick' sets are a little on the small side. Does this matter? Not too much. The main things that we want from our onions are tastiness and the ability to keep, in that order. We certainly do not

want them too big nor too small. The size of a smallish apple or cricket ball is about right. At the moment they are still in the greenhouse, drying on slats. After about ten days of this they will be stored on racks in the potting shed and should last us through until about March. If I do grow enough to last beyond this they always start to sprout, so there is not much point.

Damsons are not grown widely enough. How often do you see the fruit in shops? But if I could have just one tree, I would choose a damson over any plum every time. This part of England, along the border with Wales, has a long tradition of damson-growing. All members of the plum family like our rich, rather wet soil, although only damsons, by far the toughest of them, are untouched by our strong winds and very cold snaps of winter weather.

Damsons work well in pies and crumbles as well as being delicious on their own, stewed. Pickled damsons, swimming in red liquor in a Kilner jar, make a wonderful accompaniment to any cold meat, but we

14 August 2004
Damsons

. . . .

Freshly lifted garlic drying in the sun. //

turn most of our fruits into damson cheese, a very intense conserve that goes well with game of any kind and is superb with lamb and, ironically, also very good with a strong cheese.

Damsons are not difficult to grow and, because they come true from seed, have quietly carried on down the years so that the fruit you eat from your slightly scruffy tree in the back garden tastes the same as the fruit the Crusaders brought back from Damascus. You need not worry about cross-pollination with most damsons. Of the self-pollinating varieties, 'Merryweather' produces the biggest of all fruits and is a heavy cropper, the fruit lasting well into autumn on the tree. 'Bradley's King' was first recorded just over a hundred years ago, has fruits sweet enough to be eaten raw and is covered in bloom when ripe from mid-September on.

I have planted 'Farleigh Prolific' and 'Merryweather' in an existing hedge of natural damsons on one of our boundaries. Damsons lend themselves to this kind of informal planting, but I also put 'Shropshire Prune' in my orchard and already it is growing into a handsome tree with fruits that have real intensity of taste. There is a lot of debate about

// *The plum (or possibly damson) 'Shropshire Prune' ripening nicely.*

this variety. There are those that swear it is a plum and others who put their life on it being a damson. For what it is worth, the evidence suggests to me that it is actually a plum. It is damson-like in the smallness and darkness of its oval fruits, although the ends are usually more pointed on a damson, and it is very sweet and plum-like to eat when ripe. The fact that there is such doubt or debate merely shows the closeness of damsons to plums. Whatever you like to call it, it is a variety known since the sixteenth century and is perhaps the nearest taste we have to the fruit of the Tudor dining table.

I have been filming all week at home, which means I have been in limboland. I am actively being used perhaps half the time but am on standby for the remainder, unable to go out of earshot or make a noise lest I spoil recording, yet in my garden and free to potter about. We film a series of jobs, taking them just as far as the camera needs to before moving on to the next one. This means that by the end of the week there are twenty things half done across the garden which then need finishing off. I easily accept this – it is my job – but it is an odd, even confusing, state of affairs.

It has also been blisteringly hot. Which has been a joy, especially as the nights have been cool, but it has meant that the overriding concern has been watering. However, we could not water anything that was to be filmed for at least four hours before the camera rolled in case it was flattened or sodden. This added logistical complexity to what is already a laboriously inefficient aquatic set-up. When we laid the garden out, we neither had the money nor the forethought to put in standpipes in all the useful places, and although we have added a couple, watering still means lugging yards of yellow hosepipe along paths, with a cricket stump at each corner to protect the plants. (I knew there would be a use for the three cricket sets given to and abandoned by the children.) We have found that a round sprinkler (the kind with a spike that you jab into the lawn) tied on to a tall pole is the best for the borders. It throws up a fine spray that falls almost as a thick mist and doesn't bash everything down too much. A system of leaky pipes would have been much better, of course. But then, after the kind of weather that we had all last year, who would have thought that we would be complaining now about irrigation?

The hot weather has meant that we have had a big basil harvest and frozen lots of pesto. The tomatoes are ripening by the dozen daily, and the borders are, I think, three weeks ahead of themselves. We keep deadheading madly in order to sustain things a bit longer, but it will be interesting to see how the garden is in mid-September.

One of those high-sided, free-standing circular swimming pools arrived the other day, ordered by Sarah for the children. It has been put – as the only viable place – in the middle of the walled garden. It is bright blue and hideous and sits in the midst of that genteel order like a spaceship from planet Marbella. I hate it. But I love the way that it makes the children so happy and, in a small way, returns the garden to them. And it makes a very good water butt to dip into.

16 August 2004
Tomatoes

This morning I got up, walked up to the top greenhouse, picked three 'Black Russian' tomatoes (vermilion skin clouding alarmingly to a greeny-chocolate top – it looks like it's dying but tastes like it's gone to heaven), cut them in half and fried them in olive oil with some finely chopped fresh garlic. I toasted a couple of thick slices of sourdough bread, put the tomatoes on these and scraped all the sticky, tomatoey, garlicky juices from the pan. Lots of salt. A cup of tea. An hour or so later the ghost of that fruity, savoury taste remains like the refrain of a song. Throughout the day the children will nip in and out of the greenhouse to pop a warm cherry tomato into their mouths. So, I hope, will I. That is why I grow tomatoes.

18 August 2002
Sweet peas

Leaning silkily over the angle of my computer screen is a vase of purple sweet peas. I think they are 'Purple Prince'. Their colour is in fact a red so infatuated with blue that it loses itself within it. It is red that has crossed the divide. From above, the bunch looks like a floral brain. Below, the petals gleam impossibly. The folds of flower are fiercely frilly and yet in that fragility is something as hard and brittle as coral. It is a strange thing about sweet peas – for all their soft prettiness they inspire fanaticism. There are men who devote the meaningful part of their lives to growing perfect sweet peas with a rigour that has all the characteristics of a special-forces assault.

Not me of course. We grow them enthusiastically but lazily and probably badly, although well enough for us to enjoy them, which is all we ask.

This year we have grown most of our sweet peas in a long avenue, thirty-two wigwams, following on after the wallflower 'Blood Red'. I dig a pit under each wigwam, fill it with compost and try to give the plants as much water as time will allow, which, although it takes ages to

// *Sweet peas and clematis 'Perle d'Azur' entwined in the jewel garden.*

give thirty-two wigwams a soak, is not nearly as much as they would like. The Sweet Pea Walk (obsession is breeding pretension) has been only a partial success. The concept is great – a deliciously scented walk with height and colour. But – and it is funny how there is always a 'but' – the execution has not quite worked out as it could.

There is a bundle of reasons, good and bad, for this. For a start, although we chose the varieties for scent as well as colour, not all the sweet peas are equally scented. So instead of wafting down a path swoony with sweet pea fragrance, you dip in and out of it, rather like a radio signal.

But the biggest problem with our mixed bag of sweet peas is what is happening – or not happening – beneath them. Sweet peas are best growing up or through a support that masks their rather threadbare bases. A really vigorous plant smothered in flower can have a bottom two or three feet that looks as though it is about to wither away completely. In the jewel and walled gardens, this is not a problem at all – they haul themselves up through all kinds of other plants. But in this walk, after the wallflowers were cleared, they went into completely bare ground. I under-planted them with squashes hoping that these would quickly provide a lower storey of interest. But because it was cold and miserable in June and early July these grew very slowly. About a third got eaten by slugs in their semi-paralysed state. Experience tells me that they will come good but probably not until well into September – by which time the sweet peas will be gone. This highlights one of the great truths of gardening: it matters not so much what you do, or even how you do it, as *when* you do it.

20 August 2000
Slug dog

I have made autumn salad sowings of rocket, mibuna, mizuna and 'Little Gem' lettuce. In practice this means sowing in soil blocks and plugs and then trying to protect them from slugs. This is the hard part. A couple of times in the past week I have been out after dark and noticed that the ground – predominantly the grass – was literally covered in small slugs. Tens and tens of thousands of them. What can they all be living on? In light of this it seems a miracle that so little of the garden is devoured by them. Scary. Certainly they are on the offensive in the greenhouses, eating great beef tomatoes overnight and grazing off trays of seedlings at a pass. I don't want to sound calm about this because I hate what they do with a deep loathing, but I am happy to concede defeat. However, we would like to install a batch of hedgehogs in the garden, situated at strategic points, so that they can eat themselves almost to explosion through a choice range of slugs. The only problem is that Poppy, our Jack

Russell, cannot resist trying to kill them (hedgehogs not slugs), a result she all too often achieves, digging enormous holes in the process.

Mind you, a slug terrier would be a thing. Small, lives exclusively on slugs which it devours by the thousand without damaging the garden in any way: there's an opening for some enterprising breeder.

At this stage of the year dusk creeps forward week by week. Strange to think that only two months ago was the longest day, light by four in the morning and still light enough to water the garden at ten in the evening. In June the sun sinks down in a notch just by the church tower that sits to our north. Now, almost daily, it is edging back westwards across the sky until by the winter solstice it will dip below the hedge almost at right angles to its midsummer high-tide mark. The quality of the evenings has changed too, the light becoming thicker and velvety. This is when white and its shades look at their best, shimmying out from the shadows like a barn owl slipping across the field.

You can see why the concept of a white garden or border is attractive. However, as soon as the two words *white* and *garden* are conjoined, the spectre of Sissinghurst looms over them.

The truth is that Vita Sackville-West's white garden is one of the world's great horticultural masterpieces and should be celebrated as such. It is an icon of everything that most (British) gardeners aspire to. It was one of the last pieces of the Sissinghurst garden to be made, in the early 1950s, and was a long time in gestation. It was hardly an original idea. Lawrence Johnston had made a small white garden at Hidcote and there was also a white garden at Tintinhull, and Vita knew both these gardens well. But her interpretation of the theme surpasses anything done before or since.

There is a longish parade of white flowers here in this garden. The first snowdrops in January, 'White Triumphator' tulips in April, the spring joy of damson, plum and pear blossom, the many white roses (of which *R. rugosa* 'Alba' and *R.* x *alba* 'Alba Semiplena' are my own favourites), white lupins, *Nicotiana sylvestris*, white poppies, white sweet peas, the floating haze of white flower from *Crambe cordifolia* and *Thalictrum aquilegiifolium* 'White Cloud'. Then the final autumnal flowering of white snapdragons, white cosmos and iceberg roses and the white stems of *Rubus cockburnianus* in midwinter. But all these apparently white flowers hint at other colours, and all need green to seem as white as possible.

Green is the context that makes white look simultaneously rich and ethereal. White flowers tend to have less form and bulk than darker

colours – this is because white bleaches out into the space around the plant, whereas a rich red or purple creates a clearer volume – so a dark background crispens up the edges and creates volume. It also means that white looks better within defined green shapes and contained areas. At Sissinghurst this is done by edging the smaller beds with box hedges that are higher than the paths that divide them. This creates an effect of boxes out of which the white planting erupts and doubles the amount of green in the garden. It is a detail but one of real genius.

24 August 2002
Topiary
· ·

My garden is nearly all out the back. There is a path to the front door flanked by yew cones and a high yew hedge that is one of the walls of the walled garden. I know that it's a cheat – only two sides are actually made of stone – but there you are. Names have a habit of sticking even if inappropriate.

The yews in the front were based around ten cones that I bought dirt cheap in a sale nine years ago. Since then I have added another sixteen, half via reshaped hedging plants and half – huge extravagance – bought in already shaped. We hardly think of this as part of the garden – it seems to belong to the path in an odd sort of way – yet it is one of my favourite bits. I am always pleased to walk down to the front door because of the yews as much as the welcome of my own house. Occasionally I look out of the window in the middle of a moonlit night and relish their shadows and silhouettes. They are very beautiful.

I always cut them at this time of year. Any later and a mild autumn will stimulate new growth which will be vulnerable to a hard November frost, any earlier and they will not stay crisp through the winter. I have never been scared of topiary – although my cones and the pebbles in the back garden are obviously easier to cut than peacocks, or the horse and hounds that a friend of mine has in his garden. In general, curves are much easier to cut than straight sides. I use an electric hedge-trimmer for the initial cut and then tidy up with shears. I give each bush a little feed of seaweed meal afterwards to encourage it along, but other than that this is the only attention that they ever receive. Initially I wanted the yews to grow fast and assume their shape as quickly as possible, but now I cut away all new growth every year. Yet they are still getting bigger and bigger. I remember filming years ago at Powis Castle near Welshpool where they have fantastic, huge box and yew hedges. The man who had clipped them for the previous twenty years told me that he cut away all new growth every year and still they became inexorably bigger. That is the way with hedges and topiary.

There is a holly hedge dividing the drive (more of a scruffy car park really) from the front garden. The idea is to keep cars out of sight of the house, and the house and us out of sight of any lookers in. On the road side I put up hazel hurdles to protect the young hedge and to establish an instant barrier, just as I did for all the hedges in the garden. Unfortunately this was the south-facing side. So, eight years on, the hedge has grown to about seven feet tall with a thick north face, but the south side of it, shaded by the now crumbling hurdles, is thin, etiolated and frankly pathetic. So we removed the fence and cut back the weedy side as hard as it would go to provoke new, thick growth. The result is harsh and shockingly transparent, but I have every faith that it will work. The only compromise has been to put up chicken wire to stop the dogs getting out and attacking or mating with passers-by, depending on sex or breed.

Gareth is building a wall in the walled garden. It is not a big thing, just three feet high to mark the boundary between paving and lawn, and as much for perching one's bum as for the pots that will languish on it. I know that they will languish because I am terrible at watering pots of any kind. I get bored with it and forget and then feel defeated and then give them an apologetic soak and so the cycle goes all summer. The truth is that I am not a pot sort of person and there's an end to it.

But I am a wall person. Had I the money I would build walls all over the garden, as much for their aesthetic values as for the shelter and warmth they would provide. I like brick and stone equally and we are lucky in that there is a good local supply of both, the clay providing the bricks and the local red sandstone the stone. Whereas brick walls are business-like and constructed, however mellow and soft the colour, stone walls cannot help but feel more organic. Our sandstone is soft and splits so the stones tend to be large and the walls thick, and this adds to the effect of them welling up fully formed from the earth. Yup, fanciful to the point of indulgence, but it's my garden, my fancy, and I'll shape my mental walls as I like thanks all the same.

There was a wall on the spot where Gareth is working and it was not a very good wall, an apology in stone. But it had been low priority and we had lived with it, meaning to rebuild it every year. The odd thing is that I almost miss it. The new one is sleek and chichi and not at all wonky. It will soften just as the holly will grow back. But for the moment it stands out like a sore thumb in this very wonky garden.

27 August 2000
Geard
. . . .

It was 4.35 a.m. May. Long ago, perhaps '74. At nineteen I had discovered that getting up early, really early, exactly fitted my rhythm and psyche. The early morning was mine and like any coloniser I felt that I alone owned this territory. I would quietly slip out into this private world, feeling like Columbus.

Dawn in mid-May is, without question, the best place there is. It bubbles with birdsong, not like March's shrill, almost hysterical dawn chorus, but wave upon distant wave of fading, gentle song. Now, at the end of August, this last May – any May day – seems another country. But that particular May morning a repetitive metal clicking drew me down the road. Click click click pause, then more: Mr Redman is cutting the hedge at 4.30 in the morning. He is a dapper man, lean, with white moustache, cap, shirt and tie even at this time of day. For all his slimness, his forearms are beefy and his hands like great hams. In one of them is a pair of clippers. He has already done a few yards and has perhaps another hundred or more to go. We greet each other warily, me scarcely more than a boy, him older than my father but almost apologetic. 'Thought I'd do a bit before it got too warm.'

// Late-summer sunrise. The back yard waiting for light.

I knew his story. Mr Redman had farmed a small dairy farm all his life. A hundred and twenty acres on the border with Wiltshire. Small fields, all hedged, and a coppice and a stream. His father had farmed it before him. He slept in the room he had been born in surrounded by the land he cared for. This is the patchwork of fields that you fly over and glimpse on a clear day, this is what people sentimentalise as 'The Country' – only he had not an ounce of sentiment. He loved it, deep in the bone and hardly ever expressed.

Then the farm's ninety-nine-year lease expired and was not renewed. He had to sell up and get out in three months. A lesser man would have pined publicly, bitterly. I would have. But he took the job offered him by the man who threw him off the land and became his gardener. He was a refugee, watching his new employer come home each night in his Mercedes from his agribusiness that had an office but no farmhouse, grew crops that no one loved, used land with every hedge of the two thousand acres grubbed out. Mr Redman was polite and worked hard. He laughed and was delighted at little things. He had dignity.

And he got up at dawn, just as he had done all his life for the milking, to clip the hedges of the man who took his farm from him.

The hedge that he was cutting that morning was mixed, hawthorn, hazel, ash, blackthorn, oak, elder, dog rose, holly and ivy all growing indiscriminately. It was a rolling, lumpy thing, a bit open at the bottom, and Mr Redman did not try and impose any particular shape on to it, merely going the way it inclined so that it ran round the garden with an organic flow to it rather than a fierce boundary. It was a marker more than a fence. Of course, cutting a hedge in May is likely to disturb nesting birds and probably not a good idea, although his clinking shears and light trim were not as hostile as the four-square levelling of a power hedge-cutter.

I often think of Mr Redman, particularly at this time of year when I cut the hedges in my own garden. I also often think about gardening as a substitute for farming. Our English obsession with hedges is because they are psychological remnants of the fields that time and history have made into motorways and shopping centres and that are irretrievable. Instead of thinking of the garden as a series of outdoor 'rooms', perhaps we should more helpfully see it as a jumble of small fields, carved out of the wildwood that is our cities and suburbs and housing estates. The etymology of 'garden' is the same as 'yard' and 'garth' and derives from the Old English *geard*, which means a hedge or enclosure. A hedge enclosing a space is the exact definition of a garden, just as it is of a field.

We are all on a ninety-nine-year emotional lease. So instead of connecting the garden to the house by making it into a roofless living room, better to think of it as our land that we tend. We crop contentment, beauty, privacy, some prized bits and pieces of food, and maintain that direct link to our own private farmed countryside.

28 August 2005
Garden party
....

If you don't think that climate change is damaging the world, try Malaga airport at ten on a summer's evening. The herded horror of cheap travel is God's revenge for buggering up his planet.

We arrived home from a fortnight's holiday at three in the morning, but daylight revealed the full extent of a fortnight's neglect. It reminded me of the first time that we left our children in charge of the house. Promise us that you won't have a party, we said. Oh come on, they said with Oscar-worthy solemnity, what do you take us for? Of course we won't. It was not so much the inevitable party that followed our departure but the sheer inventiveness of the mess that was created. Like teenagers, the garden, in our absence, had been partying long and hard.

The grass had been allowed to grow longer than it has since 1993. There is a moment when lawn and grass paths become something else completely – but there is only a millimetre or so of grass in it. You go to bed with a lawn that needs a trim and wake up to a meadow in the making. All our grass had evolved from napped velvet to rich Herefordshire pasture that the cattle eyed over the fence with wet tongues flicking. The hedges seemed to have grown with a kind of surreptitious spurt, and the limes in the lime walk were almost meeting across the path. The topiary yew cones in front of the house had, I swear, grown six inches in a fortnight and become shaggy caricatures of themselves. It was like finding that your bank manager has turned up for work having spent the last fortnight at Glastonbury without a razor.

The jewel garden looked rather lovely, all morning-afterish, tousle-haired and slightly bashful. The bronze fennel had become monstrous and fuzzed with tiny lemon flowers, and the cannas were twice the size that they were last year. Dahlias and tithonias were flowering riotously, and the clematis and crocosmia were all at their very best, although the cardoons and hostas had been terribly ravaged by slugs. Bindweed, thistles and nettles nestled insouciantly with their carefully cultivated cousins. The party had been a good one.

Unlike the ravages of a teenage jamboree, this cannot be put to rights in one session. And all the frantic reparation in the world will not bring August back into the garden.

September

I have just been away for a week, camping in the Outer Hebrides. We were on an island, and the only mod cons were a fresh water spring where we collected our water in a bucket. No people, no cars, no telephones, television or radio. Just cliffs, seabirds and the sea. Heaven. Of course it is one thing to dip into this kind of world for a week's holiday but quite another to live in it, which people did until the beginning of the last century. It must have been a fearsomely harsh existence for all but the summer months. They grew their crops on lazy beds, raised beds mounded from the very thin topsoil and bulked out by seaweed. They seemed to grow very little other than potatoes and oats, and the beds would have become exhausted very quickly so would have been rotated to allow some to go fallow and recover fertility. Every possible site was cultivated at some time, and the sheer human endeavour needed to cultivate the island landscape is awe-inspiring.

1 September 2000
Lazy beds

Returning to our very easy, domesticated patch has made me realise how soft we have all become. In reviewing my own vegetable production, I think that I have become unnecessarily hung up on large harvests. We do not need to grow as much as possible in our brief productive period and then store it for the winter but to try and have a wide range of crops throughout the year. This is better suited to our needs, which are about as diametrically opposed to those of a Hebridean crofter as could be.

At the beginning of this year I resolved to try and use less mechanical gear – all the toys-for-boys that fall somewhere between invaluable aids for coping with a large garden, and the absurdly expensive, unnecessary kit that splashes the user with testosterone like cheap aftershave. Much of this is the equivalent of using a large four-by-four with bull-bars to take the kids to school. It does the job but with farcical and damaging over-specification. Yesterday we were clearing an overgrown corner of the orchard. My son used a petrol-driven brush-cutter, and I had a long-handled slasher that I bought from a farm sale for one pound fifteen years ago. Despite being unfit, unskilful and not having bothered to sharpen the slasher properly, I still cut and cleared more ground in the same time than he did with his machine, for all its roaring noise and gas-guzzling specifications. A curved blade on an ash handle that made a slightly damp whoosh as it fell through the nettles was all that the job actually needed.

4 September 2005
Gear

But I confess that I have not done very well in keeping to my good intentions. The growl and whine of mechanised gardening still shatter the quiet for us and our neighbours far too often. I am using an ethanol mulching mower which works well and certainly is much more environmentally friendly than a standard petrol-driven mower. The two drawbacks are that it leaves the grass rather longer than is aesthetically and practically pleasing (it is American so designed, I imagine, for a drier, less lush grass-growing season than ours) and that grass clippings are an important part of our compost heap.

We have miles – literally – of hedges, and all the hornbeam has been cut with big petrol hedge-cutters. I like using electric ones, but they quickly break under the strain of heavy work, and a two-hundred-foot cable is unwieldy and dangerous in the wet. But I have cut all the box, hedges and topiary alike – with shears. This is slow, with a clip-clip-clipping rhythm, and it makes your forearms burn with lactic acid like nothing else, but it is very satisfying and, significantly, much easier on my back. I was brought up with shears as one of the key pieces of gardening kit. We clipped edges and hedges, banks, round trees and shrubs where the mower could not get to them and even paths too narrow or awkward for a machine. But the strimmer has ousted the shears, and hardly anyone ever uses them any more. This is a real shame. They work well, cost next to nothing, are quiet and good for you.

6 September 1998
Illumination
. . . .

It is hard to be angry about plants or gardens. I do try. God knows that anger is necessary to confront the injustice, incompetence and general dreadfulness of life. But whilst other people's gardens often bore me, my own invariably draws the sting from any accumulating venom. Gardening makes me easy, bland and very happy. I feel a bit inadequate about this – I want to make words that slice through complacency and philistinism – but my cutting edge has been blunted by flowers. I had planned to inject a shot of vitriol into the weekly column that I write, but went outside for a moment and was ambushed by the garden. I punctuate my work by walking round the garden most days when I am at home and as often as not get nothing from it other than a sense of business, a mental list of jobs to be done. But what I am after is illumination, that way of seeing the world anew which the combination of weather, seasons and growing plants bring about more often than anything else I know of.

Anyway, I was looking at the shape of things, lemon sun canting in across the fields by the river, trying to see the world with that mixture of intimacy and fresh eyes that only loving familiarity can bring. Then I noticed a corner of the flower borders as though coming across all of its components for the first time. These beds are planted as a loose, wildly overspilling arrangement of harmonised intensity. In places it is not so intense and in places not so harmonised, but that kind of failure is part of the fun of it. When it works, it works good. This patch caught the morning sun with plum-coloured splendour where the dahlia 'Bishop of Llandaff' is growing amongst a huge clump of self-seeding purple orache. This dahlia is almost a cliché nowadays but was considered groovy a few years ago, at a time when grooviness and dahlias formed as unlikely a conjunction as New Labour and free thought. There are two great things about 'Bishop of Llandaff': the flowers, which are a wonderfully rich red, crimson at their centres (flecked, as the flowers mature, with bright yellow anthers) flowing out to vermilion at the ends of the petals, and the stems and leaves, which are a chocolatey-bronze. The combined effect is as rich as a second helping of Chocolate Nemesis.

A few weeks ago I visited the Royal Welsh Show at Builth Wells, and in the flower marquee (curiously anticlimactic, a sideshow to the relay wood-chopping races, prize cattle and parachute drops) by far the most exquisite thing I saw all day was a class of pompon dahlias. There were three entries, each consisting of three perfect balls of burgundy petals balanced on long stalks. To my dazzled and oafish eye all nine flowers looked identical. But only one exhibit had won a prize of any kind. It turned out that each flower had to pass through a metal ring of a specific diameter, and if one of the three blooms failed this test then the whole entry was deemed unworthy of a prize. It was a charming display of horticultural insanity, harming nothing but the feelings of the losing competitors, but also a case of gardening disappearing yards up its own backside.

As we approach the high point of our tomato harvest, I am already thinking about next year in light of this year's batch. It has been good. I have grown 'Roma' (excellent for making into a sauce but not great for much else), 'Shirley' (dependable, healthy and unspectacular, ideal texture for frying – my breakfast this morning was three of them, cut in half, fried in olive oil with a clove or two of garlic for about twenty minutes and served on well-toasted white bread with lots of salt), 'Black Plum' (another very good sauce tomato), 'Britain's Breakfast' (another plum, although less inclined to dissolve in the pan than 'Roma'), 'Tigerella' (first time I have grown them and they seem to be good – lots of flavour) and some rogue 'Gardener's Delight' that were, I seem to remember, planted as 'Roma'. It is surprising how often a packet of seed will contain one or two intruders like this. No problem.

9 September 2001
Tomatoes
....

They are welcome. For the first time in ages there are no beef varieties in the list. I have grown disillusioned with the taste of the ubiquitous 'Marmande'. In past years I have grown and liked 'Costoluto Fiorentina', which is very heavily ribbed, and each fruit the size of a cooking apple. For reasons I forget – probably all bad – I did not get any seeds this year.

All these are cordons and are grown up canes to the roof of the greenhouse. Summer would not be complete without the lines of tomatoes growing inside, their hot, musty smell essential to the season. And their paraphernalia is a comfort. The twine for tying, the weekly ritual of pinching out side shoots, fingers stained yellow and reeking of tomato, watering, removing lower branches – all in the ordered jungle of the cordons. It is a good place to be.

But tomatoes bring out the worst in men. There is a type of gardener (always male) that just loves fiddling about in the greenhouse with tomatoes. The growing of them is much more interesting to these people than the end product, so the more arcane and mysterious the process the better they feel about themselves. Given the way that tomato seedlings spring up all over the place via the compost heap (I found a seven-footer just yesterday in the jewel garden growing gracefully through a clematis), it is perhaps salutary to let a couple of plants grow untended each year as a reminder that we need them much, much more than they need us.

11 September 1999
Oak

Seven large blocks of oak were unceremoniously rolled off the back of a lorry yesterday. Sarah had ordered them weeks ago and we both silently admired them, enjoying that sensation of expectations being exceeded. Six are eighteen inches square and intended as seats at the end of each dead-end path in the jewel garden, and one, a few inches bigger, is to stand alone on the new paving in the yard. The idea is simple enough, but a large block of wood or stone is surprisingly rare and transforms and enlarges all preconceptions of what our lives might reasonably contain.

They were all cut from the same tree in the last few days, and still smell of oaky sawdust. Over the coming months they will buckle and warp as they dry out, losing their four-squareness but gaining unpredictable character. Comfy as seats, they are absolutely beautiful as objects. This is gardening and inspired gardening too, on Sarah's behalf, tying in all the non-vegetative pieces that make and sometimes break a garden.

We have given the spring garden its Late Summer Clean, weeding, digging up barrow-loads of the lamiums, geraniums and vincas that we use as ground cover in the dry summer shade, cutting back all the new hazel growth, mulching with mushroom compost and leaf mould, and generally giving it some love after a few months' summer neglect. It sleeps for July and August, with only the hostas performing, as these are its dormant months.

But new growth is starting, and we have to get it ready now to see where the gaps are and to give everything the best start possible so that when January comes it is roaring away. I have had a close look at all the hellebores and start taking off browning leaves now, picking over them every month or so until February. It is odd to see a piece of the garden so spruce and scrubbed at a time of year when everywhere else is looking overblown and jaded in rather a nice, dissolute kind of way.

12 September 1999
Clean
....

Show dahlias are like Ascot hats. They come out only for the big occasion. But they got a bad reputation amongst those who care about reputations for being somehow a bit naff and lacking in the subtlety necessary to appeal properly to sophisticated tastes. The truth is probably cruder. Dahlias were considered common and vulgar in the same way that gladioli, hybrid tea roses and hanging baskets are still frowned upon. Nowadays 'Bishop of Llandaff' is allowed within the inner circle of good taste, and perhaps 'Arabian Night', but as exceptions that prove the ghastly rule. This is, of course, pure snobbery, and stupid snobbery at that. For all the democratisation of gardening through television, there is still a ridiculous streak of aspirational snobbery that runs through too many back gardens. I hate it.

And I love dahlias. They are undiluted fun. The deep, dark ones are velvety and voluptuous like the inside of a bordello, and the bright, garish pinks, yellows and oranges have the 1950s sumptuous joyfulness of Monroe or Bardot. They come as tight, minimal pompons of flower or clumsy starbursts of petal. They can be childishly simple or mathematically complex. They are busy plants, giving out more energy than almost any other.

13 September 2003
Dahlias

I love September. I love the chill mornings and nights with the hot midday sun, and the garden loves it too. We came back from holiday to find the garden in a surprisingly soft, benign mood, a gentle place to be with that dusty, well-worn feeling, like an old shoe, somehow so much more attractive than August's tired valiance.

I left for holiday feeling disillusioned with the garden but have returned with fresh impetus. My main concern is to simplify the place – or at least to create the impression of simplicity – which might be quite complex to achieve. I want less of the cluttered, busy mass of very English borders and more rigorous blocks and spaces, which feels more American or European to me. Pretentious stuff? Who cares? The one place where you can pretend anything is in your garden. It is, after all, only a game.

The first stage in this transformation will be to create new raised beds in the orchard for veg and to use space in the existing veg garden for simpler blocks of crops. Not a vast change in itself, but it will make a big difference. I am also going to remove all the woven hazel fences from around the vegetable beds and replace them with oak boards with a box hedge. The hazel is picturesque but needs replacing every two years otherwise it just looks tatty, and it harbours millions of snails. I know that box does too, but I want the blockiness of the green hedging.

14 September 2000
Pretentious? Moi?

September light is thin but the colours are the richest of the year. //

15 September 2000
Chicken run
. . . .

I have been blaming slugs and snails for the past two months for eating our tomatoes. Dozens have been gnawed into, starting with a hole which is then raggedly widened around the softer edges. The beefsteak tomatoes such as 'Marmande' were worst hit. My hatred for slugs tightened another notch.

But I owe the slug population in all its rich diversity an apology. Yesterday I walked into the tunnel and discovered half a dozen of our hens happily pecking away at the tomatoes. A light clicked on in the dim recesses of my frontal lobes. It was them all along. The *bastards*! Seething, I went into full-blown Basil Fawlty mode, frog-marching them back to their run. As if my life wasn't complicated and fraught enough. Anyone who keeps hens knows that each egg costs about as much as a dozen prime, organic, free-range eggs from a supermarket and that the chickens demand constant, unreturned attention. At bottom (especially the bottom of a scraggy old hen) they are vile, malicious creatures. So Tom and I wasted an hour or so making screens to go across the greenhouse and tunnel doors, to keep hens out and ventilation and lovely, harmless slugs in.

16 September 2000
Gold
. . . .

Metal colours were part of the jewel garden from the outset. But it has not always been straightforward. When is gold not gold but yellow, for example? Yellow – real, unarguable yellow – is no good. You cannot get away with it. So most of the wonderful luminous lime greens and acid yellows of spring – think of *Euphorbia polychroma* or *E. characias* subsp. *wulfenii* in April – are not appropriate. Golden flowers are thin on the ground until midsummer. There are a number of crocus that are golden goblets, and the species tulip, *Tulipa sylvestris*, counts as golden for me, as definitely does 'Golden Apeldoorn'. The wallflower *Erysimum* x *kewense* 'Harpur Crewe' is also a good gold.

Later in the year it simply becomes a matter of trial and error. All the buttercup, egg-yolk-yellow flowers are perfect. There are marigolds (with the amazing calendula 'Indian Prince' as deep as gold will go before it becomes orange), the California poppy, *Eschscholzia californica* (which, within its own variations, is as near as any flower gets to true gold), *Lysimachia punctata*, heleniums, sunflowers, *Achillea filipendulina* 'Gold Plate', the imperial fritillary, and the *Ligularia przewalskii*, *L. dentata* 'Desdemona' and *L.* 'The Rocket'. Like ligularia, the North American daisy, rudbeckia, is another border plant that secretly pines for a nice soggy bog. Their daisy flower heads have golden petals around curiously cone-shaped black centres. Chard usually lives in our vegetable

garden, but 'Golden Chard' is true gold. We grow the hot crocosmias, like 'Lucifer' and 'Firebird', but species *Crocosmia × crocosmiiflora* has rich golden flowers and is very good. We started out with the pale yellow potentillas, self-seeded rocket, variegated comfrey, thalictrums and variegated sages but after a year or so realised that the pale gentleness simply does not work. It is false gold. You might think that plant names would be a pretty foolproof guide and that 'Aureum' would be as good as gold. Not so. Bowles' Golden Grass (*Milium effusum* 'Aureum') was too yellow and had to be taken out. Golden hop, *Humulus lupulus* 'Aureus', is dodgy in spring, but it comes good later in the year as it matures so can be forgiven a month of what my American friends call 'chartroose'.

Grasses are a significant contributor of gold to this bit of the garden – perhaps the most important, all things being equal. The wonderful waving wands of the giant stipas are molten gold in the evening sun, and if you look at any summer meadow it is actually hardly green at all – more every shade of fawn. (How come fawn is suddenly allowed and bracketed under gold whereas a decent yellow is summarily ejected? It is all to do with light. Trust me.) *Calamagrostis × acutiflora* turns from an

Miscanthus nepalensis leaning under the weight of its plumes. //

orangey-brown to gold with the light behind it, and *Carex elata* 'Aurea' has enough intrinsic gold to need only sun to enhance rather than create its golden tones. We grow the bamboo – just a big grass – *Phyllostachys aureosulcata* 'Aureocaulis', whose golden stems gleam through the plants before it. *Miscanthus nepalensis* produces plumes like delicate strands of gold thread. It is a good one.

17 September 1998
Fall
····················

When I went away at the beginning of September, I left the garden at the end of summer. I returned in autumn having been away for all of six days. No one thing confirms this but the quality of light and intensity of green – or lack of it – in the foliage. Certainly the weather is no worse than it has been all summer, and on Thursday it was as good as it ever gets with an exquisite buttery, light, warm sun and a sensation of the year gently falling away. 'Autumn' is clumsy and inarticulate beside the wonderfully expressive 'Fall'.

The first job of this Fall has been to take up all the sweet peas and bundle the pea sticks up and stack them away until next year. The dried-up

// *Cardoon flowers evolve into fantastically fluffy seed heads.*

haulms are good for mixing up with grass cuttings in the compost heap to stop it getting too soggy. This has left holes in the borders that are actually a delight – the sweet peas had been hiding too much. There is always the temptation to cling to growth whereas cutting back usually improves things. Nothing can hide the leonotis, which are definitely the stars of the borders now – all grown from seed collected from last year's plants. In a week or two I shall sow next year's sweet peas and have thought of keeping seed – there were certainly plenty of plump pods – but they must have cross-pollinated, and we try hard to get the sweet peas to come true.

Before I went away we dug up a couple of ash trees in the process of laying a water pipe to a new polytunnel. They lay in the route of the trench and it was a good excuse to move them. They were temporarily put into plastic containers with the intention of planting them into their new sites in a month or so. This was a mistake. We should have transplanted them immediately. They have started to turn yellow and droop badly, so we have now planted them (each one fifteen feet tall and with a big root ball – a two-man job), leaving the hose on both for fully an hour each. I shall water them weekly and think they will survive. My experience is that transplanted trees over about ten feet tall take a year to establish new roots and another year to start new growth and do not get back to the point they were at when moved until the third year following. For small hedging plants it is nearly always better to plant new, small plants than move larger ones.

I took our last batch of box cuttings – there are five hundred in total – and put them in pots in a cold frame. This is long-term gardening, but every year I mean to do it and for the past four years have missed the boat. They are the easiest cuttings in the world to take and will save a fortune three or four years down the line.

Figs

I have just eaten the first ripe fig of the year, guiltily because there was no one else in the house and I did not wait to share it, and yet with such pleasure. It has not been a great year for figs, yet it is never a bad year for fig trees. We have nine 'Brown Turkey' growing in this garden, yet it does not feel as though this particular pudding has been over-figged. I love everything about fig trees, from the elephant-trunk stems with their curious wrinkled bark that looks as though it has rucked and slipped a little down the wood it encases, to the huge concealing leaves and, of course, the voluptuary promise of the fruit.

In this country there is a myth tagged on to figs that if they are to fruit at all, they must be planted into a rubble-filled hole. Not true. But some restriction on the roots will limit the growth of the tree and stimulate a higher rate of fruit. Most people see figs as fruit trees, in the same way that they would grow a plum or gooseberry, but their fruiting is pathetic in this country, and they are best grown as lovely living objects with the fruit as a bonus. When I was in Spain this summer there was a large fig in the courtyard of the house that was laden with hundreds of fruits like plums in an Evesham orchard. You never see that in this country because outside of a heated greenhouse they simply do not have the sustained heat for the succession of fruits to ripen, whereas the tree grows just as well in our climate as on the most baked Andaluthian hillside.

19 September 1999
Courtyard

The main story in our garden this week has been the completion of the courtyard. Bloody brilliant. It is now all laid with local flagstones with a five-foot square in the middle filled with big pebbles. Sarah's big oak blocks are placed around the edge. A great big stone ball she bought at a sale years ago (which curiously enraged another bidder and prompted him to march up to her and say, 'If you were my wife I'd give you a slap for bringing that home' – nice man) sits on the stones. Nothing else. No pots, plants, nothing. Just stone and wood bounded by stone walls, all browns, pinks, greys and the ochre of the oak. We love this space.

20 September 1999
Slugmare

I cut the grass this week on one of the lovely days we have had – hot day, last of the summer wine, orange sun slipping down over the trees, the smell of grass holding regret like a sweet threat – and walked out in the dark in bare feet, enjoying the dew like iced water.

Then I squished on something and realised that the entire surface of the mown paths and lawns was mucilaginous with thousands upon thousands of slugs. It was Hitchcockian, unbelievably repulsive. They have eaten off all the autumn salad crops as the little seedlings emerged and are covering the mature vegetables like maggots. They don't seem to like chard, though, whether in its white (Swiss) or ruby form. All the more for those that do, as my horrible grandmother would say.

21 September 2001
Equinox

I've been ill. It all began with a terrible meal in an overpriced, trendy restaurant in Shoreditch and has resulted in considerable involuntary weight loss. And precious garden time loss. I have occasionally drifted downstairs and outside, looking at the shape of things, wondering when on earth it is all going to happen. The dog finds me and bounds up carrying three tennis balls in her mouth, carefully popping out each one at my feet. Look! Not one, not two, but three! In my mouth! All together! Usually I admire this trick unreservedly, but now it seems a reproach. Look, each yellow ball says, not one acre but two. Abandoned! And too late to retrieve it. The harvest is in and you are not saved!

Perhaps I am overplaying this. I have been feverish. But for certain, whilst I have been abed, summer has slipped me by. Today is the autumn equinox. As with everything, we have had a tendency to simplify the seasons, demanding nothing much more from our autumns than yellow leaves, mists, apples and leaves rattling around the place. This is a kind of Disneyfied vision of autumn, made patronisingly easy to digest. The fact is that we are at that thinning stage of the year as things gradually lose substance, marked as much by the angles of light as by leaf fall.

I like this a lot. More than at any other moment in the year, the combination of emaciation and low light means that you can look through everything. The process of reduction will carry on, of course, and the light will steadily get lower and lower, but it is only for a few weeks now, balanced astride the equinox, that there is enough left to give real interest to the picture.

The dominant plant in our borders at this time of year is *Verbena bonariensis*. It loves this garden and grows, self-sown, everywhere. It is unexceptional, of course, even ubiquitous, and has taken on a kind of stock role defining late-summer/early-autumn teatime good taste. But that does not diminish it at all.

For a start, it is too big to be insipid. Standing up to eight feet in rich soil, it is immensely strong without overwhelming any companion. And this is its special contribution to any garden. It is tall and yet blocks practically no light; it has shimmering colour and yet works perfectly with rich browns and crimsons just as easily as the yellows, pinks and tawny softness of autumnal colours. It looks good backlit by the sky and it looks good as an open fringe through which to see other plants.

All the hundreds of individual specimens that are growing in this garden now originate from one plant that we bought in 1984 from a National Trust garden in Cornwall – Cotehele I think. This was carefully brought back to our London garden and spread, albeit modestly. Along with all our favourites, we brought it – or scions of it – with us to Herefordshire. We planted perhaps three individual plants seven years ago here and it has spread everywhere, loving the rich clay loam and the open site. For a few years we took this as an untrammelled gift and savoured every plant, but now we weed it ruthlessly, especially as it has a habit of getting in amongst the young box hedges.

As I trudged round the borders in nightshirt and slippers this morning, I noticed the way that it draws the butterflies to it. This has been an astonishing year for butterflies and moths, and *Verbena bonariensis* attracts them as much as any other plant. We have soft clouds of Red Admirals, Tortoiseshells, Painted Ladies and other small, anonymous butterflies sipping at the verbena's nectar as though it was the most precious, most delicious thing on earth.

22 September 2003
View

The ideal view is one where you can look out from the privacy of your garden but no one can look in at you along the same line. However, for most of the year I have curious eyes peering in at me. At this time of year they are particularly interested in the garden, although their fascination is not entirely horticultural. They are nearly always large, gentle, round and attached to a body with four legs. Cattle, of course. These are put out on to the water meadows that bound one side of my garden and have a seasonal migrational shift. They start out right at the other end of the twenty-acre field, spending almost all of their time up there where the grass is juiciest and only coming down near us for an occasional visit just to see how we are getting on. By the end of the summer the grass has all but disappeared, and they mill around on our boundary casting envious glances at the vegetation and leaning far enough over our boundary fence to chew on our hedges and trees. I don't mind this at all and welcome their presence, although it does mean that I have to mend my fences pretty assiduously.

In ten years the cows have only once got into the garden. I was getting into the bath at about nine o'clock on a summer's evening and as I lowered myself into the water I looked outside and noticed half a dozen friendly brown faces looking at me from the vegetable garden. I don't know if it was my skilful herding or the shock of being chased by a wet man naked save for a pair of wellies that sent them back through the gap in the fence as quickly as they came, but since then they have restricted themselves to merely looking in at us as we look happily out at them.

23 September 2001
Buzzards

The other day I wandered idly into our wild garden (it's not at all wild now but was once upon a time, and you know how names stick) hoe in hand and lunch on my mind, and surprised a buzzard that was sitting on the bench. I admit that he surprised me too. Actually, if I am strictly honest, he was not so much sitting on the bench as standing. And panting. He took a second look at me, outrage and horror all over his face, and lumbered off through the willows with all the ease of a twenty-stone man performing a *pas de deux*. It was a thrilling moment.

Our sky above this garden – and in gardening terms it is ours – is filled with buzzards, particularly at this time of year when the young are fully grown but hopeless at hunting and spend most of the day mewing and screeching, frightening away all potential prey as they lurch around learning their trade. I remember one tried to catch the terrier once, made an abortive pass at it, then saw the cat and stalked it by hopping from tree to tree in the hedgerow. The cat in turn stalked the bird. Sarah and I watched, horrified but transfixed. I put my money on the cat, but she had visions of it disappearing into the sky in the buzzard's talons. The upshot was that the bird bottled out first and wheeled away with more plaintive crying.

Last week as I was weeding the celeriac (very good this year, down to a steady water supply, I think), I caught just a hint of power out of the corner of my eye, looked up and right overhead saw a tiercel flying in a purposeful straight line, broad wings beating just like a scull in full flow. Brute power and artistry combined.

24 September 2000
Cones

I cut my cones yesterday. These are twenty-six yews flanking the path down to our front door in a double avenue, six of which are now about two metres tall and absolutely dense, and twenty are shaping up nicely, thank you, but are much younger. I bought the older ones at a Wyevale tree sale from their base in Hereford in April 1993. It was a filthy day, pouring with rain, and the Grand National was on, so the combination of the elements and entertainment thinned the buying field.

I bought a lot of stuff that day, but half a dozen mature yew cones at twenty quid each were the biggest bargains. I also bought two dozen three-foot hedging yews which are now a dense two-metre hedge flanking the cones. Although the rest of the cones have been trained from various bits and pieces of yew I have had, I cheated and bought in eight last summer, already shaped. That is the kind of extravagance I never would have indulged in before television went to my head. Every time I look at them I feel a little bashful, as though I have been caught cheating.

25 September 2000
Silver

There is a problem with silver if you are trying to introduce it as part of a controlled colour theme in a garden. There are no silver flowers. They mimic gold via yellow and do some good imitations of copper and bronze, but that silvery sheen, which you might think would be well

suited to the satiny texture of many petals, simply is not found. When we started our jewel garden we thought that we could get round this by using suitable shades of white. But it doesn't work. White is never silver.

In fact for silver you have to forget flowers and look to foliage and bark, hunting amongst the blues and greens. Of course there is no silver foliage either, just shades of grey at its most silvery when polished with moisture. Walking round the jewel garden in mid-September, there is actually surprisingly little silver to be seen. I suppose that we could have incorporated water into the garden as a silver foil (ho ho) and there is an attractive logic to that, but it would be quite a radical, expensive development. This is a time of year when the colours tumble softly from their perch, richly jaded, and for the moment all silveriness must come from plants.

There are the leaves of the weeping pear, *Pyrus salicifolia* 'Pendula' (although that is a bit denuded) and the stems of *Knautia macedonica*, silvery blue perfectly setting off the burgundy flowers. This combination you see throughout the summer, with perhaps the best being the darkest opium poppies opening like plums frozen into a moment of frilly

Morning mist shrouding the fields in front of the house. //

explosion. The leaves of the annual *Salvia viridis* – which has been fantastic this year, adding amethyst bracts deeper and longer lasting than any flower – fade to a lavender-veined silver before turning strawy. Silver for just a week or so, but the phase adds much to balance the garden. The blue grasses like *Festuca glauca* and *Miscanthus sinensis* 'Morning Light' are still going strong, although to get a decent silver-blue from the festuca at this time of year you must be tough and cut it back in early August. *M. sinensis* 'Silberfeder' has silver-pink plumes that look very good next to the plume poppy, *Macleaya cordata*. The blue oat grass, *Helictotrichon sempervirens*, has glaucous leaves and silvery plumes and is evergreen. 'Morning Light' is my favourite grass at the moment, with very long, languid leaves holding an exaggerated arch of grey-blue. Not silver at all really, but in this never-never land of the garden it works as silver.

Another silver thistle – perhaps the best silver thistle – which also needs really serious support (but which has not got it from us this year, so is falling hysterically all over the place) is the fantastic *Onopordum acanthium*, or Scotch thistle. Like the cardoon it is now a ghost of its

// *The hornbeam hedges are still green walls, but starting to fade now.*

former self and is so top-heavy that unless it is really securely staked it is best cut down now. But I would always want some onopordums in my garden, and in June and July they are top of the silver league, by far.

Running a close second is the equally prickly, equally biennial *Eryngium giganteum*, or Miss Willmott's Ghost. It got its vernacular name from Miss Willmott's habit of dropping its seeds in all the gardens she visited in the conviction that it was an essential component of any garden. Miss Willmott was from Essex, lived about a hundred years ago, was very, very rich and sounds a bit of a pain. Despite this, it is a fantastic plant.

There is no doubting that the garden is running gently out of steam and so am I. The equinox was last Wednesday and for a day all things were equal; the see-saw hung perfectly level for a few hours. Now we must wait until 21 March for the balance to be restored. It is officially autumn, rents are due, and the moon tonight is sliver-thin. Time to pay your dues and start anew. A time of reckoning.

I was listening to the radio the other day, driving home in the dusk down brambly lanes, and heard an American priest talking with wonderful poetic rhythm of ethnicity and of how all the many waters run down to the sea. Rather ponderously I hoiked this thought into the garden and all the varieties and variations upon the plant themes that we pore over. In this autumnal slipping state of mind, I started thinking about elder. Not *Sambucus* this or *Sambucus* that but the common, rank-smelling elder that muscles into wasteland, hedgerow and untended woodland. It follows humans like nettles, growing in middens, drains and where humans and animals have peed, tangling round crumbling buildings, pushing its gawky branches into gutters and between the remaining roof tiles. It is the sprawling memory of uncomfortable humanity.

In the border its less feral cousins are highly prized, and rightly so. This year the *Sambucus nigra* 'Guincho Purple' in our jewel garden has put on yards of growth, the deep purple leaves holding their chocolate depths throughout the season in a way that so many purple-leafed shrubs do not, getting greener as the summer progresses. 'Guincho Purple' actually does the opposite, starting greenish and progressing to a deeper colour as it cooks in the sun. I prune ours back to a bony bunch of knuckles each spring to encourage lots of vigorous new shoots that will have bigger, better-coloured foliage than those left unpruned. The flowers have pink buds that open white with a pink wash, which for us is a pity as it is the only white we allow in that piece of the garden. But the stalks are a good, rich purple. It would be a truly fabulous plant if the flowers were plum-coloured like *Angelica gigas*. There are dozens of elder seedlings growing far too lustily all round it – these are not from 'Guincho Purple' but from the elder in the hedge beyond it that has promiscuously put itself about. If I don't whip these out, they will be a thicket with awkward, deep roots, so well do they grow in our fat-earthed beds.

A few years ago we lost *Sambucus racemosa* 'Plumosa Aurea' to a fungal attack that gradually worked its way up from the base, reducing its leaves to grey rags. This left a huge hole in our affections as well as in that corner of the garden. It is a really good foliage plant with, in April and May, leaves of an intense yellow that shifts to acid green in June when exposed to full sunshine, and a clear bracken-green on the under branches that are shaded. The leaves are delicate and finely cut and, when young, edged with a browny-crimson line, picking out each reticulation like lip liner. It produces yellow flowers – almost exactly the same colour as the leaves – which in turn become bright red berries. We did not replace it exactly but planted *Sambucus racemosa* 'Sutherland Gold', which is similar, with the same finely cut foliage and yellow leaves inclining to green in the shade, but a bit more robust – coarser even – and perhaps better able to cope with the hurly-burly of the border.

27 September 1999
Orchard

I spent the better part of last weekend sussing out the orchard. Forty-two trees, all carefully chosen for their regional relevance and idiosyncratic qualities of taste, all planted with labels and – this is the bit that really galls me – all mapped out on a beautiful and neat plan. Then I lost the lot, plan, labels and all. I ransacked the same drawers and files countless times but couldn't find anything. The labels had rotted and faded. So I went back through planting diaries (this I can be smug about: for the past two years I have recorded everything planted, all weather, flowering and harvest details in a desk diary – it is proving invaluable) and reference books and identified all but four of the trees, from rarities like 'Tillington Court' and 'Stoke Edith Pippin' to hoi-polloi like 'Blenheim Orange' and 'Newton Wonder'. I loved it. The orchard on a sunny early-autumn weekend was as good a place to be as any, and painstakingly identifying fruit, bark, leaf and shape of tree to match an identity parade was fun.

28 September 2004
Grasses

We have used grasses here for the past five or six years and they are now a fixed reference point in our jewel garden and in the dry borders that we made this spring. We have made every kind of mistake during that period, but the major lessons seem to be these:

Stipas do not like being moved. They have very shallow roots and take a while to recover from the shock of upheaval, especially when at all mature.

The astonishing *Stipa gigantea* throws its oaten heads into the air like tracer trails and catches the midsummer setting sun like burning brands. It is worth growing for those few evenings alone. It does not like wet, heavy soil, and we lost five in one winter.

Stipa arundinacea, or pheasant grass, is a star. We began growing it in an informal, loose-ish sort of a way because, in late summer at least, it is a very loose plant, but a couple of winters ago we replanted our dozen or so plants as formal marking points (I suppose that makes them 'architectural plants'; you never hear that expression nowadays), and this works very well. What makes them special is the leaves, shot with pinks and russets, and the hairy flowers that flop and fall everywhere – two quite different modes. Unlike their gigantic cousin, they move easily and seed everywhere, and the seedlings are easy to pot up, grow on and replant strategically.

Stipa tenuifolia is delicate and dramatic and good for a container or the front of the border; it has amazing longevity throughout the growing season. In February it is one of the brightest things in a border, and the feathery heads are silkily, fetishistically irresistible.

Panicum miliaceum 'Violaceum' (millet) has the loveliest flower head of all grasses with the seeds hanging like a plum-coloured mane off each stem. But it seeds so freely and so fast that it can easily become an annoying weed. Quaking grass, *Briza maxima*, falls into this category, and we have stopped growing it for that reason.

The miscanthus family is our banker. They are spectacularly drought-tolerant but will also perform well in soggy conditions. They are upright and elegant, which makes them good for the middle or back of a border. We grow *Miscanthus sinensis* 'Silberfeder' with flower heads that start out pinkish but take a distinctly silverish turn in autumn. 'Strictus' and 'Zebrinus' both have banded stems. Were I to order again I would take 'Strictus' because it is more upright and taller. But both are good. 'Malepartus' has flowers that are plum-plumed and open out with a golden thread. 'Ferner Osten' flowers especially early and has russet flowers with white tips. It is medium height so adaptable in a border. *M.* 'Purpurascens' does not really flower with us because it is too cold although, ironically, it is one of the hardiest of all grasses. It has the best orange-bronze foliage of all grasses in autumn but needs moisture to thrive.

At the moment I have two favourites amongst the delicate grasses. *Deschampsia cespitosa* 'Golden Dew' is like a mini stipa, but its flower

heads gently jangle with gold. We have a couple, but one is rather hidden. I must move it. The other is a moor grass, *Molinia caerulea* subsp. *arundinacea* 'Windspiel'. It has oaten heads on elegant six-foot golden stems that gently move with the wind without – apparently – getting bashed about. Eventually the stems self-prune by snapping off at the end of winter. It is probably happiest in acidic bog but will grow almost anywhere. At the moment we have just two very young plants, and I am looking forward to seeing them grow up.

I spent four days the other week filming *Gardener of the Year 2003*. No one in their right mind believes that this represents *the* gardener of this or any other year even if such a measurement were possible, but it was surprisingly good fun and interesting to do. We had five 'finalists' who had jumped through their horticultural hoops sufficiently well to get to the point where they had to build show gardens in Birmingham Botanic Gardens over four days as well as take part in various gardening tests. For amateurs who had never done more than tend their own patches it was very demanding, and they created gardens of astonishingly high standards.

29 September 2003
Celebrity

At the end of this ordeal I asked them all why they had put themselves through it (apart from anything else, there was no cash prize of any sort). One woman, whom I noticed had been eyeing me oddly all week, confessed that she had entered primarily so that she might meet Alan Titchmarsh. I retreated to my garden suitably chastened and yet also more glad than ever to have somewhere to go that is a million miles clear of the bonkers cult of celebrity.

We were talking, in the aftermath of the catastrophic events in America, about how much, if anything, had changed. Someone said that things like gardening and cooking seemed unbearably trivial at times like these, almost disrespectful. (I write this with fighter jets screaming across the night sky, preparing for vengeance.) But I am sure that this is not just wrong but a real misreading of the times. America has been shoved from the age of innocence into the Age of Paranoia, and although where America stumbles we are sent flying, it seems impossible to judge where this will take us. I am sure that certainties will now seem doubly precious. Verifiable honesty matters more than ever. The flash, the glib and all things phoney will be exposed in this new, rawer light as the dross that they are. Growing things, making something beautiful, eating

30 September 2001
Wallflowers

simple, fresh food – these things matter now more than ever. I often think of how Aldous Huxley, after years of intense exploration, came to the conclusion that all religious and spiritual learning could be summarised into two words: 'Pay attention'.

I have no embarrassment in elevating the goals and rewards of gardening to the spiritual. It seems self-evident in the sheer power of the life force that fills every cell of the smallest back yard to great estates. The trick is to pay attention to it, to notice things, to be fully alive yourself. I always know I am not functioning properly when I lose the rhythm of the garden. This is a hard thing to define as on the one hand the garden gets along fine without me and on the other there are plenty of still moments to relish. But it is not enough just to wander around admiring the catch of light on a leaf or the arch of a stem against the green. There has to be a commitment to the rolling future of the place. The best way that I know how to do this is a kind of controlled business where one is always spending time, effort and perhaps money in making the future. It seems better to deal with where we are going rather than where we have wound up. Which is why I have been planting wallflowers.

I have grown wallflowers before but have never really paid attention to them. In the way that lots of things in my life do, they just sort of happened. But this year I have paid attention to them. Sowed them, pricked them out and transplanted them to various points of the garden to mature. They are, of course, biennials. You sow them in May/June, plant them in autumn, and they flower the following spring.

I have a friend who has a castle – very ruined but dead cool all the same – and the wild wallflowers – gillyflowers – grow thirty feet up on the sheer sides of the keep. Although it is said that these were sometimes planted deliberately in the walls of grand medieval houses so that the scent would waft through the windows of the bedchambers, these ones are obviously not freshly sown nor are they a new batch of seedlings every year. The truth is that wallflowers are really perennial, but it suits gardeners to treat them as biennial to get the best from them, otherwise they tend to get leggy and sprawly and the florification diminishes. The fact that they find themselves into the lime mortar of old walls is a pretty good indication of their preference for chalky, very well-drained soil. They seem to take the warmth of the sun on an April day and process it into fragrance.

October

It is apple season in this the applest of all British counties, and I have spent a lot of time over the past week identifying the apples in our orchard. If I had kept a proper record of what was planted where when I did it – which is what I do nowadays – then I would not have had to do this, but I didn't and there it is.

The trees are still very young, but we are getting dozens and dozens of apples. Knowing where and how to store them is a bit of a problem. A dedicated apple store seems to me to be a lovely thing and I am tempted to build one in the orchard. It need not be much bigger than the chicken shed, and as long as it was frost-free and dry could be very simple. It would be a kind of grown-up Wendy house, dressed in the solemnity of a purpose. I can smell it now, that slightly musty, cidery tang that stored apples with crinkly skins give off, each variety in its own rack or shelf, all labelled but slightly scruffy. Bit like the orchard itself.

The beginning of October and here we are at the end of something, facing the empty quarter of the year, speeding along, barely noticing the passing of time, getting older and more infantile along the way, and the world is turning brown. I think that brown is a deadly colour in the garden. It must be used very carefully indeed, especially in winter, if it is not to weigh too heavily on the eye and spirits. Copper and bronze, on the other hand, add richness and depth. The trick is not to confuse either with brown.

For the last month the best examples of this distinction have been with the fabulous sunflowers 'Velvet Queen' and 'Prado Red'. The yellow shining through the brown tint with orange bits of pollen in the central discs, as well as the deep, almost burgundy colour of the stems and rims of the leaves, give the 'brown' a burnished coppery tint that electrifies it. These two dominate the September garden. The heleniums 'Moerheim Beauty' don't overwhelm in anything like the same way but are just as powerfully, if more modestly, effective. Their russety-bronze colour comes from the brown central cone combining with the orange petals. We also have the helenium 'Red and Gold', which is less known but works equally well at creating the dispersed russet burnish. *Rudbeckia hirta* is grown as an annual (although it is actually biennial or even perennial in the right conditions), while 'Gloriosa Daisy Mix' has wonderful rich, orangey-copper tones, as does 'Rustic Dwarfs', although this might include the odd truly yellow flower, which, in a fit of puritanical zeal to retain metallic status, can be smartly snipped off.

But that is last season's story. The reality of the garden now is that it is dying quietly on the vine. And dying as well as anything are the grasses, and of all the grasses, *Miscanthus sinensis* 'Malepartus' is relishing the hour most gloriously. As the plumes are opening they are gathered in an extraordinary concertina of zigzagged thread which then becomes the familiar bronzed, plum-feathered pennants.

If you think that it is stretching things too far to call the 'Malepartus' bronze, then there can be no argument with *Miscanthus nepalensis*, whose plumes are always described as gold but which are actually more a brassy colour. It is ravishingly beautiful. *Carex buchananii*, which is similar but which has charming wiggly bits at the ends of its leaves, is a useful component of the metallic kit, as is *C. flagellifera*, which has a more ginger tint to it than *C. comans*, which it resembles.

3 October 1994
Bulbs
·····················

It is time to be getting on with bulb-planting. One reads that you should plant bulbs at the end of August/beginning of September, to give the roots maximum time to grow, and yet every year I have a pile of

// *Picking green tomatoes is a kind of surrender. Summer is gone.*

unplanted bulbs into November, by which time I think that it is too late. Half of them are palely sprouting and the other half are reproachful husks. My guess is that bulbs are a bit like the mustard left on a plate: more are piled up in the corners of sheds or surreptitiously ditched than actually get planted.

This is odd, because bulb-planting requires absolutely no skill and hardly any knowledge. The rule of thumb is to allow twice their own depth of soil above them and to put them pointy end up. That's it. Everything else is fine-tuning.

If you have heavy, wet soil like my Herefordshire clay, grit helps but does not change the prevailing conditions. However, fritillaries, snowdrops, anemones and the summer snowflake will thrive in the damp, so choose your plants for the conditions. I remember peeing into a hedge on my first day of farm work, three of us with our backs hunched against the cold breeze. 'First rule of nature,' the oldest told me as he buttoned up, 'is don't piss into the wind.' First rule of gardening too.

I love a good pear more than any apple. Not one of your supermarket numbers, all glowing green skin and gentle swell on the outside with not enough juice, not enough taste and never – this is the real offence – *never* the right texture. A fresh, perfectly ripe pear is firm-fleshed with a closely grained texture, and intensely sweet.

And you get the tree. Pear trees are glorious objects. A mature one can stand fifty feet tall and in full early-April blossom makes the best flowering plant on the planet. Of course to do that it must be grown as a standard on its own roots and with no intention of seeing its maturity in your lifetime. Pear trees live much longer than apples. Do not build up the expectations of your children either. Pear grows slow and long. It belongs to bigger time than people. Planting a standard pear is like planting an oak or at least a beech. You are making landscape, making the future.

My pear trees are prized beyond price. This is not because they are particularly good pear trees – they would win no conventional prizes for anything other than affection received – but because I can watch the fruit develop from the stunningly beautiful white blossom to that moment when they are ready to pick or have just fallen to the ground. I test the pears every day as they approach ripening, lifting the swollen hips of each fruit in one hand and gently tilting it at right angles. If it comes away then it is ready. Not, you understand, ready to be eaten. First there must be a period on the windowsill (east-facing, not too hot), checking it twice a day, turning it as the skin turns more yellow. Then, after perhaps four days, if I gently press my thumb at the base of the pear there will be a slight yielding. Not a soft squidginess, just a bit of gentle give. Pears have a tendency to ripen from the inside out so that the flesh immediately beneath the skin is the last to be ready. They often fall before they are fully ripe where birds and mammals can chew at them, eat the seeds and cast them in their perambulations with a convenient supply of manure. You want to eat a pear as soon as there is any softness to it at all. When that moment comes you have to act fast. Get your priorities right. Take the phone off the hook, let the kettle boil itself dry and the bath overflow as you cut it into quarters, peel it, slither the core away and eat the firm, slippery flesh.

5 October 2003
Dry
....

It is dry, dry, dry. This is the first time that I have seen ash trees so stressed by drought that their leaves hang like rags. The walled garden normally has a second flush at the end of September, with a gentle mix of cosmos, evening primrose, verbascums, geraniums, roses, fennel, figs, acanthus, melianthus and borage entering autumn with a swing. This year it will have none of it and has packed up shop altogether, with only the figs and rosemary looking at all happy. As soon as it has had a week or so of rain I shall clear it and mulch it thickly with some good manure as well as its normal spring mulch of mushroom compost next March, which should beef it up a little and extend next year's season.

The grass in front of the house has not been mown for nearly five weeks and has not grown at all. Not a millimetre. The orchard grass, which at this time of year is normally due for its second cut of the year with much attendant raking and carting of hay, is only inches long. In fact I mowed it yesterday with the lawnmower, collecting the cuttings as I went, which is a first. As a result there are parched grass stripes beneath the apples, giving it a tremendously chichi air.

The reason I cut the orchard grass at all was not for tidiness's sake – I like my orchard to look and feel as though a flock of sheep would be at home there – but to provide a clean fall for the apples, which are ripening weeks ahead of normal schedule. It is useless trying to store windfalls as the smallest blemish or bruise invariably spreads and overtakes the fruit, but equally my trees are too small and young to have enough fruit to carelessly discard.

I have put an empty vegetable crate by each tree, and every time I pass I pop windfalls into them so the slugs and birds don't have a go before we do. So we are eating apples for every meal in a rather self-

// The sedum 'Herbstfreude', still standing in the dry garden.

conscious way. I am very aware that none of this will last. A few days' rain and a more comfortable shagginess will return but without the lushness that can reassert itself after a spring or summer drought. The garden is like a door left ajar waiting for the movement that can only close it.

I have not done very much outside at all. This is partly due to a general listlessness – energy levels shockingly low – and partly due to the pressures of catching up on work after a week in bed. When this situation is allowed to ride for a few days it is a bit like facing housework when the place is a tip. Where to begin? I have a fallback position, which is to blindly stumble into the vegetable garden and start weeding. I don't rationalise this or plan it or work in any kind of systematic fashion. First weed I see gets it. From that crouching position I work outwards, spreading my destructive aimlessness like a weed-blight. It works wonders. The important thing is to get on to your knees and use your hands. Gloves act as a prophylactic to the true effect. Dirty and perhaps stung hands are necessary. Then when a cleared patch is self-evident the motivation to continue in a more structured way kicks in.

6 October 2001
Getting going

I finally got round to cutting the box pebbles. That they are in an active state-of-becoming-pebbles gives me a huge amount of excited pleasure, I must admit. Once a year, when I cut them, I know for sure that I am doing, conceptually, exactly the right thing. I suppose that the real mark of this is if you feel it and don't give a jot if no one else agrees with you.

7 October 2000
Pebbles

I have put off the job for months – I would normally expect to do it in June – because of the palaver of clearing the clippings up. Not because I am too grand to do that part of the chore but because the sixty-three box pebbles are set in cobbles. Big green living cobbles set in small stone ones. Everything all of a piece. However, the thousands of knobbles of stone make sweeping or raking up a nightmare, with box-leaf confetti wedged in the cobbled interstices. So I put off cutting the pebbles until I could get hold of a garden vacuum cleaner. I had one years ago and it was useless for me then in a brand-new garden made up of a bare field, dreams and eighteen-inch hedges, so I gave it to my father-in-law. But over the years I have secretly hankered after one again, and the other day I finally got round to hiring one for these box blobs. It worked a treat. Fantastic. The only fly in the ointment was that the electric hedge-trimmer decided to stop working whilst I went and had a cup of tea.

The last flowers of Cosmos bipinnatus 'Purity' in the herb garden. //

It worked beautifully when I stopped it and put it down, but when I started it up again refused to cut a thing. I fiddled with it for an hour, made it worse, and did the rest with shears.

Before I started I took a few hundred box cuttings from the most vigorous of the box ovoids, lining them out directly into the seed bed in the vegetable garden. I shall keep them cloched over the winter, and they should form the stock for my plan to line all the vegetable beds with box hedges. I like the idea of these vigorous spheroids spawning sharp-edged boxes of box-edged vegetables.

8 October 2000
Paths
· ·

When we first moved in eight years ago, I believed that we could simply cut beds from the grass of the field, mow the bits in between and call them paths. It is not a bad policy if you have limited funds, and half our paths are still just mown field and need only a pass with a mower once a week to keep them that way. I especially like the paths made by cutting the orchard grass at different lengths with the mown, gently curving strip fringed by the tall meadow grasses. Dead simple but dead lovely.

But grass is useless in the rainy season, which, with the unstoppable roll of global warming, is at least eight months of the year. And even in summer, every time you set foot on the path, let alone wheel a heavy barrow on it, you are compacting the soil, worsening the drainage and increasing the subsequent winter quagmire.

OK, I speak from jaundiced experience, living in one of the wettest places in England with heavy soil to boot, but even the fastest-draining ground loses some of its allure after a week's rain in November. Certainly in my own garden the lovely, springy grass paths of summer are just a photograph in a book. Feet can't remember them. Going outside to get a sprig of rosemary or to shut in the chickens means taking off your shoes and putting on wellingtons. Only frost brings sufficient hard dryness to walk unprotected.

So over the years, as money and time have allowed, we have been converting our paths from grass to hard surfaces. The luxury of walking dry-shod is worth the work and expense. It also opens up a whole range of colours, textures and structures. A brick path is a wall on edge. The first paths we made were intended to be all stone, but after the first few yards it became apparent that what seemed like a huge pile bought as a random job lot at a knock-down price was not going to fill anything like the required stretch. So we started mixing in cobbles to fill the gaps and make the stone go further. It worked very well, despite the fact that

cobbles do not make good paths. They are too knobbly and slippery to walk on with ease. But if you have sufficient stone they are fine.

Then we progressed to brick, with Sarah giving me the bricks for a path for my fortieth birthday. She hunted for ages until she found second-hand ones from the same brickyard (small, local, closed down in 1884) as those at the back of the house where the path leads from. Choosing bricks that relate to those of the house or any existing walls is the most important aspect of any brick path. Ours was laid basket-weave fashion and I love it, although the shadiest bit gets incredibly slippery.

George made what I think is our best path. It curves through the spring garden and is made entirely from the leftover bits and pieces of the first phase of building work. The only consistent materials are concrete blocks, which are laid sideways a block's length apart. The gap between them is infilled with anything that could be used.

In the vegetable garden we now have brick pavers. These are like bricks but baked much harder so that they take more wear and tear and, crucially, will not break up or split when they freeze. The downside is that they are very brittle and prone to cracking when you lay them. We

Fallen leaves and light spangling the lime walk. //

have also used pavers as narrow paths-within-a-path down the centre of some of the grass paths. We can mow over them and yet walk and wheel a barrow down the centre in the slushiest of weather. The plan is to continue this throughout the garden.

Our jewel garden paths are topped with a material called 'Redgra', a kind of pink sand mixed with clay that binds it solid when laid. It is much cheaper and easier to lay than paving or brick, but we have learnt that if it doesn't have really sharp drainage it turns almost to mud in very wet weather.

My week has been dominated by one major job. When we first came here the only garden was a smallish walled area that had been the farm's vegetable patch. The builders used it as a dump for all their rubble. Nevertheless we cleared that and made four large beds, which I rotovated. Then Brian, the Bobcat driver, was doing other work out the back and I got him to make inter-crossing paths between the beds, shifting the topsoil from the paths on to the beds. He and his tiny bulldozer tore over the site furiously and it was done within the hour.

It turned out to be a disaster. While the top nine inches of the beds were lovely, crumbly topsoil, the layer below had been compressed into a hard, rock-like pan by his machine. I have since seen this on a number of estates of new houses where all the building materials are handled by forklift trucks, zooming over the site, which is rotovated and turfed before the houses are occupied.

To make matters worse, the ground was – still is – infested with bindweed, couch grass and horseradish, the roots of which are deep under the pan so cannot be forked out. From May to July all looks great but from July to October it is a disaster zone. For a couple of years now we have been meaning to take out all the plants from the four beds, including forty large shrub roses, weed them thoroughly, break the pan up, manure it and put everything back in. So far three whole days have cleared one of the four beds. Every plant has had its roots hosed down to get every millimetre of bindweed root out. Everything, once cleaned, has been put in pots packed in sand or heeled into the veg garden. On Sunday I dug the border and found the only way to break up the pan was with a pickaxe. It all looks a horrendous mess and at this rate it will take until November to get done. The moral of the story is: Whatever it takes, however long it takes, do it right first time.

9 October 1998
Pan
....

Miscanthus sinensis 'Silberfeder' flying high in the jewel garden. //

12 October 1998
Sauce
....

Sarah pushed a wheelbarrow into the house the other day with thirty kilos of red tomatoes – there are as many green ones still to pick – and spent two days working on different tomato sauces with different varieties of tomato. All were frozen. I don't mind the odd glut when you eat far more of one fruit or vegetable than normal for a month then do not taste it for ages, but there are very few things that cannot be stored or frozen to be eaten across the year. The one question always asked when we show someone round the vegetable garden is what do we do with all the food we grow? The answer is simple. We eat it.

15 October 2000
Ethics
....

In the recent petrol hysteria created by, depending on which side of the political fence you sit, a group of decent upright citizens or a self-serving pressure group of polluting hauliers and highly subsidised farmers, I thought that the green movement were pretty pathetic and missed a clear trick. We all use far too much petrol and are all guilty of being utterly wasteful of it. We drive big empty cars on journeys we could share or walk. I certainly do. We gardeners mow millions of acres of lawns to within a centimetre of their lives and use fuel to strim and hedge-trim, chainsaw, suck up leaves, vibrate paths and God knows what else besides. Practically all gardening mechanisation, unlike half our car journeys, is entirely unjustifiable save on grounds of labour-saving and the fun of operating a big noisy machine. The latter reason, of course, is hard to deny.

Even organic gardeners are often guilty of using up vast amounts of the world's limited resources just to fulfil the organic creed. Is it better to use a certified organic mulch transported expensively from abroad or a bark mulch that is not organic but that comes from just down the road and would otherwise be dumped? It is not easy.

You may not be able to square your use of the car, but when it comes to the garden you must look your conscience in the eye. The buck stops in our own back yards. This is gardening shaping the way that we mean to live.

16 October 1999
Nettles
....

We have now finished with the film crew that has been coming here every few weeks since February. Although we grew to be great friends, there was a sense of relief because we could revert to being the real slobs that we are. One of the restraining factors was that we had to keep the vegetable garden looking fuller than perhaps it needed to be. So I had a clean-out the other day, brutally clearing all excess leafage from the various manifestations of chard, chicory and cabbage. I pulled up the sweetcorn and the acorn squashes that I under-planted them with (squashes good, sweetcorn bad), cut the hedges behind them and planted out excess strawberries on the patch. It is a bit late for this, but they should develop root growth before winter sets in.

The river burst its banks again at the beginning of the month, slinging a lovely cloth of water across the meadows and lapping into the orchard. I can forgive it flooding into the garden for the brief watery beauty, but the price is a million nettle seeds washed on to the margins of our ground. I spent a few hours slashing back all the nettles that were a result of this spring's floods. They grow eight feet tall in the silt with stems as thick as my finger and fall in on you so you are wrapped in nettle. I managed to get stung inside the mouth in the process, which was unfunny, but it at least gave a huge pile that will make really good compost.

I was collecting the last barrow-load of mushroom compost from an enormous lorry-load that had been tipped on to our driveway last spring when I realised that the lush growth of horseradish in the drive was because of the compost dumped on top of it. It had wonderfully long, clean roots. Maybe this is the way to treat horseradish: bury it beneath a heap of manure and let it fight for survival – as it surely will.

17 October 1998
Empty
. . . .

The yew hedge in front of my house is turning coppery, yellowing and dying. I think it is something to do with the extensive building foundations below this part of the garden. So last weekend I decided to move the survivors and dug a new trench only to come across yet more walls, paving and stone drains a foot or so below the surface. This is fascinating, but the place looks like an archaeological dig, and my poor (very expensive) yews are still unmoved.

The clearing of the walled garden continues. Halfway through this excruciatingly slow process (which should have been finished weeks ago) Sarah stood looking at the site for about ten minutes and then announced that she 'had had an idea'. This is a coded message for change. Radical change. Why not clear the whole area and turn it into lawn? We could keep a long border against the walls around three sides and open the rest as a child-friendly play area?

At first this struck me as madness. Keen gardeners are always looking to fill more ground with plants, not less. But it very neatly solves one big problem. The children have long felt ostracised from the garden by plants. There is not enough dedicated space for them anyway, and what space I have grudgingly allotted to them is miles from the house, which they hate. This would be a private, screened play area near the house that they would feel was theirs and which could still look fine. And, thank God, it means we don't have to double-dig the rest of it. If at a later date we want to plant it up again it will be easy enough to do so. So four large, wonderfully rampant, square flower beds become empty lawn. No, not empty: lawn for filling with play and mucking about and laughter. This kind of decision-making feels liberating, like knocking down a wall between two rooms.

18 October 2003
Cuttings
....

I planted out a batch of rooted box cuttings this week. Having taken them last September, I'd left them for twelve months stuck directly into a 50:50 perlite/coir-based potting compost mix laid on the floor of a cold frame. About twenty per cent died back – which is too many for box – and not a single cutting showed the least hint of growth all year. But when I lifted them out (lovely soft mix through the fingers), nearly all had got bushy, clean white roots.

I lined them out into the nursery beds, where they will stay for perhaps another three years. I have found that it is far better to wait until each plant is strong enough to look after itself before planting into its final position, otherwise there are unacceptable losses from smothering by over-vigorous neighbouring plants. It is a slow business, but I now have about a thousand box plants at varying stages of maturity. Somehow their slowness is a kind of perverse pacemaker for the garden – slowing things down to the speed at which they need to be.

It would probably have been best to have left the box cuttings where they were until next spring, but I needed the space for overwintering pelargoniums, dahlias, agapanthus, brugmansias and the various cuttings that I've taken this autumn. These are all tucked up snug as frost has already come with a sharp edge for a few nights. I have no objections to this at all – the more frost the better really – but I like to mollycoddle the tenderer things. The citrus plants are always a problem in that respect. They are not hardy enough to leave outside but rather big for the greenhouse. They look lovely indoors but hate the central heating and get scale insects in a bad way. A cool porch or conservatory would be ideal, but neither is to hand, so they sprawl and bush in the greenhouse, perfectly healthy but wasted to the eye. The apples are almost all in too, satisfying my control-freak tendencies, variety by variety on their slatted shelves. I have resisted the temptation of keeping any with the tiniest blemish and at this early stage of

autumn they all fairly gleam with stored health. And has there ever been a year in living memory when apples have generally been so red?

I have been cheated of *moyesii* hips this year. When they are there they are orange flagons, long and waisted like gourds and covering the big, fine-boned bush. I have two groups of five bushes of the plain species *Rosa moyesii* and a solitary *R. moyesii* 'Geranium'. Both have wonderful single crimson flowers that speckle large upright bushes in a curiously scattered but deeply satisfying distribution (one of my annual treats is to crawl behind one of the large clumps of the *moyesii* when in full flower and peer back at the garden through the veil of delicate leaves and blood-red flowers, seeing the world for a moment through that particular mirror), and I would – do – surely grow them for the flowers alone, but the hips are just as good. Last year they fell short on flowers, so of course no hips, but this year they flowered beautifully so I have waited for the fruits with bated breath. Two. Just two sodding hips are there. Two hips may work well for people but are just not enough on a rose.

Raindrops bejewelling a fennel seed head. //

Last night I jogged around the Herefordshire lanes and came home almost drunk with the scent of apples. Every breath was a slug of strong cider, at once sweet and dry, fizzy and still: all the contradictions of smell bundled into easy associations of taste. Not enough mention is made of the way that smell is such a feature of the countryside, such as the foetid sweetness of the May blossom, the chaffy greenness of haymaking, the strawness of harvest time and the hard boniness of frost on the nose. I know that this might seem like a catalogue of rural elitism, but city gardens serve as *rus in urbe* now more than ever, and for most people the closest contact with the earthiness of country matters is through our gardens. That tang of apple from the little tree in your garden at this time of year is the same experience as mine last night.

This is reason enough to grow apples. The reason has to be good because for such ubiquitous plants, apples are surprisingly tricky to grow healthily. They hate wind, need plenty of sun, good drainage and good soil; they grow much better below five hundred feet than above; they do not like too much wet, which causes scab, mildew and canker; and the buds from which the apples stem are destroyed by spring frost. Given that you can buy an apple in any greengrocer and supermarket in the land for a few pence, you might wonder why bother with them.

For a start they hardly smell at all in the supermarket. Without that October scent the experience of growing and eating is cut short, and both are diminished. You never tasted an apple aright until the tree itself groweth in your veins … Apologies to solemn Thomas Traherne (who walked these same Herefordshire lanes), but I am not being entirely facetious. There is room for an apple tree in almost every garden, however limited the quantity of crop that you might harvest, just so that you can experience directly the intense appleness of a good apple off the tree, be you in city or remote countryside.

Last Sunday, for the first time in my life, I found myself longing for Michaelmas daisies. Let's put this into context. I hate asters. That has been my official line for ages. They are a waste of space, spending most of the year creating boring foliage, then doing flowers that get mouldy and insignificant, then they are a nuisance to cut back because the stems are so ridiculously tough. And, adding insult to injury, they take ages to compost down.

It is, like everything else that is wrong, all everybody else's fault. The realisation of this asterless aspect of my life suddenly hit me when showing some friends round the garden the other day. I am not cool about this. I long to let them saunter round the garden, taking it as it comes, just as we all drift round public gardens in every corner of Britain. But if I know that someone is coming, I cannot resist the urge to impress them. I get into a pre-emptive fluster. (I don't even do the tidying and primping myself any more. Sarah said the other day that I had become an 'executive gardener'. Ouch.) I immediately want to start a running dialogue with the visitors-to-be explaining away that gap in the hedge or the border, the way the nettles are romping gleefully over the pond-to-be. You know the story. It is depressing in its predictability.

The good side of this is that it makes you do what a friend used to dismissively call 'park-keeping'. I like park-keeping for exactly the same reasons that I like the house when it is clean and tidy. I will admit that the sheer novelty of the experience has quite a lot to do with this pleasure, but it is like having a haircut and putting on a suit fresh from the dry cleaner's. You feel up for it and ready for the fray. So I enjoy the edging and collecting of leaves, the weeding of the paths and the general face-scrubbing that goes on. No shame there. Of course when the visitors do finally get their guided tour no mention is ever made of the extraordinary preparation done entirely on their behalf. The rig of the garden in all its scrubbed shipshapery is worn as lightly as vanity will allow.

But on this particular occasion all nicety of pretension and detail was blown away by the rain and gales. The rain washed out what colour there was and the wind mussed up the crispness of the edges that we carefully contrived. As we reached the jewel garden I was aware of the brownness of the earth and the drabness of the green. The urge to apologise had to be knocked back. But there were no good excuses. The borders in October ought to be strong. The dahlias look OK if a bit thin by now, the grasses are good, and the *Buddleja* x *weyeriana* is at its best. But the colour gaps are screaming in their absence. More purple, more violet and more gold.

It was then I realised that asters were the answer to our autumn gap.

23 October 2005
Chestnuts
· · · · · · · · · · · · · · · · · · · ·

I have been assured by a number of people that it is going to be a hard winter because the squirrels have been exceptionally active hoarding nuts. I want to believe this kind of observation because I want to tap into a knowledge that transcends and subverts the stultifying logic of measurement and science. I suppose the antithesis of this is the council goons who order chestnut trees to be cut down in case a conker falls on a passer-by or someone slips on a leaf.

A fully grown horse chestnut, *Aesculus hippocastanum*, will be more than thirty-five metres tall and almost as broad, and is unquestionably one of the finest flowering trees in the northern hemisphere as well as being all those grown-up things that anybody in their right mind should celebrate (but conkers belong to children). Our own horse chestnut has not produced any fruit yet, but it is only six years old, and they normally start to flower around their seventh year. We moved it three years ago, which effectively set it back two years, so it may be a year or two yet before we have the good fortune to be hit by falling conkers. The flowers, balanced like pyramids of ice cream or white candyfloss, are at their best in early May, but the sticky buds break into glowing leaf in early April and the whole tree is a delight all spring and early summer. In the hot dog days of high summer no tree casts such a congenial shade.

The sweet chestnut, *Castanea sativa*, is a southern European tree and was almost certainly introduced by the Romans. It is happiest on well-drained or sandy acidic loams. So whereas the horse chestnut grows almost everywhere, its sweet counterpart tends to be very localised. The wood is fast-growing, hard and extremely long-lasting in the soil – so ideal for fencing. The reason for this durability is that it forms a hardwood heart at a very early age. It is this that makes it able to cleave very cleanly and straight. I once bought a hundred eight-foot chestnut stakes, each about eight inches in diameter, and split them all into quadrants to use as the uprights for the woven hazel fence that went right round the vegetable garden to protect the hornbeam hedges that I then planted in their lee. These hazel fences have long disappeared inside the hedges but the chestnut stakes are all still good. Almost without exception these stakes split straight and clean using just an axe and a wedge. It was one of the most satisfying couple of hours of my life.

What happens here in the confines of the garden is my base reality and, when it happens, my only seasonal yardstick.

This, above all else, is the apple season. My favourites are the local apples, some of which are hardly known beyond a twenty-mile radius of where I live. They belong to this place. These include 'Doctor Hares', 'Tillington Court', 'Madresfield Court', 'William Crump', 'Stoke Edith Pippin', 'Crimson Queening' and 'Herefordshire Beefing'. I make no apology for the roll call of names – it is music to my ears. It immediately adds character and personality to the orchard exactly because it is – like my private weather and private seasons – so very local and parochial. They belong to this piece of England. They give the place meaning.

25 October 2002
Floundering
. . . .

There are times when I seem to lose the gardening habit. I want to do it but have forgotten how to. I know the motions – could tell you all sorts of stuff about gardening – but then I get outside and flounder.

I have been doing bits and pieces – mainly planting for the instant fix of soil on the fingers and the easy sense of contributing something useful – but without much conviction. Part of the problem is that I have spent so much of the past six months writing a big gardening book. Because it is very practical, writing becomes a substitute for actually doing. For the past few months it is as though I have been on a dream journey, visiting my own garden at every stage but never actually being there.

I am lucky in that I have new help in the garden, a husband-and-wife team – Norman and Jayne – who are so energetic and competent that in the two days they come here each week they achieve huge amounts, all immaculately done. The place has never looked so tidy or had such a sense of confidence. I only wish I had a rather larger part in it.

So now, just as the clocks are going back and the light really starting to fade, it is time to renew my acquaintance. It is no bad thing this, to walk round the garden with the eyes of a traveller, taking stock, seeing the growing year slip gently away. The garden seems to thin, to waste a little, and you start to see through spaces that you have been accustomed to consider solid. Of course there is no surprise to this – the leaves are falling and that's the amount of it – but it changes all the shapes and volumes, and this alters the whole world. Because the weather this autumn has been so exceptionally dry – by far the driest that I can remember here – there is that combination of intense autumn colour and tiredness. Things are not so much parched as worn out. But it was wonderful whilst it lasted – to be able to step out to any point in the garden in indoor shoes, to go and weed or dig on dry soil, even to lie on dry grass at midday in October – these are real luxuries and were not taken lightly in the Don household.

26 October 2002
Squashes
. . . .

We usually harvest our pumpkins and squashes around the end of the first week in October, by which time their foliage has become either a mildewy grey shadow of its luscious self or else been blasted by frost. There is also a point at which the squashes, sitting on wet soil, become damaged and therefore keep badly. Not this year. As I write they are still sprawling over the sweet pea walk like teenagers watching Saturday-morning telly, growing more orange by the day and still with a shine to them, which means that they are not properly ripe. This lateness is not

all down to the Indian summer but partly due to the fact that I sowed them too early. It is an oft-repeated mistake. They all – 'Baby Bear', 'Etamples', 'Jack Be Little', 'Butternut', 'Early Acorn', 'Uchiki Kuri' and 'Turk's Turban' – went in on 29 March and were ready to plant out by the beginning of May. But it was cold and the risk of frost real, so they sat in the cold frame being eaten by slugs and did not get finally planted until 15 June. Nothing wrong with this last date although if it had not been a cold June it would have been a fortnight earlier. But I shall not think of sowing them before May in future.

Last year my single fruiting quince tree produced four precious fruit. This year it is quince jelly all round as I have just picked forty-seven fruit from the same 'Leskovac' tree. We have also planted 'Portugal', 'Vranja' and 'Champion' trees in the same spot down in the damp garden, so it is now a little quincey orchard under-planted with hostas, primulas, ligularias and royal ferns. To make this space, Norman and Jayne cut down the willows that I had planted nine years ago as rooted cuttings

27 October 2002
Quince

Squashes laid out in the back yard to ripen in the last of the sun. //

no thicker than my finger but now thirty feet tall, fat-trunked and needing a chainsaw and ropes to shift and drag them out – somehow without so much as damaging a leaf of the tightly packed planting – to make a vast bonfire. This is a new experience for me, seeing trees that I planted outgrow their welcome. It does make the point that gardening is always a process of renewal, but what comes back is never quite the same as what it replaces.

28 October 2005
Light

· · · · · · · · · · · · · · · · · · ·

We had a light fixed up in the greenhouse yesterday. It is the first time that it has ever been lit. Not a big deal perhaps, but I think that it will transform the coming months. Over the last several weeks, I have been working harder than I think I have ever done before in my life. It is entirely my own fault – one of these days I will learn to say no – but it has meant working from very early till too late for an average of twenty days out of every twenty-one. It is mostly interesting and rewarding and it pays the mortgage, but it is a pretty stupid way to live. Hard work never harmed anybody, but overwork will always end in tears. However,

// After a hot summer the field maples turn a brilliant yellow.

things will ease off a little over the winter, and I should be able to spend a whole day every week with my family and my garden.

It is the garden that has suffered most. Like any gardener I tend to measure the quality of my life by the amount of time that I have to spend in my garden. I find that there are two phases to this. The first is when you book in regular 'garden time' like an appointment and then scurry around being busy and getting things done. Sometimes it has to be like this, and I am happy to boast that I am good at it. I can get a lot done in a short amount of time. But this is a bit like that terrible expression 'quality time'. What it really means is guilty-inadequate time. You do the best you can, knowing, as you do it, that it is not going to be enough.

The best time in the garden, as perhaps with all things that you care a lot about, is time that is easy and even a little wasteful. Children like parents who are just reliably there, as happy to do nothing with them as to bombard them with 'quality' events. So it is with a garden. It is necessary to give yourself the time just to mooch about, looking with keen eyes but not necessarily planning or conventionally working at all. Just being there.

Now I have had a very small garden and a very big garden, and I love the luxuries of the latter – it was one of the main reasons for moving back to the country, having endured ten years living in London in the 1980s. But it is a much more unforgiving place. Leave the jobs unattended for more than about a week and it becomes almost impossible to catch up without spending extra time – the lack of which caused the problem in the first place.

I have the winter to catch up on myself so that I can reach the point where I can stroll slowly around the garden without feeling that I am wasting precious time. But it is a bit of an irony that this time is just coming available the weekend that the clocks go back and we lose that precious evening hour. This is where the little light fitting in the greenhouse comes in. A flick of a switch will buy gentle hours of extra gardening. Not 'quality time' necessarily, but so much better than no time at all.

Over the weekend I cut the box balls. In the process I cut through the cable of the electric hedge-trimmer and blew up my main hedge-cutter, but despite these minor distractions, the job was done. Our collection of box balls grows in number as well as size each year. At the moment we have 113 of them although thirty are not really balls yet and need pruning rather than trimming. Still, it is quite a business. But I love having done it, when the box has been transformed from a shaggy set of shapes into

29 October 2004
Evergreen
....

a crisp interplay of curves and spaces. It is like wiping a foggy glass and seeing what had been blurred outlines leap out clearly for what they really are in all their detailed glory.

And yet – nothing could be simpler. Just rounded shapes in a grid. No two are alike, nor do I want them to be. I like the way that they are all individuals and resist any attempt to make them conform too much. As winter approaches – much too fast for me – this kind of crisp evergreen living sculpture is just what the garden needs to retain its presence.

30 October 1994
Pumpkins

I sowed some pumpkin seeds this year, partly because I thought their great orange footballs would look jolly, partly because I have loads of space so anything that grows dramatically is needed to add substance to the place, but mainly so that I could earn brownie points as a good father come Hallowe'en. The idea was that there would be at least a pumpkin per child, preferably two pumpkins each – a fleet of pumpkins – which we could cut and carve into toothy candlelit grins. General delighted spookiness all round.

Well, here we are, almost, and I do not have a single pumpkin to my name. I have lots of marrows, great whopping jobs, but everybody has marrows. Marrows are one of those crops that, if they grow at all, inevitably produce a glut, and a little marrow goes a long way. Or is treated as a courgette. But the pumpkins all failed to germinate. I sowed them in April in an unheated greenhouse and then again in May outside, directly into an old compost heap. I now know, having done my research, that both procedures were doomed.

Pumpkins need heat of at least 16 degrees to germinate and must be kept dark. If you sow them in individual pots or modules filled with a general-purpose compost and then cover these until they have germinated, they can stay in the pots until planted out. William Cobbett, writing 175 years ago, observed that 'about the middle of May, the pots should be taken out and sunk in the natural ground, and a frame set over them, or they should have a covering of hoops and mats for the night time, just to keep off the frosts'. This sounds elaborate but contains the essential wisdom of hardening off plants grown in indoor sheltered conditions before putting them out in their final position. Otherwise, however healthy, the culture shock is too great and they give up the ghost.

It is odd that such a robust thing as a pumpkin should need mollycoddling, but they are not natives and have not got used to our climate. It is easier to understand if one thinks of them as close relatives

The stark stagheads of onopordums dominate the jewel garden sky. //

of cucumbers. They should not be planted out until the days – and, critically, the nights – are warm. In this garden that is never before mid-June. They are not fussy about soil but like a well-drained, rich root run, so the technique used for marrows of digging a shallow pit filled with compost and planting them in that is a good one. They should then romp away with no assistance at all other than regular and plentiful watering.

I have told the children this – weeping in the corner and throwing me recriminating looks – and promised them pumpkins the size of coaches next year.

31 October 2004
Last light
....

Sarah and I were speaking the other day at Cheltenham Literary Festival, and the chairperson asked about the effect of the seasons and how important that was in the garden. For a moment I was flabbergasted. It is such a fundamental and essential aspect of gardening that it dominates everything – every tiny detail of everything. My eventual response was to wheel out the stock phrases along the affecting-everything theme. But it made me realise that for some people the change in seasons might not be of fundamental importance.

There are only two possible reasons why this might be. The first is that some people are unaware of seasons or the natural world at all. The second is that modern life has so blunted the edge of the seasons for most people that they just slide by in a smooth, well-blended continuum. For myself, I find the seasons' teeth bite deep. And even with climate change, even with freak flowers and blossom appearing out of season like Christmas cards arriving in May, there is no way out of this one. We are staring November in the face and winter lies unavoidably ahead.

The key moment, of course, was at two this morning, when the clocks changed their time by deed poll. Two became one and things got half as good. Only an hour gone but the heart and soul of the day lost. However, there is nothing to be done beyond endurance, getting outside as much as possible and making the most of what is there.

But there is not a lot. Every day brings less. Of the very few flowers in my garden at the moment, the best is the monkshood, *Aconitum carmichaelii*. We have an unknown (or at least unremembered) variety which is probably 'Kelmscott' because the flowers are pretty dark – almost purple – whereas 'Barker's Variety' is a paler blue. There are some who find both colours a little insipid, but I am grateful for the best we can get. Certainly there is no other blue flower that can equal it at the end of October.

November

One day it has been violently stormy and the next clear as glass with blue skies and frost. The dahlias are frozen black, as are the nasturtiums and squashes, whose leaves had held on to the semblance of summer. I have dug up the dahlias, cutting them off just above the ground, and put them upside down in a box in the greenhouse to dry off before storing them somewhere dry and cool for the winter; last year it was in the downstairs loo.

The rain has made all our grass paths slimy on top and like well-worked plasticine below the surface. They will stay this way except in hard frost until next April. It will not do. So we have begun the enormous task of digging them all up and replacing them with hard ones. So far this means grey chippings, which look pretty brutal, and we will have to top them with stone or brick – which will be ruinously expensive. Good, well-drained grass paths are a great luxury.

A silver lining to this process is that we will create a large stack of turf with which to make our own loam-based potting compost. We are stacking it in a block of grassy sandwiches and by next spring it will be ready to use, slicing down through the heap with a spade. We mix it with grit and some sieved garden compost, which works very well and has a kind of organic self-sufficiency that I like.

We ate the last of the artichokes this week, and the first of the 'Red Treviso' chicory. The latter has exquisite leaves, green on the outside and deep blood red on the inside, this pattern repeating to the tiny heart leaves when split open. A joy.

We cleared out our cold greenhouse, which is used for tomatoes, melons and peppers. The tomato harvest from this has been astonishing – by far the best ever – and has meant days of work processing the damn things into storable forms.

But the most surprising harvest was the peppers, especially a green variety whose label has been lost and whose provenance I have completely forgotten. They were grown in Gro-bags, and when I emptied the bags the roots had completely filled them – there was no spare soil at all. These peppers look like chillies but are sweet, not hot. We have a rule of thumb that we do not attempt to produce exotica of any kind – we only grow what wants to grow in our conditions without any special treatment – but these acted as though they had found their spiritual home, with six small bushes producing more than a hundred small peppers.

4 November 2000
Worms
....

It is the knobbliness of the grass that I notice first. Around the middle of October, worms start leaving casts on the surface of the lawn and grass paths. Walk across the lawn in the dark and the ground skids away from under you exactly like dog turds on pavement. (And it would be tiny, lapdog turds. Somehow nastier for that.) You step on the neat piles of worm excretion and smear it across the grass. Relief. It's only mud. But mud is awful. Mud is brown, wet lumps of despair. You can brush worm casts away if they are dry enough. But they will not get dry enough until spring.

I like worms. On the whole the more worms a garden has the better. They are a measure of healthy soil. But these casts are the price you pay for the few months that the worms turn.

5 November 1997
Shit
....

It is strange how autumn surprises you every year, even though it is as predictable as a birthday. You are conscious of summer stretching itself so thin that it is transparent, hardly any substance to it at all and yet enough colour in the garden, enough fragile heat in the sun to cling to. And then you turn away for a moment and it's gone, autumn in its place, lumpen, damp and chill. Overnight you can hardly recall what summer was like. Yet something positive – if rather intangible – takes its place. It is the scent of apples and wet leaves, the amazing sight of cobwebs suddenly strung from branch to branch like a string of delicate seaside illuminations, and a mouthful of tastes that have lain dormant or inappropriate for two long seasons.

There are enough features to celebrate that belong exclusively to autumn to enjoy it for what it is rather than bemoan what it is not. For example, I love the display of onions arranged in rows in their racks at the back of the potting shed. It is a simple but immense satisfaction to go there to bring in a couple of onions as and when you need them, long after the growing season has gone. It is funny how onions become something else after harvest. They are as polished as an apple when first dug, but this dulls within days, and then they adopt the dry, tissuey skin that characterises an onion. How many people ever know that sleek onion smoothness?

Autumn in the garden is like the aftermath of a party. In all the clearing and tidying and putting away, you need the slow absolution of a bonfire, dealing with all the things that have no neat role in the overall scheme: the perennial weeds, broken canes, prunings and woody stems of plants that will not compost for years. Whilst bonfires are frowned upon by those who would have us encourage insects by

// One of the (many) joys of living in the country is a proper bonfire.

leaving rotting wood, piling up our prunings for the same purpose and shredding woody stems before adding them to the compost heap, I think that a bonfire is a human need. It belongs to the season as much as blossom comes with spring. The combination of the thrill of flame and the lazy melancholy of slow smoke is a horticultural treat. And if you need more justification than the pleasure of watching the flames leak from the bottom of the pile as dusk closes the day down, smoky tang in your hair, then you can salve your conscience by spreading the ashes around your soft fruit.

Less easily melancholic is the business of digging that cannot now be delayed. In principle I relish it, love the slog, love the earthy manifestation of struggle in exactly the same way that I love splitting wood or scything hay. Sweat and skill always make good travelling companions. The secret is to start early and just do an hour here and there from now until the new year, and gradually it all gets done.

I find that well-rotted cattle manure is ideal for autumn digging, with a mulch of mushroom compost added in spring. I ordered some manure months ago, so it would be all ready for the autumnal campaign. Having almost given up on it, it arrived out of the blue a couple of days ago, two ten-ton loads brought by tractors that could not fit through the gate, so we had to dismantle the fence to let it in. The farmer who delivered it leant against his tractor admiring the monstrous black heap, smell oozing from it like lazy bonfire smoke. 'Good stuff that,' he said proudly. 'Fair old tump mind.' As I silently converted the muck-mountain to barrow-loads of manure pushed skidding along muddy paths, I responded with a thoughtless boast, telling him that I'd probably want another couple of loads before winter was out. He smiled and said all I had to do was give him a call. Shit was something he was never short of.

I was lunching with a garden designer yesterday and he said that it was always a bad sign when he paid his initial visit to a client and was greeted with a pile of garden books, each adorned with a fringe of yellow page-markers. My own garden is riddled with a ragbag of ideas and constructs filched from dozens of visited gardens and thousands of pored-over pages. But I cannot feel too bad about the way that this garden treads a well-worn design path. It would be like feeling downcast at one's lack of originality in serving a meal that included dishes first conceived by someone else.

And so I have pleached limes. Not that they were always so. I bought them as a job lot of trees, labelled *Tilia cordata*, in a tree sale nearly ten years ago, these twenty ten-foot ones for £60 and another bundle of five-foot ones for fifty pence each. As it turned out they were none of them, big or small, *Tilia cordata*, the small-leafed lime, but some were *T. platyphyllos* 'Rubra' and others *T. p.* 'Aurea'. At first I felt ripped off – although I had never grown limes before, I had done my homework and discovered that the small-leafed lime was the ideal garden lime. It is fairly restrained in growth, does not produce the mass of bristly side shoots that the common lime, *T.* x *vulgaris* (aka *Tilia* x *europaea*), is prone to do, and does not attract the aphids that produce the black goo that drips on everything beneath the leaf canopy, which *T.* x *vulgaris* and *T. platyphyllos* do. (Although, to be fair to the unwanted *platyphyllos* lot, as far as I have noticed, mine don't.)

I planted them, put up a crude framework of three tiers of hazel sticks between each tree and, as they grew, inexpertly pruned them into shape. The fresh young growth of limes cuts in a particularly satisfying manner, as Grinling Gibbons found and exploited with such sublime skill. Every snip of the secateurs has a muscular and curiously pliant, elastic pleasure, rather like hitting a cricket ball in the sweet spot of the bat. The stems of 'Rubra' are brilliantly scarlet against a frosty sky, and 'Aurea' are olive-green, so I wait until I have seen their performance against a clear blue sky before I start cutting. Sometimes this can be as late as March.

I have spread the pleaching so now it goes right round the vegetable and jewel gardens, with hornbeam hedging underneath it, reaching up to where the bottom level of the limes begins. There is another long pleached avenue between the two pleached 'boxes'. It hardly notices as such on the ground but looks good if you crane your head sideways from the attic loo window, which is the only place from which you can see the whole garden. It also acts as another piece of protection from the wind and creates a microclimate within each boxed area.

I have a theory that this kind of intensive tweaking and training in a small(ish) back garden is a kind of mad aspirationalism, because it is a proper avenue *manqué*. If you visit any of countless grand houses they all have vast avenues of limes marching out – sometimes literally for miles – across the fields that approach the house. This use of the lime as the archetypal avenue tree really took hold in the late sixteenth and early seventeenth centuries – the period when people started to express their domination over nature rather than just fence themselves off from it. These limes are the ingredients of Power Avenues. We now pleach and prune our limes as a kind of desperate inward-looking rage against the constraints of the garden fence.

We got off lightly with the storms last week. All the wigwams for the various clematis in the jewel garden blew over, but the plants lay on the ground like drunken revellers with their legs in the air, not seeming to mind too much. Quite a few of the supports for the pleached limes broke and sagged like distressed rigging, but that is a fairly frequent price for using hazel bean sticks instead of a proper system of tensioned wires. Too cheapskate you see. Always watching the short-term penny rather than investing in the long-term pound. Would that I had the long-term pound to spend.

The river that runs a hundred yards from our back door burst its banks and flooded the whole area but no more dramatically than it has done a few times over recent years. If you were not used to it, that would be alarmingly high – just six inches from our back door and from there through the whole house – but those six inches represent trillions of gallons of water across a whole flood plain, so gave us no real cause for alarm. Given the incredible wetness that we have had, my only surprise is that it did not flood earlier. I love the flood. It puts this house at the edge of a vast lake, with swans and ducks sailing into our garden and

Flooding means that for a few lovely days the meadows become a lake. //

a huge, shiny peace that is infinitely better than the rather drab brown and grey of winter. The greenhouse and cold frames were flooded but harmlessly so.

Sarah and I cleared the greenhouses of tomatoes while the rain pummelled the glass, making wheelbarrow forays to the kitchen with 'Shirley', 'Gardener's Delight', 'Marmande' and, my favourites, 'Burpee Delicious'. Next year I am going to grow fewer plants (I say this every year) and a higher percentage of beefsteak tomatoes. They are better raw, better cooked and ripen more slowly, which gives us more time to use them. But I don't remember our tomato season lasting into November before. One of the upsides of global warming.

8 November 1994
Berries
. . . .

Bonfire Night is a pyre for the passing year and marks the descent down into a grey dampness that hangs over Britain until proper winter weather comes. Guy Fawkes Night for me is always to do with gardens, the smell of brown earth and worm cast before cordite buries it, and the sudden silhouettes of vegetation as a backdrop to pyrotechnical wonder.

// At times the garden floats like an island for weeks on end.

After Bonfire Night it seems as though it is the gardening closed season, and all one's jobs are geared towards what will happen when it starts up again next spring.

But the berries shine brightly. Of course to get fruit you must leave the flower to develop, and for many gardeners that goes against the puritanical grain of tidiness as well as the more reasonable practice of cutting back faded flower heads to stimulate more to follow. It is a payoff between fewer, bedraggled flowers followed by berries or more flowers but no fruits of this particular season. Summer has plenty of flowers, but November needs all the colour it can get, so I plump for the berries every time.

The most obvious candidates for this harvest of neglect are roses. Not all roses produce hips (just a berry by another name), but most do, and some almost more spectacularly than they flower. In the main the species roses are more prolific and interesting hip-bearers than hybrid roses. *Rosa caudata* has flagon-shaped hips covered in bristles, while *R. moyesii* and its various hybrids all shine with orange bottles in autumn. The burnet roses, *R. pimpinellifolia*, produce dark hips ranging from chocolate brown to black. The hips of *R. rugosa* are globular, with those of *R. rugosa* 'Alba' and 'Blanche Double de Coubert' almost tomato-like, although the latter does not always set fruit.

Hips have an unbreakable link for me with haws, the fruit of the hawthorn, *Crataegus*. Town-dwellers miss the beauty of haws, but I love them, turning a dark red as they ripen and become irresistibly delicious to the birds. We have a number of overgrown hawthorns in our boundary hedge, beyond the reach of trimming and thus free to flower and fruit at will.

Hips and haws framed against bare twigs or yellowing leaves are part of the pleasant melancholy of the season, but the bright red of a berry against an evergreen leaf is a laugh in the teeth of the encroaching gloom. Holly is best. Nothing else quite hits the button in the same way. The oddest of berries out now are those of *Callicarpa bodinieri* var. *giraldii*, which have an almost metallic sheen to their purple shanks. I have one in a new border I made this summer, but I think it would look better on its own in a pot and exhibited at berry time before being stashed away out of the limelight for the rest of the year.

I am ashamed to admit that until recently I have had a snobbish attitude towards pyracantha and cotoneaster, regarding them as suburban and dreary. I have now seen the light. I like pyracantha's common name, firethorn, as it perfectly describes the way the berries blaze out from the unexceptional matt leaves.

My feelings are that with pyracantha one should be as brash as possible, and 'Orange Glow' is as brash as they come. Cotoneaster is slightly more subtle and slightly less dramatic but still jolly. There are far too many different cotoneasters to get to grips with unless you have a particular bent that way. I like *Cotoneaster microphyllus* because the berries are as big as the leaves. *C.* 'Rothschildianus' has yellow berries, and one could have a yellow-berry corner with this, *Pyracantha* 'Golden Dome' and the holly *Ilex aquifolium* 'Bacciflava', which has masses of yellow fruits like tiny lemons. I unwittingly planted one in the hedge bounding the field and was astonished by its unhollylike yellowness in its first winter. We have now become used to each other.

I always read of the long list of gardening jobs that should be done in autumn with a mixture of profound admiration and disbelief. All that digging and planting, splitting and replanting, cuttings to be taken, pruning and tidying to be done gives the impression of an orderly progression through the days up to Christmas as though – leaving aside the assumption that you are sufficiently organised and motivated – there was no *weather*.

9 November 1998
Weather

Well, I'm looking out of the window at the kind of weather that makes a trip to the garden shed into an adventure-training master class. Weather has made the grass shaggy and dishevelled because the ground is too wet to get a mower on to it although the temperature is not cold enough to stop the grass growing. The path to the front door is slippery with leaves and a gutter is leaking on to a lavender that will drown if the rain doesn't stop before I fix the gutter. That is what weather does to my best-laid gardening plans and, I suspect, to most other people's too.

But I like weather. Weather is change. The variety sharpens your experience of the world both seasonally and from day to day. That is why so many of us felt cheated by this last summer, not just by the cold greyness but by the predictability of it. One of the great virtues of modern gardens, in an age when most experience is vicarious and people pay to go on holiday under a dome, is that it brings you back again and again to the irrefutable actuality of the weather.

Perhaps this is a country thing. In a town you can treat your garden like a cinema that sometimes shows a film you don't want to see so you give it a miss. It is not umbilically connected to indoor life like it is here in the sticks. This garden was made out of a field and a few weeks of bad weather show how quickly it would return to one. Every day here is measured by the weather and directly affects what we wear and eat, let alone what we do out of doors.

Over the years I have wasted days braving the elements, trying to wheel barrows through mud lapping about the axle, digging soil when more was sticking to my boots than to the spade or, on one embarrassingly memorable weekend, bullying house guests to help me plant a long beech hedge in constant torrential icy rain. Total waste of time. Not one plant out of two hundred survived six months.

There is no need for heroics. Gardening can be grim enough. There are days when the wind cuts straight through you yet it is not raining and certain jobs need to be got out the way. There are always a couple of weekends in February or March like that, when I prune our lime trees, constantly dropping the secateurs from the top of the ladder because my hands are too cold to feel the bloody things. But I associate the job – all cutting and fumbling with twine to tie in the whippy, sap-filled branches – with a particular season, and the pleasure I get from the avenue of trees is in part down to that annual chilly experience. The weather is part of it.

11 November 2000
Remembrance

When I was a young boy there was an old man who worked as a gardener in our village. He seemed impossibly ancient to me then, but I suppose that he must have been only twenty years older than I am now. He always worked in a suit and had a watch on a chain that he kept in his waistcoat pocket. He always wore a collar and tie to work, even if it was to shovel muck all day. He had fought in the First World War and returned home after 11 November 1918 to the village. He was lucky to have survived. He had a brother who was killed; his name was carved into the pillar by the pew we always used in church, along with such a very long list of other names from that dreadful war.

The old man is long dead now, forty years on. He was a quiet, gentle man who lived in the same village all his life and never did anything other than garden from the day he returned. He hardly ever said a word to anyone much and certainly never more than a greeting to me. But he is somehow deeply connected to the reason that I garden. His passive, distant presence influenced me and influences me still. I believe in the healing power of tending the earth, of growing things and of learning about a place intimately, over decades if necessary. I love the way that this old gardener used a spade or a hoe like a craftsman, and took such slow care and pride in even the most menial of garden jobs.

I have just been looking at pictures of the garden in late September and early October and had forgotten how summery it looked – all bright and full and soft. Outside the window the bare branches have a black, rain-whetted edge. Only the weeds are growing lustily, with the stinging nettles adding a weather-hardened edge to their sting. If they were jellyfish we would fly a red flag in the cabbages and employ Gareth to sit on a high chair to check that no one ventured into them.

As it was I wore a glove and pulled them all out, ripping the woolly yellow roots from the ground like pulling off a scab, with all the pleasure and disgust that goes with it. I hate gloves and – if I am remotely honest – think them unmanly. I want the scars, calluses and engrained dirt that hand-weeding and hoeing bring, partly to validate to myself that I walk the walk and to convince others of the same. Not noble but true. But winter stinging nettles are stronger than even my vanity, and anyway, I find that the bastards always get me in the face first. I am bending over, grasping the nettle with one gloved hand whilst the other, naked and suitably scuffed, works its way under and around the roots ready to rip, when my tugging bends a stem that is growing unnoticed from the same roots to gently brush my face. The funny thing is that you feel nothing for a moment or two. At least one of the great advantages of this garden is that I can bellow my angry profanities at the top of my voice. Perhaps that is the mark of privacy.

Stingers

Today we did a momentous piece of gardening. I say 'we' but in fact no one in this household had anything to do with the process. BT engineers did it all. Today we buried the phone line into the house and removed the telegraph pole. At last, after exactly thirteen years, the front garden is done.

When we came to this house it had no phone, and when we were connected they linked us by twin curving wires to the nearest telegraph pole, which meant cutting diagonally right across the front garden. For years we accepted the wires as a fixture. They were, after all, not a terrible eyesore. Yes, they were the first thing we saw every time we walked down the path to the front door and yes, they would get blown down every few years so that they flapped amongst the yews, but in the scheme of things we had bigger things to worry about. One day, we thought, one day we will get them buried and clear the airspace to the front of the house. And today is that day.

This rearrangement is all part of the garden space and affects it, in its own way, as much as the plants that we lovingly tend below the wires.

Phone line

Of course now they are noticeable only by their absence. We have all been going to the front door and taking a good look precisely because there is nothing to see.

Mind you, I do have one regret. Every September the swallows would line up on the telephone wires, swinging in the wind like trapeze artists, ready for their journey south. Now that perch is gone. But their forebears were leaving from this house many years before the wires were put there, and I fervently hope that their descendants shall continue to do so many years after we, and our telephones, are a distant memory.

14 November 2005
Warning

The meteorologists keep 'warning' of a cold winter. (Why is everything perceived as a threat? What climateless, health-and-safety-checked yardstick is used to measure these fears? Tsunamis, earthquakes and hurricanes are a *threat*. Everything else is just weather.) I have been waiting for a long time for it to happen. The colder the better.

We have had our cold moments over the past few years. I see from my garden journal that on 29 December 2000 it was minus 13 overnight and never rose above minus 5 during the day – the pipes froze and it took all day fiddling with blowtorches to clear them – and on 1 January 2002 the ice was four inches thick on the water butts and it measured minus 11 overnight. There were other cold snatches but nothing sustained. Nothing to be warned about.

15 November 1999
Archaeology

The morning after we moved into this house, I innocently set out with my spade intending to dig a pair of borders either side of the front door. Within five minutes the spade was abandoned for a pick and within a couple more for a pointing trowel, hand shovel and bucket. After three months of careful and timorous excavation we had uncovered a large area of early medieval paths, drains and walls, shot through with later planting holes. Up until that point I had thought of 'my' garden as a construct entirely created by us. The newly occupied territory was a *tabula rasa* blankly accepting whatever expression of horticultural creativity we chose to put on to it. This archaeological world sitting inches below the surface blew all that apart. I had at least seven centuries of garden history before I was aware that I even had a garden.

None of this, of course, is new. Garden history is a thriving branch of historical research. To know our gardens is to know ourselves.

No archaeology or visible history should be damaged or lost in any way, you have to start anew. So I stopped digging with a pointing trowel

Just some of the things that we have dug up from the garden. //

and took up my spade. (Although not before everything was reported to the County Archaeological office, drawn, photographed and recorded. Then twenty tons of sharp sand, four inches of topsoil and turf were spread back over it so that it might lose itself again for another hundred years or more.)

I was thinking the other day that it is strange how we celebrate growing anything edible at all in our gardens without applying much consideration to its quality as *food*.

Men are mostly to blame. In primitive societies the growing of vegetables is left to the women, who are also expected to cook them. There is therefore an inbuilt relationship between horticulture and gastronomy. But in post-industrial Britain men muscled into the kitchen garden without setting foot in the kitchen. Vegetable growing became another division of the inexhaustibly interesting subject (for men) of penis size – measuring success against the dimensions of a marrow, carrot, cabbage or leek or, slightly more subliminally, against the sheer quantity of potatoes, peas or tomatoes. Can one imagine women in all seriousness devoting hours and days to growing parsnips three feet long or gooseberries the size of rams' testicles?

I was brought up on *The Vegetable Garden Displayed*, and as a clear manual of basic vegetable growing it is yet to be surpassed. But nowhere in the entire book is taste mentioned. Recommended varieties are described as 'trustworthy' – which accurately describes the mistrust with which the average British male before the last decade or so eyed food of any type that strayed from his childhood norm.

This schism between vegetable growing and the result on the table is barmy. Luckily women are entering the field as authorities, concentrating on their qualities as tasty food rather than displays of maleness. During the summer I visited Joy Larkcom, who has become the guru of vegetable growers; her Suffolk garden is an incredibly pretty jumble of a huge range of edible plants (although highly organised and meticulously monitored) without any of the rigid ranks of vegetables one associates with many allotments or walled kitchen gardens that we pointlessly romanticise.

Even after an hour spent out of the ground a lettuce loses some of its savour. So I stroll the paths of the vegetable garden like the aisles of a supermarket, picking here and pulling there, building a dish from a dozen salady ingredients. Now, at the beginning of November, I have radicchio, rocket, chicory, curly endive, winter purslane, 'All the

Year Round', corn salad, 'Lobjoits' (bolting a bit), red and green 'Salad Bowl', 'Lollo Rosso' and a mixture called 'Saladesi', which contains a bit of everything.

The edible gardening process must begin at the dinner table and work its way back via the kitchen to the garden, not the other way round. Grow what you like to see ending up on your plate, not what happens to flourish in the garden or allotment.

23 November 2002
Yellow

I am struck by just how yellow my autumn has been. I say 'my' autumn because it has been strongly influenced by the plants in this garden and anyway, I don't get out much.

The best yellow has been from the field maples, which turned the most lovely buttery lemon just before the leaves finally fell. I planted a whole load as hedging around the perimeter of this garden and have allowed quite a few to grow out into good-sized trees, which, being bigger, blaze out more. Can buttery lemon blaze? Shine then. They shine and shine. Actually the very best autumnal yellow of any plant comes

For some years a tunnel was the main source of winter salads. //

from the elm hedges along the lanes. But you never see this on a tree because by the time the elms reach twenty feet or so they die, whereas the hedgerow elms, being cut every year, remain lustily alive.

Our hornbeam hedges turned the most unexpected yellow this year, making a really significant difference to the amount of light in the garden, almost as though they were reflecting sunlight. I planted them just eight years ago, and this has been the first year of their maturity when we have had a suitably hot dry August and September to intensify the sugars in the leaves and induce this intensity of colour, but I know that they will turn their normal coffee-brown in a few weeks. The hazels in the coppice did the same trick. They are always inclined to yellow in November but did so this year with a will – although not for long, falling thick and fast a few weeks ago.

For about five days there was a wonderful yellow combination of my redcurrants and one of my neighbours' lovely *Rosa rugosa* 'Alba' hedge, which froths over the top of the hazel hurdles on our boundary. It is not a planting pair that one would immediately think of, but for a few days at the end of October it was hard to beat.

// Just before they fall, fig leaves are gloriously translucent.

A storm has left the garden looking like a moulting chicken. In fact we got off quite lightly compared to the tales of destruction that unfolded around us. Not a pane of greenhouse glass was broken, only a few roofing tiles lost and the electricity, although fluttering like a trapped butterfly, never quite gave up the ghost. But a robinia was snapped clean off at the base, 'William Crump' and 'Bramley's Seedling' apple trees were knocked over to forty-five degrees, hazel hurdles flattened, and Tom and I had a tree fall just in front of the Land Rover which took an hour's sawing to clear before we could get home. So fun and games rather than disaster.

But the real change was that we lost a lot of leaves. Overnight the contours of the garden were stripped and altered. The odd gleam of light that fights through the clouds highlights the astonishing intensity of yellow leaves, but that will go any moment. I wish I could enjoy them more – they are there and I know it is a wonder, but the sky sits on me like a lid, closing down on all sensation. This is not such a good time.

Best, as my mother used to say, just get on with it. There is much to do. The storm has put paid to the last floral vestiges whose crumbs we had been feeding on. Everything that can be cut back has had the chop. The result is a lot of bare earth, hidden since the spring. This, then, is the time to get our bulbs in.

November and December might seem late for bulb-planting, but it is the only viable time in densely planted borders, and I have never found it causes any problems. We had a delivery last week of seven and a half thousand bulbs, piled on the doorstep in eight large boxes. Buying plants by mail order is a wonderful thing – everything, despite having been paid for, arrives as a present. The quantity is bulked out by two thousand crocus ('Purple' and 'Tom's Purple') for the orchard and spring garden and a thousand *Allium sphaerocephalon* for the jewel garden. We have some there in one patch already and they make a tawny and purple tapestry, simultaneously soft and rich. They are a meadow plant really, but then the jewel garden is a bit like a berserk meadow, so they fit well enough.

We have other alliums too, predominantly 'Purple Sensation', which is a clone of *A. aflatunense*. It is the richest, most intense purple of all alliums and flowers early, at its best in this garden in the middle of May, when there is so much yellow and fresh green to contrast with it. Five hundred might be a bit of overkill, but you never know if you have enough until there is too much, so we shall see. There are a hundred *A. schubertii* with mad exploding heads whose floral units, instead of making a neat globe, fire away at different lengths. *A. cristophii* is another whopping drumstick onion, although the heads are loose but perfectly round. We have a hundred to add to some in our walled garden, where they are at their best in the middle of June. We also have forty *Eremurus* 'Cleopatra' and twenty *E. himalaicus* to go in with them which should (once they have got going) flower at the same time.

Finally there are a hundred imperial fritillaries, *Fritillaria imperialis* 'Aurora', which is a rich orange-red and which will increase our current stock to a hundred and one. If they all flower – I will put them in the spring and damp gardens – they will be an amazing sight.

26 November 2000
Trenches

We don't just need wellies to walk to the end of the garden but special trousers too as the mud is so thick and splashy that we get spattered in the stuff just from walking.

We extended the land drains by digging another overflow soakaway because the existing land-drain soakaway has given up soaking. This meant another very handsome trench and hole. I seriously find holes in the ground exciting and beautiful and, if only they could be kept dry, can conceive of enormous aesthetic pleasure from a series of interconnected trenches and pits. But perhaps that trespasses beyond the realm of gardening.

27 November 2005
Moles

I don't like cities and avoid them whenever possible. But I know I am in a minority. Most Britons live in towns or suburbs and most get their countryside from a car window, *Emmerdale* or *The Archers*. I am out of kilter, unrepresentative and hopelessly marginalised.

This does not bother me in the least. But I do have to restrain myself from time to time from writing about things that have a major impact on me and my garden but which probably have no relevance to the majority of people's lives. I often get asked about 'pests' (not a word I like – it has a slightly dismissive, irritable ring to it and has become jargon, used unthinkingly by hacks with 'diseases' usually yoked sullenly to it) as though these were a common plague that every gardener had to equally bear and share. But I have never come across a vine weevil in my life. It is simply not a problem, let alone a pest. In this garden pigeons pose no threat whatsoever, yet in the *Gardener's World* garden at Stratford pigeons will strip a patch of cabbages overnight. We share our outdoor space with millions of other creatures and despite the attitude of many of the more conventional garden sages, they are not put there deliberately to interfere with the horticultural scheme of things.

I bet moles don't feature much in Hackney or the middle of Manchester, yet round here they are a major problem. I have just walked

up to the end of the garden and counted seventeen separate molehills, all fresh from last night. The cats occasionally catch a mole and present us with their poor charming snouty bodies. It is awful. But they are destructive little bastards. At the moment they are particularly keen on burrowing a few inches below the surface of the beds in the greenhouse, which is planted out with winter salad crops. This means that the soil is riddled with holes and every now and then, when watering, it collapses like a disused mineshaft, taking the plants with them. In practice this means that the roots are dangling below ground in thin air, and whilst it rarely kills the plants, it severely disrupts and stunts their growth.

On the grass paths and lawns (such as they are), moles do not just create absurdly large heaps of soil but also have underground hollows. These do not collapse like those in the greenhouse but merely sink to become ruts and dips. If the mower is not becoming clogged by wading through the heaps of soil then it is bucking and dipping like a boat in brisk chop. Repairing this subterranean damage is really quite a business. The only consolation is that molehills, mixed with garden compost and sharp sand, make excellent potting compost.

Lapwings sharing our northern sky. //

28 November 1999
Seeing to

. . . .

It has been a lovely autumn. We have had a series of glowing days, and the garden has seemed to welcome us with open arms every time we set foot outdoors. This is also a quiet(ish) time of year for me, so there has been a chance to do some regular daily work outside.

The main project for the past week has been giving the jewel garden a good seeing to. Because it is fairly new and we had to have it looking busy with plants for a photo shoot in August, we filled it with annuals (mainly cosmos, marigolds, nasturtiums, sunflowers, tithonias, leonotis, purple orache, snapdragons and purple millet), and these have all been pulled up and carted off to the compost heap.

Instead of leaving the area looking bare and winterish, this has created good space and uncovered forgotten gems. A big (but flattened) *Salvia guaranitica* came blinking into the thin sunlight, in flower in mid-November. We put in a box hedge in midsummer and this was all but smothered, but we can now see that it has grown remarkably vigorously despite this blanket neglect, which means that all sorts of things are planted much too close to it. Dozens of purple plantains, oriental poppies, sweet Williams, *Knautia macedonica*, sedums and geums have been dug up and moved back. The dahlias have all been dug up and stored in vermiculite (the earwigs were terrible in October, ruining all the young plants we had put in, but the tubers are healthy and the older plants shrugged them off). Do we dig up the chocolate cosmos or leave them to overwinter in the ground? We have lost a lot in storage in the past, so we've decided to risk leaving them be. I must remember to put extra mulch over them.

We have failed to properly mark the spots of herbaceous plants like the various ligularias, delphiniums and aconites which have now completely died back. As we are starting a mass of tulip-planting in these beds we should have marked out the no-plant areas more diligently. The grasses are all still very much in evidence and looking fantastic. The melianthus and banana (grown from seed I got in Tenerife in March and now six feet tall) have got their own wigwams covered in fleece, although I think I shall move the melianthus to the pastel borders. They are wasted in the jungle of the jewels. I have cut back hard two of the best lime-green shrubs, *Rubus cockburnianus* 'Goldenvale' and a lovely cut-leaf golden elder, *Sambucus racemosa* 'Plumosa Aurea'. The rubus has become hugely tangled, with dozens of its stems rooting where they touch the ground. It is not really suitable for these types of mixed borders, but it is such a wonderful backdrop that it will stay. Another thorn, *Ribes sanguineum*, which has blood-drop flowers in early spring, has also had a crop. I love it, Sarah hates it. The debate ended with it staying put. For the moment.

December

We are tulip-planting in a big way. Thousands of the things. This is a lot of holes to be dibbed, but it will go a surprisingly little way, and we are having to plan their positioning carefully to make the most of them. The majority of them are to increase the ones that we already have growing in the jewel garden such as *Tulipa acuminata*, 'Abu Hassan', and 'Black Parrot', which is not black at all but a frilly deep blackcurrant explosion on a stem.

We have especially increased our oranges. 'Generaal de Wet' is simple-flowered and orange over a yellow background. We have two other oranges, 'Orange Artist' and 'Orange Favourite'. The former is (confusingly) one of my favourite of all tulips, a pale orange washed with claret stains on a thick chocolate stem. 'Orange Favourite' is much pinker and a parrot – although not nearly so burst asunder as some of that ilk – with a distinctive jade flare running up the outside of its petals. But it is not all bright and brash. A mass of primrose-yellow 'West Point' for the spring garden perfectly pick up the colour of *Euphorbia polychroma* and have long gaping beaks of petal; while 'White Triumphator' will bulk out the ones that we already have lining the lime walk and are serene and cool and surprisingly leafy; and finally there is 'Carnaval de Nice' for the walled garden. I can never decide whether its resemblance to a raspberry ripple is amusing or alarming.

They are all going in very shallowly as we intend to dig them up after they have flowered. We have never done this before – always trying to plant them as deep as possible – but I am assured by those who have that it is not such a big deal. You simply dig them up and store them on racks until they are completely dry and then store the largest for replanting. The bulbs you dig up, of course, are not the bulbs that you planted, which disappear, but new ones. Anyway, that is for an unimaginably distant future. For the present it is dib dib dib, getting the little sods in the ground. To get it right we have divided each bed into metre squares marked by string. In consequence we trip and stumble over the gridlines, pulling the canes out of the ground and swearing at each other. I think that we are having a good time, but you can never be quite sure of these things.

Yesterday I broke my best spade. You might think this a pity rather than a disaster, but it is possible to love inanimate objects and easy to love tools that have made things of which you are proud. A great chunk of my love of gardening is the unthinking sensuous pleasure of using hand tools that have evolved to an exquisite adaptation to specific work, that are made by hand for the hand and enable the work and the worker and the tool to seamlessly merge into a rhythmic flow. I went to the foundry in Wigan to watch how it had been made from the boiling metal through every stage of forging to the sanding of the ash handle by a northern girl with the sexiest wrists I have ever seen. That heavy industry was a kind of digging too, and a thousand pieces of the thread joined up, a spade linking me to the world like a metaphorical internet. I remember that at lunchtime the news came through that Mrs Thatcher had resigned. The whole foundry cheered.

It was expensive, nearly £100, but I dug for hundreds of hours, months, with that stainless-steel, ash-handled Bulldog spade, and it was bought as part of the exhilaration of an intense (and ultimately ruinous) love affair with a patch of England. Later there were times when my mind was so at odds with itself that I did nothing, no work, no gardening, nothing at all for months on end, but even then to take my best spade from the wall and just swing that balanced purposefulness from a clenched hand was enough to raise hopes, enough to mend.

3 December 2000
Sex
. . . .

At this time of year the specifics start to fade from the garden, leeched out by low light, short light and hibernation. The garden goes into a completely reasonable spell of introversion. There are very few gardens that would suffer anything from a regime of complete neglect throughout the month of December. The gardening world falls into two camps at this point. I will plant things together to see if that is where and how I want them. The actions shape and inform the thoughts which in turn set up a reaction and response that I was incapable of thinking up initially. Sarah would rather do nothing (in the garden) for a long period than do what she thought was the wrong thing. Yet when she has thought things through she acts decisively and with conviction. We both tend to reach the same place at the same time via these wholly different routes.

I would hesitate to make a clear split down gender lines but, for what it is worth, I do think that there is a real and important difference between masculine and feminine gardening.

Masculine gardening likes measurement. The central male ontological question is not 'What or who am I?' but 'How do I measure up?' This inevitably leads to competition, and masculine gardening is forever looking over its shoulder at other gardeners and their sets of measurements. Flower shows to the masculine gardener are not a celebration but a competition. It is no surprise that most entrants for the prizes for biggest bloom/vegetable are men or that men become obsessive about a particular tiny aspect of horticulture that bears as much relation to gardening as collecting ketchup bottles does to gastronomy.

The feminine gardener sees the garden as an extension of domesticity. In gender terms the stereotype dictates that men are outdoors, women in, and that inevitably informs the roles that we enact. So femininity tackles the skills and characteristics of indoor homemaking and carries it outside too. There is a stronger level of maintaining domestic order – cleaning and tidying not as an attempt to order the landscape at large but to keep on top of the household.

I read in the paper today that old canard that women take up gardening when they give up sex. It was, of course, written by a man. I would suggest that the truth is made up of two aspects of 'feminine' gardening. The first is the realisation that the garden offers a wonderful escape and relief from the demands of the household. It is time on your own without children or spouses making demands on you. The second factor is known by feminine gardeners of all ages (and sexes), which is that the garden is an intensely sensual place. Put simply, a lovely garden on a lovely day, however modest, can provide the richest range of sensual experiences that daily life has to offer.

I think that the real essence of feminine-attitude gardening is that it is responsive and reactive rather than proactive. It lets things accrue and interact and create their own balance. That balance – of colours, structure and a sustainable, holistic ecosystem – is at the heart of all really good gardens.

Neither pure femininity nor unalloyed masculinity make good gardens or gardeners. You need a balance of both. The truth is that they are usually mingled within all of us to a greater or lesser degree, but I think it no accident that the men who are most comfortable with their femininity and the women with their masculinity tend to make better gardeners than those who are locked into gender roles. Sometimes this can come from two people combining the rigour and broader vision of one with the sensitivity and subtlety of the other to create a complete skill and is an incredibly satisfying way of expressing a relationship. I know that Sarah and I together make better gardens than either of us could do on our own. But of this you can be sure: The deity of the garden is a goddess, and she is not mocked.

After a year of negotiations and snail-like legal activity we have just bought a string of barns next door to this house. What we really bought them for, all five thousand square feet of them, is garden sheds. You might ask why I could not have bought a normal six-by-four-foot wooden garden shed like everybody else without taking out a new mortgage (literally) to achieve the same end, but if you did you would be an unromantic misery. To have a sprawl of outbuildings is one of the main reasons I choose not to live in a town, and to let them remain as working sheds is true luxury.

I love all garden sheds, be they big, small, made up out of stuff from skips on a windy allotment or the magnificent suites of grand Victorian kitchen gardens. I love their dark recesses, musty with clay pots and dry potting compost, oiled tools, seeds in packets and jars on shelves, along with labels, twine and pots of rooting powder.

An object of early envy was the potting shed at my friend's house. He lived in a Victorian rectory with purpose-built outhouses sprouting round it like a satellite village. The potting shed was brick-floored, and once a year their gardener would wheel a wooden barrow of molehills, another of fine leaf mould and another of grit and mix the three together on that floor with a shovel to make his potting compost. It was also where he went for his lunch, sitting in an old ripped leather armchair next to the surprisingly smart fireplace. When it rained we would go in there and play, and I still associate the sound of the rain on the hipped roof with the smell of the potting-compost mixture engrained into the worn bricks. While other children hankered after train sets and Scalextric, I yearned for my very own potting shed.

5 December 1999
Wind

A northerly is slicing through the garden, hustling through the cracks and gaps (plenty of those) in the house. It's a sunny day and I'm at my desk in two shirts, a cashmere jersey and a fleece. If it wasn't for that nagging, rushing shakedown of the branches snagged by the wind I would think I was ill. Mercifully north winds are almost as rare for us as the bitter easterlies that we occasionally get in spring. On this side of England our prevailing wind is from the west and comes wet and mostly warm. The southerly winds bring dry weather and the gagging stench of concentrated shit from the turkey factory at the end of the lane.

The shape of the wind is as important as the direction and strength of it. It can come in so many forms. A wind flowing as straight as an arrow will tumble over walls and fences, crushing and flattening plants like a boisterous wave. A mild breeze can be funnelled down alleys and the gaps between houses, and in the process become a rapier, bayoneting a few choice (and usually slightly tender) plants. It can pick up a pile of

leaves in the garden and swirl them round like a spoon in a cup of tea. Wind bounces and rebounds off solid surfaces like a ball, hitting crazy angles and causing weirdly unguessable microclimates. One of the most common effects of this that often surprises people is the damage that wind causes at the base of a wall because the force is directed downwards just as strongly as it is pushed up over the top.

I guess that wind is the gardener's biggest problem. I was about to write 'enemy', but it does have its virtues. I love the way that the south wind dries up our soggy ground, transforming slippy squelch into firm turf and workable soil. A gentle, ruffling breeze is always lovely. (Except that even on the seemingly stillest day, whenever I take the newspapers into the garden, there is always just enough wind to flick and tug annoyingly at the pages.)

Wind cools the air around plants as they grow and in spring will often be sufficient to drop an otherwise mild day below the critical growing point of 6 degrees. In the past few years we have had weeks of just this situation, where at a time when it would normally be changing from day to day, the entire garden is locked into stasis by a dry wind.

On frosty days the winter tangle of the borders becomes magnificent. //

6 December 2003
Snowfall
. . . .

Just for an hour or so, it snowed. The day had woken with that leaden quality in the sky that threatens snow, but such threats often pass without a single flake drifting down from the cloud. However, this time it did perform, albeit briefly, and the evidence only stayed for about an hour or so. It is extraordinary how a snowfall reduces the garden to monochrome, smoothing out all the subtle gradations of colour and making everything a series of white spaces and shapes. It would take a horticultural heart of stone not to love it even though it can cause much damage – let alone muddy mess – as it thaws.

The last time we had a proper snowfall here in Herefordshire was back in December 1990 and it lasted, with a few days' remission here and there, right into March. It started as I was driving Sarah to hospital to have an emergency Caesarean for the birth of our third child. It took me three hours to drive the ten miles home and another three days until the roads were clear enough to get back to the hospital to see them. Since then we have just had these occasional powderings that are beautiful but undramatic and pass through very briefly.

Mind you, it is astonishing what even a light fall of snow can do. A few years ago I bought – at vast expense – an aluminium fruit cage and foolishly left the netting over it on the basis that it could easily be taken off if heavy snow threatened. Overnight we had one of these typical half-inch smatterings of powder snow which then froze hard, and the locked-in weight of the snow and ice buckled the aluminium frame as though it had been hit by a falling meteor. I could only salvage about two thirds of it. Another year we had a similar passing snow shower that landed heavy on the box bushes that I was training as pebbles. These bushes are now tightly clipped and you can practically sit on them without causing damage, but back then the branches were young and soft and the weight of the snow damaged a lot of them.

But it always seems vandalistic to go round the garden systematically knocking snow off the evergreen hedges and topiary. With global warming, each snowfall, however slight, is starting to feel almost precious.

7 December 1999
Borage-mare
. . . .

Gareth was clearing the walled garden the other day. It was one of those clean-scraped early-winter afternoons where the light is so thin that you feel a puff of wind might blow it out altogether, and he was pulling up barrow-loads of borage, which had all summer towered over and leant on the roses.

Then he came indoors, knuckling his eye. We bathed it and had a look. (I'm lying – I am far too squeamish in all things ocular to even

// *Previous. The winter borders are unfettered but hedges and edges kept crisp.*

think of peering into the damaged wastes of an injured eye. Sarah did. I hovered uselessly.) His eye was red and swollen and he was in agony. Only by holding it open between thumb and forefinger and not turning it in its socket could he bear the pain. So I drove him to the local community hospital. This is a wonderful place that cheerfully and promptly patches us all up from time to time. They put saline solution in his eye and then sent us to the eye hospital in Hereford, twelve miles away. By now it was dark. Gareth held his eye open and chatted about the planting, with occasional gasps of pain. I prayed that the opportunity would never arise for me to display my total inability to be so brave.

We parked right outside the front door, they greeted us by name and saw Gareth within one minute. Whilst he was being tended, the nurses told me garden/eye horror stories with lip-smacking relish. Apparently the really scary plant is blackthorn. Their advice was always to wear goggles if you do any hedge cutting, shredding or strimming near blackthorn. One little piece in your eye and the chances are that you will lose the eyeball. But no one likes wearing goggles. They mist up and make any job feel more dangerous.

A light fall of snow makes the simplicity of the yew cones stark. //

Anyway, after various inspections, mechanical and human, it turned out that Gareth had got a borage hair in his eye and as he'd rubbed it had made dozens of tiny lacerations to the eyeball. The nurse told him to go home, take a couple of painkillers and then go down the pub and have a drink or two. He was fine, had a drink or three, had a day off and no harm was done. But who'd have thought it? A borage hair!

When I went out this morning the garden was laced with countless thousands of spiders' webs. This is one of those phenomena that I realise are simultaneously both common and rare. By this I mean that it is common enough for most of us to have noticed days when the dried heads of flowers or the bare branches of trees have seemed unusually cobwebbed but also, if you analyse it, these days only happen about a couple of times every year. This is because the spiders only make webs *en masse* in autumn, when the young that hatched in spring mature, mate and then die.

You need either frost or mist to see them properly, and this was one of those mornings when frost and mist joined to make every dancing mote gleam with a core of ice and every stick and blade of grass seemed to be joined by a million webs. Although I am, of course, aware of spiders around the place, there must be tens of thousands of them to produce so many webs overnight. The garden must be positively jostling with them. They eat flies, of course, but also aphids and other flying bugs and in turn provide an important source of food for wrens – which this garden is also full of. So they are a good thing.

Spiders like cover in any shape or form, and I suspect that they particularly like the cocoa shells that are part of my mulching regime because they take a long time to rot down, each shell acting as a mini umbrella for a waiting spider. Many of the spiders that you see in the borders in summer are hunting spiders which do not build a web. In fact I have just looked spiders up and discovered that there are nearly six hundred species of British ones, most of which are webless, although the majority of the garden lacework is, appropriately enough, down to the garden spider, *Araneus diadematus*. Money spiders also spin, and it is they who are responsible for the gossamer sheen that seems to coat a whole area of lawn or hedgerow. I know that arachnophobia is a kind of social norm, but I think that they and their workings are wonderful.

It always astonishes me how many cobwebs winter reveals. //

Maurice is a rat-catcher. 'Pest-control' is the official name of his game, and he will deal with anything from wasps to starlings, but rats provide the bulk of his business.

We have a simmering rat population in our barns, and Maurice comes regularly to put down and check the poison. This autumn there has been an influx and we have found a few dead ones in the garden. This is a bad sign. Maurice reckons that for every one that you see, dead or alive, there are at least another fifty in the vicinity and probably more like a hundred. Maurice says, with bleak delight, 'Lot of rats at the moment. Lot of rats. It's the mild.' I am always prodding him for rat horror stories but what comes through is respect rather than disgust. He knows the ways of rats and gets them by out-thinking them. 'It's no use just putting poison anywhere. Creatures of habit, rats. What you've got to do is find their runs – I look for the grease they leave.' He shines his torch along the walls and beams of the barns and I look with disgusted fascination for rat-slicks in the spotlight. 'A rat must have fresh water every day, so that's the first thing to check. A leaking drainpipe will do or a puddle. But no water, no rats.'

Not only do rats need to drink fresh water but they are also strong swimmers. He told me that he had been called out in the middle of the night to a 'domestic' where there was a rat in the bathroom. When he went in he found it swimming happily around the bath. 'But if you get a domestic you can usually guarantee that it's either the garden shed or the compost heap.'

The rats like the subterranean cosiness beneath the floor of modern kit sheds and use it as a dry base-camp for forays into the garden. Because we tend to come across them inside buildings, it is easy to think of them as indoor animals, but most rats live perfectly happily in the fields and hedgerows, coming inside as winter approaches. To the undiscerning rat-mind, an inner-city garden is a patchwork of fields and hedgerows, so it will feel quite at home there. A badly made compost heap is another ideal environment, warm, dry, full of rotting food and easy to burrow into. The secret is to 'make' your compost properly. This comes high on the list of all-time boring topics, but you want to make sure the heap gets really hot so that everything rots much faster and no mammal can survive.

Mice are a bigger problem because, unlike rats, they burrow into the soil and eat seed. This time of year mice can be particularly destructive, with the absence of other food sending them to crocus corms that you have tediously and carefully planted and to the early broad beans which should be sown now for a crop next June. In spring they eat early sowings of peas and apparently have a taste for sweetcorn seeds. You can tell if mice are the problem because any top growth will be ignored and only the seed eaten. Maurice reckons mice are worse than rats to have in the house because they are incontinent, dribbling urine over every surface. Lovely.

Go outside as the dawn lifts on a cold morning and everything is sheathed in white. Every tiny component of the garden is made precious and fixed, from spiders' webs wrapped around the yew cones to the tiniest details of all the plants in the borders. The fennel heads are best, delicate three-dimensional cobwebs – worth keeping – in fact, worth *growing* – just for this effect, even if it is only one day in December.

The other day I went out on just such a morning and there seemed to be an exceptional amount of rustling of birds, but in fact it was leaves falling off the trees. Thousands upon thousands of leaves all falling at once although there was not a breath of wind. It was as though they had all lost their balance and were slipping off, bouncing on the branches, knocking more free as they passed, rocking and zigzagging down to the ground.

When I took the dogs out last night there was a swirl of snow falling from everywhere, blowing down the back of my collar, harrying the torchlight. It did not last for long, but this morning it had been frozen into place, poised on every twig and leaf. Our little terrier, Poppy, who has been ill for a few weeks, did not come with us in the late-night snow. She always hated the cold at the best of times. I came down this morning to find her stretched dead in her bed. As soon as it was light I buried her in the coppice next to my big old Blackdog Beaufort who died nearly seven years ago and whom Poppy adored. So did I.

I love digging and take pride in doing it well. I love the soil and particularly our rich Herefordshire clay loam. But I didn't want to dig that hole and put the little stiff body into it and most of all did not want to cover it up again with earth. She moved into this house with us almost thirteen years to the day so she has always been part of this garden.

The death of a pet that has long been part of the household throws things out of kilter and leaves a bigger hole than the space that they occupied in life. But today is also my daughter's eighteenth birthday and, amongst that celebration, another big change for parents. A letting go, and what is left behind largely belongs to this house and garden where most of those years have been spent.

Change is the only constant. Much of the comfort of a garden is that change is slow and intimate. At this time of year it feels more like

hair growing than transformation. That is fast enough for me. I like the humanity and accessibility of it. Anyway there are enough odd things going on and irregularities to provide all the excitement I can bear. Everyone has noted the violets, primroses and cowslips that were flowering in October. This recent cold snap has put a timely stop to that unseasonable behaviour, but even ten years ago it would have been considered freakish. There are less dramatic but significant differences too, even in the Christmas department. Last year the mistletoe berries were notably untranslucent in December, reaching their milky best at the end of February and even March. This year there was a full bunch of squidgy white berries three weeks ago.

I have been in bed for days. I would love to confess that this was a kind of sybaritic indulgence and that the time was spent eating truffles, indulging in casual but complicated fornication and drinking brandy and champagne. But no such luck. I have had flu. For much of this time the rain slapped against the windows and what I could see of the sky was leaden. There was a smug comfort in this. It is bad to feel ill but far worse to do so when all the other circumstances draw you to a celebration of vitality and health.

But one day – I can't honestly remember what name of day it was; sickbed, fevered time merges into restless days and sweat-drenched nights – there was a hard frost and I crawled out of bed to photograph it. I take hundreds of pictures of the garden on my digital camera every week, almost all bad, although (proving the chimpanzee-and-typewriter theory) every now and again I surprise myself by taking something half decent. But quality is not really the point. The pictures are not intended for publication any more than my garden journal is. They are just a record.

This, of course, means lots of boring words, files of boring pictures. But I love them. I love the way that the record is being meticulously kept, certainly from week to week, and at times from day to day. So I have lain in bed, laptop on my knee, playing through thousands of pictures from the past three years, dipping into July, comparing last November, rummaging through the tulips in May.

The leaves have clung and clung, but now the significant ones have finally gone. The big hazel outside the back door is the real arbiter of the season and its nakedness can spell only winter. But the most beautiful

The midwinter jewel garden is a place of spaces. //

leaves this sodden autumn were those of a rose, *R. willmottiae*. This has a shimmer of tiny leaves the colour of beaten gold that lasted for weeks, carried on plum-red stems with weird and beautiful thorns when bunched all together, each zigzagging away from the one above and below, making a graceful geometric pattern. In summer it has small, fairly modest lilac-pink flowers.

It is one of a batch of species roses that I planted a few years ago and which I love. They include *R. hugonis*, *R.* 'Cantabrigiensis', *R. moyesii*, *R.* x *wintoniensis*, *R. sericea pteracantha* with its shark-fin thorns, and *R. moschata* and *R.* 'Complicata', which are both green-stemmed, even in the heart of winter. They are all tough and loose and pretty unsuitable for a small garden, I suppose, which – had I a small garden again – would instantly make me want to grow them. They prune with a pair of shears, and their laxity and sprawling nature encourage a general freedom and unlacing of the garden spirit. Long may they sprawl.

14 December 2000
Injuries

I have had an injured shoulder for months now which has severely limited my horticultural activities, and last week I added to these restrictions by dropping a paving slab on my foot. We were shifting stone that was laid this summer in the jewel garden for a patch indoors, reasoning that it was less work to redo the work outside than to go and find a new source of slabs that will match. Anyway, this very handsome square of York stone landed on my instep, which made it swell dramatically and turn black, reducing me to a hobble for a few days. Entirely my fault. Of course a psychoanalyst would say that these things are never accidental and that what I really wanted was an excuse not to garden. And with the rain tattooing the windows, the sodden ground that is not actually submerged slicked with mud, the light almost gone by 3 p.m. whilst I lie with my foot up on the sofa watching the rugby on television, I can believe that, subconscious or not, there might be a grain of truth in that.

15 December 2004
Digital memory

I was on my hands and knees, tidying up the walled garden, when I suddenly had to rush indoors for a dose of sanity. I had, for a terrible moment, forgotten what it looked like. Not that I needed any reminders of what was staring me in the face. The stark, brown winter garden is only too present and visible. But in a way, the garden is like someone that you love when they are behaving very badly. You forgive them, love them all the same, but hate what they are doing and saying at that moment.

// Unpruned knobbliness of espaliered pears in the vegetable garden.

A December garden is at best sick and at worst betraying itself. It is not the reason that any of us garden. So I had to whiz, with muddy footsteps on the stairs, to my workroom, get into the computer with muddy fingers, load up the programme that carries the thousands of digital snaps that I obsessively take and flick the 'real' garden up on to my screen. I quite often do this, rather in the way that people might open a book at random in order to seek guidance from the first thing that they read on the opened page.

An image appeared on my screen. Thanks to the wizardry of the digital age, I was able to trace it back to 6 July of this year, taken at 7.29 in the morning. Then I looked at my digital calendar and saw that it was a Tuesday and that half an hour later I drove down to Highgrove to look around the garden as a guest of the Soil Association. So a momentous day, but what remains most vividly from it are not the princely gardens but a lovely tangle of roses, nigella, poppies, *Allium* 'Purple Sensation' going to seed, *Geranium* 'Johnson's Blue' and goosegrass already twining its sticky tendrils across the border. I would give a lot for an entanglement of goosegrass at the moment rather than the arid, sticky emptiness of the borders. The *really* spooky thing is that this is a picture of almost exactly the spot that I was clearing and weeding a minute or two ago. Is this coincidence or did I subconsciously choose it? Did it choose me, knowing that I needed that hit of summer beauty to lift my spirits?

We have been busy doing winter gardening things like planting garlic and broad beans, cleaning out the greenhouses and gathering leaves with the costive obsession of a tramp going through waste bins. But however remorselessly cheerful you make yourself, in the end there is not much for the eye. Winter is the time when the things that the eye glides over from Easter to Bonfire Night suddenly reappear in the foreground, demanding attention. Or, and this is more often the case, are shockingly noticeable by their absence.

Any garden in July can smudge over its lack of definition and shape in a welter of flower, fresh foliage and benign chaos. But you cannot cheat the raw gaze of a winter's day. It is not so much empty as absent. Empty, of course, can be good. A really well-structured garden in winter has the austere simplicity of good minimalist design.

I am feeling positive about winter starkness because of a little hedge-trimming I did the other day. As part of the general clearing of the borders to make room for bulbs, we topped off the box hedges that frame each border in the jewel garden. I had intended these to grow abnormally

16 December 2002
Structure

We cut the hedges hard in winter followed by a light summer trim. //

high – about three feet – with the intended effect of making the borders leap out above them like jack-in-the-boxes, so they had not been topped since planting in spring '99. They were growing well, but somehow it was not working. They were making a good-enough hedge and the borders were doing fine in their lee, but the relationship between the two was becoming semi-detached. So I took about nine inches off and in the process squared the top. As an afterthought I also ran the hedge-cutter down both the sides, cutting them back quite a bit. When I inspected the result of this I was stunned. Total transformation. By reducing the width of the hedges it had effectively raised the height in proportion to their length. This instantly gave me the effect that I wanted.

You might think that I would *know* this. It is certainly the sort of thing I would tell someone else about. But the opportunities do not arrive that often to cut back nearly a hundred metres of virgin box hedging, and it literally changes everything. Really quite small changes of definition can be enough to establish a space that is visually satisfying, even if it is empty of all the conventional floral necessities of horticultural life. The white garden at Sissinghurst is one of the best examples of this. If you see a picture of it in midwinter (the garden is closed from October to March), you will see that its real genius is one of structure and volume.

This is the secret of winter gardening. This is why the flat, dead spaces of grass and empty borders are a kind of winter anti-matter. But set them as one plane of defined space and their dreariness is absorbed by the satisfying qualities of empty space.

Nearly a quarter of a century ago, at about this time of year, I visited Robin Hood's Bay on the Yorkshire coast between Scarborough and Whitby. It was and is a surreally beautiful place. But it seemed more than that to me. It was a revelation. The sea had eroded large boulders of soft stone which sat on a stratum of harder rock so that they had become rounded pebbles stranded on a shelf. Every one was an exquisitely beautiful object. Some were the size of a room and others could fit in my pocket, and the spaces between them were heavy with meaning. I don't know now any more than I did then what that meaning was, but it has occupied my mind ever since.

17 December 2000
No-dig
· · · · · · · · · · · · · · · · · ·

I think I may be wrong.

It could well be that it is time for me to stop digging with muscular enthusiasm and consider the whole system of no-dig gardening. And if I am going to do that then so can you. If the Ohio State University thesis is correct, gardens are potentially a significant contributor to carbon

loss. Every time you stick your spade in the ground and turn it over you are adding a fraction to the flood in my garden. Every time that I, all spade and vigour, dig my already well-dug garden, I inch the waters nearer your back door. No-dig gardening requires the soil to be deeply prepared initially but untouched thereafter. The wetter winters and drier summers will need masses of organic material added to the soil to provide drainage and water retention when it matters – and nothing does that better than lots of organic material added annually. The solution is not to dig it in but to mulch all bare soil every year with a thick layer of home-made compost.

The research at Ohio State has shown that soil can soak up a lot of carbon. In fact it contains three times as much carbon as all the earth's forests. As a 'soak' it is enormously effective. But over the past hundred years it is estimated that around a hundred billion tons of carbon have been lost from the soil into the atmosphere through farming. Most of this has come through ploughing. The enormous extra power that has come through machinery in the past fifty years has meant that much more land is ploughed. Ploughing introduces oxygen into the soil and

Jewel garden furniture ready to bring under cover. Too late. //

helps rots organic matter. For ploughing, read digging. In gardening terms, so far so very good. But as organic matter decomposes it releases carbon dioxide into the air.

The argument is that the process can be reversed. If farmers cut back on their ploughing, added plenty of organic manure and planted more trees, the soil could soak up much more carbon than is currently being lost.

This information has made me think hard. It contradicts my empirical view of agriculture that ploughing is a good thing as opposed to direct drilling and, more relevantly, it contradicts my oft-vaunted view that digging is superior to no-dig gardening.

The no-diggers will cry victory and dance around my shouldered spade, but not disturbing the soil is only one part of the complicated equation. Bonfires should be seen as a last resort, and the ash put back into the ground. Compost everything. All of us should use as little mechanical energy as possible and as much muscle power as we can instead. Get that scythe out and whet the edge. This is not a matter of self-consciously attaining sufficient brownie points to reach an organic, recycling eco-heaven but simply a question of harnessing our resources and dealing with those things at home that we are best dealing with rather than leaving it to politicians to make more of a mess of. The spirit of Gerard Winstanley and his fellow Diggers can be harnessed (with suitable irony) to make a difference.

None of this will make the weather better. At best it will stop it getting worse. So for the rest of our lives we have to adapt and get used to it. The point is that everything changes. There is no going back.

18 December 1998
Off-season

I have been in a social funk all week. We have visitors this weekend, friends I made over the summer whose garden I filmed every fortnight for six months. Almost every visit I would tell them that they must come and visit us here and blow me if they aren't due in about an hour's time. Seeing them will be lovely. They might even be pleased to see me, but if ever I do not want anyone to see the garden it is this weekend.

The garden in winter has no airs or graces. The countryside is revealed as a bleak, selfish landscape, inward-looking and utterly refusing to charm. The structure of the hedges is reduced to a grid of dank walls with all the atmosphere of a suburban ring road. I forgive all this. I know that this is the low point of the year, and that the real garden is merely having a rest and gaining strength before it steps out into the limelight in early spring.

Gardens must be allowed to go off duty. There is a kind of horticultural fascism that sets standards for every week and month, which is a nonsense. I like what it is waiting to be and the memory of what it has been, but all in all it is looking pretty rough.

19 December 2001
Wake

Most of the past week has been a time of convalescence, trying to shake off the virus that put me in bed for days. So I pottered in the vegetable garden, stripping away dead and bedraggled leaves from all the brassicas and the radicchio, parsnips, chard and parsley, as well as gathering the fallen leaves from the espaliered pears which had fallen and blown into every crevice and fold of the cabbages. Pear leaves, once fallen, are an extraordinary colour, so chocolatey-brown as to be almost black. I filled two barrows of this casual seasonal detritus.

I picked the last of the apples. They are 'Norfolk Beefing' and by now have turned a deep browny-maroon, with really hard, solid flesh. 'Norfolk Beefing' is an old apple and was grown a lot in the previous three centuries for drying to make biffins, a biffin being, according to the *OED*, 'a baked apple flattened in the form of a cake'. 'Beefing' seems to be a corruption of 'biffin'. I love this depth of provenance.

Gareth turned a path over for me today. George had made it seven years ago out of bricks, with the frogs facing upwards for grip. Only they slipped like mad, and the frogs filled with soil and produced healthy crops of weeds. I didn't say anything lest it hurt his feelings. He is still part of this garden, his work everywhere. He tackled every part of its creation with the same calm pragmatism whether it was laying paths or mending mowers. Three days ago we went to his funeral. More than 120 people came, although he had no family at all. Grown men wept unashamedly and then went down the pub where respects were paid until the early hours. They said that thirty people couldn't go to work the next day and six not the day after either. It was a good funeral. George would have liked it.

20 December 2000
Buckets

To set the scene ... For the past month our lives have been dominated by buckets. We normally have a float of about half a dozen builder's buckets around the place which are incredibly useful in the garden for containing weeds, stones, thinnings, veg – a thousand and one things. Couldn't live without them. But, in normal use, they rarely carry water. Watering cans do that better. In this post-diluvian state that we are enduring, the first casualty is the septic tank. It is in the spring garden and is about as badly

positioned as a septic could be. For a start the floods invariably go over it and down the vent. We can block the vent, and we do. Then it spreads over not one but two manholes and gets in them. We can raise the height of the manholes, and we did. But the drainage pipe cuts diagonally beneath the vegetable garden and out towards the water meadows and river. This exactly – to the inch – follows the line of the flooding in the garden, which means that when it floods – which we normally expect a couple of times a year – the septic tank cannot drain. So it becomes unusable for a day. To counter this we dug a socking great drain right down the garden in October, with another soakaway. This eases the strain on the drain during a normal flood. But the current floods laugh at our drain. They despise it. The water rises irresistibly and then, teasingly, stops at our door.

This has buggered the garden. It is starting to look like a bunch of pot plants that have been left in a full sink whilst the owners have been for a three-week holiday. And to sort the situation out will create mess of scary proportions. We shall have to reposition the septic tank, put in new drains and all that goes with it. I would rather have a herd of cattle

// The dry garden in midwinter.

roaming about. In effect we shall have to remove a third of the garden, store what can be salvaged in containers, do the drains, clear up the inevitable mess and put it all back again. The silver linings will be that we can sort out proper paths and things whilst we are about it and that this enforced radicalism will boot any complacency into touch. And compared to the poor people whose homes are swilled out with liquid mud and ordure, our problems are minimal. The fact that my garlic has all rotted in the ground cannot quite rank as a major disaster.

But it does mean buckets. Buckets and buckets of water. We bathe in buckets (surprisingly satisfactory), wash up in buckets, wash clothes in buckets (a real pain), and the loo is now a sophisticated form of bucket. It is not so bad – we have heating and unlimited hot water, just like luxury camping really, with a touch of medieval London thrown in as every used bucketful is thrown into the flood outside the back door. One day we will laugh about it.

I bought a job lot of common hollies some years ago that I had no real place for. I find I do this a lot with plants. I buy them because I like them or the idea of them in my garden but have nowhere specifically for them to go. They tend to knock around in pots or be planted and replanted lots of times until they find their true home. But a couple of years ago I recruited these hollies to make my hedge-on-stilts-and-a-wall combo.

Holly is probably one of the more ambitious plants to use for this because it is slow to establish, whereas hornbeam would have done the job easily and by now it would be almost mature. However, holly makes a wonderful hedge of any kind and is worth persevering with. I have one at the front of the house which has grown over the past ten years from eighteen-inch plants to a robust eight feet. I love the story of the seventeenth-century diarist and gardener John Evelyn, who was the proud owner of a holly hedge four hundred feet long, nine feet high and five feet thick. He lent his house to the Russian tsar Peter the Great, who proceeded to entertain himself by sitting in a wheelbarrow and ordering his servants to push him repeatedly back and forwards through the hedge. Such larks.

One of the spinoffs of training my holly-hedge-on-stilts is that it gets its annual prune at Christmas each year when I gather holly, smothered in berries, with which to decorate the house. This ancient, pagan ceremony not only makes the place look lovely but also keeps the witches and hobgoblins at bay. Which is just as well.

22 December 2002
Grid
· · · · · · · · · · · · · · · · · · · ·

Rather than designed, our borders are made up. We order or propagate what we would like to have and then position the plants on the ground. This becomes a constant process of moving, filling gaps with fresh stuff and rearranging everything as it grows. However, we have been talking about drawing up a detailed plan of the borders in the jewel garden and putting the information into the computer, as a record of the changes and to remind ourselves what we have got. The more we talk about doing it the less it seems likely to happen. The main problem is that it is just so daunting. Although the jewel garden consists of twelve separate borders, each one is large.

But the other day, on my way back from feeding the chickens – an important garden activity because I have to walk right to the end of the garden and back, which means that whatever the weather and whatever my jaundiced view of life, I am obliged to have a good look at things at least twice a day – I started sticking marker canes in. The five-minute chore turned into more than an hour as I scavenged all the short canes I could muster and stuck them into all the borders at one-metre spacing. I made no effort to measure this, just took a pace and then squared off by eye until gradually scores and then hundreds of canes marched regularly across the garden.

It was fascinating. You would think that you knew your borders inside out, but as soon as this imposed grid appeared everything took on another context. It also enabled me to look at what was actually there, square by coldly rational square. Some of the spacing suddenly looked absurd. Gaps lurched out. It was all reduced to manageable bite-sized chunks. Now all I have to do is methodically get it on to paper.

24 December 2000
Pleaching
· · · · · · · · · · · · · · · · · · · ·

I have just spent the day pruning the pleached limes. I can honestly say that now, at 4.45 on a pitch-dark Sunday evening, boots off, hands washed and cup of tea, I feel as good as I have done all winter. There was a shower when the logs were delivered yesterday morning – a lorry-load at 8 a.m., all in six-foot lengths that had to be sawn up and stacked to keep the Christmas fires burning – and I heard the rain lash the windows at four this morning, but other than that it has been dry for two whole days. Sunshine, a wind keen enough to make the warmth of a jacket friendly and, above all, light – clear, thin light.

// Down the nave of the garden through the middle of the coppice.

What have I done in this or a previous life that merited being given spiked aerating sandals for Christmas?

What bothers me most about this present – other than the knowledge that there is someone roaming loose who devised these things – is not that they are absurd and the wearer instantly transformed into a puncturing buffoon, but that the giver might have been serious. I can stand having the piss taken out of me but dread the thought that someone thinks I would genuinely welcome a pair of strap-on lawn aerators.

But I can see that it is a problem. Gardening is a hobby. It falls comfortably into the Christmas-present category in line with any sport, fishing or brass-rubbing. Giving Christmas presents as duty is a tedious chore. Because of this, inspiration falls at the first hurdle. I know the thought process only too well: people instantly go from complex, rounded individuals to two-dimensional football fans, cooks or whatever, and I am thus labelled a 'gardener'. But I am also presumed to have everything already. Panic. Look for the unusual and amusing. But there is no time, no money, no inclination to do anything other than tick another sodding present off the list.

This is when you enter the Aerator Sandal Zone. It is not a good space. Everything within it is collapsible and plastic and comes in a kit that doesn't go together very well. It is designed to *look like* gardener's stuff rather than to be gardener's stuff. At the more expensive end it is all faded, faux-Victorian kitchen garden, where the potting shed is a lifestyle statement and men wear aprons with 'Head Gardener' wittily emblazoned. At the cheaper end it is things to put things into and useless tools, either ridiculously over-specialised or else too vaguely general.

The presents I really want are the things that get used up like good labels or a big ball of string. And how come no one gave me a stainless-steel spade? Now that is a serious present. It is not the kind of thing that you just go and buy any more than you just pop out to the shops to pick up a set of finest kitchen knives or a pair of handmade shoes. Maybe Christmas is not big enough for it. Maybe stainless-steel spades should be restricted to weddings and twenty-first birthdays or laid down at birth.

The best presents of all – at any time of year – are plants from people's gardens. Often these are no more than excess seedlings or cuttings, but they come with character and history and help build up these qualities in your own garden. I love walking round the garden and remembering the provenance of plants. It is a treat to be given something out of the ordinary, but actually it does not have to be special or rare to be treasured. The fact that plants have been grown with care and skill and are part of a household is enough to make them valuable. In my

Winter reduces the garden to snatches and glimpses. Moments. //

367

experience gardeners are extraordinarily generous and willingly give excess plants which then take something of their original garden and gardener with them to their new home. I like to think that the whole country has this interconnecting family tree of plants in gardens linking families, lovers and strangers alike.

**31 December 2001
Ever all**

I always arrive at the end of the year with the relief of a sailor turning the Cape. Actually, whilst I am usually all at sea I am the very definition of a landlubber, but the metaphor feels apt enough. For the past few months I have been battling against heavy weather, sailing into the wind, managing the garden from crisis to crisis. One day is completed in order to survive the next. But then you round Christmas, the Cape of Enforced Cheer, and the wind is suddenly tucked into your back. The currents are sweeping me towards spring like a conveyor belt. Sure the days are short, the weather vile, and good intentions undergo their own private shipwrecks, but I have a palpable sensation of heading for home, however high the local seas.

The light inevitably has a lot to do with it. Now that the solstice is past, the days are moving out in every direction, imperceptibly perhaps, but from now on the extra minutes at five o'clock matter as much as hours in midsummer. These are moments of light as precious as jewels.

I spend the period between Christmas and New Year's taking stock in the garden and preparing for next year. The first part of the process is as important as the second, although less fun. If I look back over this year it initially seems to have been dominated by the weather, and I see that exactly a year ago we were flooded, and my garden journal has the one highly horticultural comment 'No baths, washing machines, etc.' (the 'etc.' meant flushing loos).

And the best moment this year? No one thing of course – a thousand half-moments out of the corner of my eye. But flicking back through the garden journal I remember this particular entry on 9 June as both being suffused with pleasure and typical of the reason that I garden:

Wrote Observer all day. Made bread. Little Gem v. good. Broad beans lovely 3-inch pods. Jewel garden fucking good but needs working on. Played cricket with Adam 7–8 p.m. Good fun. Sarah said coppice was 'what she dreamt of' when we walked round together at 9 p.m. Lovely Prussian Blue sky at 11 p.m.

If that is ever all, then that is enough for me.

// Midday sun on the winter solstice. The year begins again.

Thanks

This book covers a period of eighteen years and a place that owes much to many people. But I would like to thank in particular my agent Caroline Michel, who read everything and encouraged and cajoled me throughout, and Richard Atkinson at Bloomsbury, who is the best of editors and a good friend. I'd also like to thank Peter Dawson, Penny Edwards and Natalie Hunt for their help in making this book the object it is.

Heartfelt thanks to George and Rose Taylor, Gareth Lorman, Norman and Jayne Groves, Fred Ellis and Jim Kelly, all of whom have worked to make this garden over the years and meant I had the luxury of writing about it. Neither garden nor book could have happened without them.

But the greatest thanks are to my family, Sarah, Adam, Freya and Tom. It is our home, and I only borrow a piece of it in these pages.

Index

First published in Great Britain 2009

Text and photographs © 2009 by Monty Don

The moral right of the author has been asserted.

Bloomsbury Publishing Plc, 36 Soho Square, London W1D 3QY

Bloomsbury Publishing, London, New York and Berlin

A CIP catalogue record for this book is available from the British Library.

ISBN 978 1 4088 0249 6

10 9 8 7 6 5 4 3 2 1

Design: Grade Design Consultants, London. www.gradedesign.com

The text of this book is set in Foundry Wilson. Created by Foundry Types, it is an expertly crafted revival of a typeface originally cut in 1760 by the Scottish type founder Alexander Wilson.

Printed and bound in Italy by Graphicom

All papers used by Bloomsbury Publishing are natural and recyclable.

The FSC logo identifies products which contain wood from well managed forests certified in accordance with the rules of the Forest Stewardship Council.

© Mixed Sources
Product group from well-managed forests, controlled sources and recycled wood or fibre
www.fsc.org Cert no. CQ-COC-000015
© 1996 Forest Stewardship Council

FSC

www.bloomsbury.com/montydon

1 July 2009
Afterword
....

This book is based upon garden journals that I have kept since 1988. In truth the first years were marked by gaps long enough to challenge the concept of a journal, but between 1995 and 2005 I meticulously recorded everything planted, sown and harvested, every job done, every thing seen or heard that I considered of note. The handwritten, day-to-a-page journal living in the kitchen became part of the evidence of the garden.

However in 2006 I began a series of journeys that took me away from home a great deal for the following two years and this, combined with an overwhelming work regime, meant I had almost no time in my own garden and little to record. The journal stopped. Then, early in 2008 I collapsed. In the months of recovery I did very little actual gardening, but I spent a great deal of time looking at my garden and a good number of the pictures in this book were taken in this period.

Eighteen years after we began here, the garden has now entered a new phase with many changes. It is an exciting time. The journal is back on the kitchen table.